RIVETHEAD

RIVETHEAD

· ·

TALES FROM THE ASSEMBLY LINE

BEN HAMPER

FOURTH ESTATE · *London*

First published in Great Britain in 1992 by
Fourth Estate Limited
289 Westbourne Grove
London W11 2QA
This edition published by arrangement with
Warner Books Inc., New York

A catalogue record for this book is available from
the British Library

ISBN 1-85702-001-4

Book design by H. Roberts
Printed and bound in Great Britain by
Biddles Limited, Guildford and King's Lynn

For
Barbara, Bernadette and Jan

ACKNOWLEDGMENTS

The author wishes to acknowledge the support and fellowship of various friends and colleagues who warrant mention for their kind assistance. Among them: Sam Goodhue, Janice Buchanan, Judy King, Jim McDonald, Robert Beach, Amy Lindman, David and Phyllis Stites, Kathy Warbelow, Charles Fancher, Alex Kotlowitz, Robert Dubreuil, Dennis Duso, Terry Ostrander, Rau Kilaru, Lenice Gregory, Dennis Fuller, Mark's Lounge, Devin Donnelly, Paul Lethbridge, Marisa Adamo, Pat Elhaje, Alex Chilton, Jack and Bixby, Glen Lash, Cathy Burlingame and Sonya Hamper. Particular thanks to David Black for his persistent optimism, to Charlie Conrad for his understanding and guidance, and to Michael Moore, who provided so much belief, a place to hide and a space to grow.

Although the tales you are about to read are, to the best of my recollection, true, the names of several individuals have been changed to preserve the anonymity of the innocent and to protect the guilty.

—B.H.

FOREWORD

by Michael Moore

MY RELATIONSHIP WITH BEN HAMPER HAS RESULTED IN MY BE-ing fired from my job, sued for libel, losing a potential friend-ship with my hero Bruce Springsteen, and now forced into writing this damn foreword so I can keep my favorite ball cap. Which is actually Hamper's favorite ball cap, but now that half the world has seen it on my head in *Roger & Me*, and, possession being so many tenths of the law, we decided to settle this with my keeping the hat if I wrote this foreword.

Let me back up for a second...

I first heard of Ben Hamper shortly after John Lennon was murdered. A columnist in the *Flint Journal*, the daily rag in our hometown of Flint, Michigan, wrote that the country was actually better off with Lennon dead, considering all of the rebellion he caused. If it wasn't for Lennon and the Beatles, she exhorted, our generation would have turned out more respectable people who held such jobs as engineers or lawyers. So this guy named Hamper sent a letter to the *Flint Journal* saying, "I make my living turning bolts in the factory. Being a devoted Lennon fan, I'm suddenly discouraged to realize that, had I avoided this scoundrel's music, I could have been a real success in some lofty vocation."

I thought about trying to find this "Ben Hamper" to see if he would like to write for my alternative biweekly newspaper, the *Flint Voice*. But that idea got shoved aside, and it was another six months before an unsolicited record review from Ben arrived in the mail with a note attached saying I could run this if I wanted to. This one-paragraph review was so wonderfully sick that I immediately called him up to discuss further writing assignments.

After a few more reviews for the *Flint Voice*, it was clear from his writing that there was more inside him that needed to come out. I asked him to consider writing a column about life in the shop—or any other subject of his choosing. So in addition to reports from the General Motors assembly line, he covered the local Elvis impersonators, faith healers and greasy spoons. It was right about then I should have pulled the reins in on this guy, but he was upsetting so many people, I just couldn't stop him.

Then one week, Hamper wrote about a bar he frequented where there were so many fistfights, he suggested a smart dentist should open an office next door to the joint. "What the place lacked in ambience," he wrote, "it made up for in ambulance." Well, the bar soon closed and the owner sued me, claiming that Hamper's remarks had ruined his business. Fortunately, the judge had been my Boy Scout advisor and firmly believed, with God as his witness, that I could do no wrong, and dismissed the suit.

Hamper's "Impressions of a Rivethead" column became the most widely read page in the *Flint Voice* and, when the paper became the *Michigan Voice*, his popularity soared. *The Wall Street Journal* ran a front page story on him, *Harper's* magazine reprinted one of his pieces and some shoe company wanted him to endorse their industrial boots (Ben knows boots). Meanwhile, he would take off work in the middle of his night shift at GM, come over to the *Voice* office, and try to get the staff to stop working and join him in his various vices. I remember one particular night watching him engage the staff in a game of lawn darts inside the building, using a poster of GM chairman Roger Smith as the target. I guess that was our version of the new journalism.

Finally, after nearly ten years of publishing the *Voice*, I was asked by a liberal millionaire to move to San Francisco and become the editor of *Mother Jones* magazine. The owner liked the "working class reality" of the *Michigan Voice* and wanted to put some of that into *Mother Jones*. It had once been the country's premier muckraking magazine, but now it was a soft, touchy-feely periodical that had lost over 80,000 subscribers. So, when I arrived in California on my mission to save the magazine, one of the first writers I commissioned was Ben Hamper. He wrote a hilarious piece I titled "I, Rivethead," and I made it the cover story of my first issue. I then told him that he could continue his "Rivethead" column in each issue of the magazine. I even sent him on a promotional tour.

Well, never trust a millionaire when he tells you he wants that "working class reality" in his magazine. As my third issue was being readied for publication, the owner came into my office and, waving a copy of Hamper's latest column, asked me if I really intended on printing this smut. Yes, I said. Bye-bye, he replied. The next day I was in the unemployment line.

I went back home to Flint, where Ben tried to cheer me up by letting me watch his collection of Charles Manson interviews. On his shelf, I spotted a ball cap that, I felt, summed up my life at that moment. On the front of the cap was a giant lake trout with the words "I'm Out for Trout." I asked Ben if I could borrow it and he said sure, but he wanted it back soon.

The next day, Roger Smith announced he was laying off another 10,000 workers in Flint. Buoyed by this development, I decided to make a film in which I would try to get Smith to come to Flint so he could see what happens to the people he throws out on the street. During the first day of shooting, I happened to wear Hamper's "Out for Trout" hat while on camera. To maintain coinsistency in the filming during the following days, I had to keep wearing that damned hat. That ball cap soon became the symbol for the film, and Hamper was not to have it on his balding head again.

As *Roger & Me* neared completion, I wanted to get permission from Bruce Springsteen to use his song "My Hometown" in the movie. I went to New York to meet with Springsteen's friend and biographer Dave Marsh to solicit his help. Instead, Marsh took me to task for once running a column by Hamper which poked fun at the Boss for being a multimillionaire while singing songs about working in a factory. Although I pleaded with Marsh that I despised everything that Hamper ever stood for, he stated "You were irresponsible for running such a thing. Ben Hamper is my ideological enemy." He showed me the door, thus ending any chance of hanging with the guys at the Stone Pony. (Warner Bros., the distributor of *Roger & Me*, and the largest media conglomerate in the world—but apparently no one's "ideological enemy"—later got permission from Springsteen for the song.)

Through his appearance in *Roger & Me*, Ben became known throughout the world as "that guy in the mental clinic playing basketball and singing the Beach Boys song." More than one person, he tells me, has stopped him on the street to comment on his pick and roll, his vocal range and the "Hinckley-like glint in his eye." With one memorable movie part under his belt, he still had not been widely recognized for the literary talent he and the nuns always knew he had, so he holed up in his backyard shed and began to write this book to set the record straight.

What has resulted on these pages, I believe, is a masterpiece of writing which paints a darkly humorous account of working class life in America. It establishes Ben as an important voice of the nineties, one which I'm sure we will hear from again and again. At the very least, it should confirm his place in publishing history as the first author to write a major book while under medical supervision—and the influence of eleven different miracle drugs. (I can hear the Regis intro now: "Please welcome author/outpatient...Ben Hamper!") And no matter what happens, Hamper still holds the free-throw record both at the mental clinic and at my house.

Of course, to read what he has to say on these pages, you may wonder who the real crazy ones are. This insane system known as the assembly line is designed to deny individuality and eliminate self-worth. Do you ever wonder who built the car you drive? Do you think about the personal toll it extracts from those individuals who spend the best years of their lives in a hot, dirty, boring, dehumanizing factory? Out there in the rust belt...the heartbeat of America...well, they're paid so well, you know, for their "unskilled" labor. Hell, they should feel lucky they even have a job! In this book, Ben Hamper tells what a lucky guy he is.

Ben and I both grew up in Flint, Michigan, the sons of factory workers. We were never supposed to get out, and you were never supposed to hear our voices. It all comes down to a matter of class, of knowing our place, and a place like Flint, Michigan, doesn't really exist in the minds of the media or decision makers. Even the country's liberals are at a loss when it comes to thinking about the Ben Hampers. They speak often, as they should, of the ills of our society, but rarely do they mention class, that growing distinction between rich and poor, between those who sweat for their money and those who inherit it or legally steal it. Do they ever give one iota of thought to what the person who rivets their rocker panels is going through. Rocker panels, you say? Huh? Exactly.

Ben and I were both determined when we left high school not to go on the assembly line. So I started my own paper and Ben made up poems while painting houses. Unfortunately, he decided one day that no one was going to see any glimmer of creativity in him, so he gave up and went into the shop. I too had similar feelings yet, after getting hired at Buick, I just didn't have the guts to go through with it and called in sick my first day of work. I never did walk through those gates. I am glad that Ben and I finally ran into each other and, in our own ways, held on to that belief that we were not invisible people with inaudible voices simply because our fathers ate out of a lunch bucket and shopped at K mart.

Both of us finally got our chance. But I still have the ball cap.

PROLOGUE

DEAD ROCK STARS ARE SINGIN' FOR ME AND THE BOYS ON THE Rivet Line tonight. Hendrix. Morrison. Zeppelin. The Dead Rock Star catalogue churnin' outta Hogjaw's homemade boom box. There's Joplin and Brian Jones and plenty of Lynyrd Skynyrd. Dead Rock Stars full of malice and sweet confusion. Tonight and every night they bawl. The Dead Rock Stars yowling at us as we kick out the quota.

We're all here. Department 07, Blazer/Suburban Line—factory outpost FF-15 stenciled in black spray paint on the big iron girder behind Dougie's workbench. We're building expensive trucks for the General Motors Corp. We've come back once again to tussle with our parts and to hear the Dead Rock Stars harmonize above the industrial din.

The music of the Dead Rock Stars bursts from a ledge on Dougie's workbench—our hideaway for Hogjaw's stereo. Just before the start of every shift, Dougie goes through the complicated ritual of threading the cords and speaker wires from the stereo down a hollow leg in his workbench and into the plug at the base of the water fountain behind his job. The camouflage must be perfect. It is against company policy to use a General

Motors electrical outlet as a source to summon up Dead Rock
Stars. Only battery-powered radios are allowed.

Originally Hogjaw complied with this rule. It wasn't easy.
Due to the enormous power demand of his radio creation, the
Jaw was forced to lug a car battery into work with him every
shift. You would see him strainin' his way through the parking
lot every afternoon, a lunch bucket curled under one arm and
his trusty Delco Weatherbeater hoisted on top of his other
shoulder. Trailing behind him would be a couple of riveters
with their arms locked around the speaker boxes—pallbearers
bringin' around the tombs of the Dead Rock Stars.

This went on for a month or so before the security guards
decided to halt the parade. Car batteries were declared illegal.
Apparently the guards had concluded that it was a mighty
dangerous precedent to allow workers to enter the plant prem-
ises with the batteries of their automobiles stashed on their
shoulders. After all, whose heads would be in the vise if one of
these sonic blasters pulled an overload up on the assembly line
and spewed a load of battery acid into the eyes and ears of the
screw brigade? Dead Rock Stars? Dead Shoprats? Not on *my*
goddamn beat.

As for the popularity of Dead Rock Stars on the Rivet Line,
I've settled upon this private theory. The music of the Dead
Rock Stars is redundant and completely predictable. We've
heard their songs a million times over. In this way, the music of
the Dead Rock Stars infinitely mirrors the drudgery of our
assembly jobs. Since assembly labor is only a basic extension of
high school humdrum, it only stands to reason that the same
wearied hepsters who used to dodge economics class for a
smoke in the boys' room would later in life become fossilized to
the hibernatin' soundtracks of their own implacable youth. Let
the eggheads in economics have David Byrne and Laurie
Anderson. The rivetheads be needin' their "Purple Haze" and
"Free Bird" just like tomorrow needs today.

It's mob rule, and the mob demands Dead Rock Stars in
their choir loft. Of course this arrangement provides for a fair
amount of bitching from linemates in our area who hold no
sacred allegiance to the songs of the rockin' deceased.

For example, there's Dick, the left-side rear spring man.
He works directly across from Dougie, travelin' a nightly path

that requires him to take the maximum dose of Dead Rock Star thud. It's nothing unusual to spot Dick takin' a deep drag from one of his ever-present Winstons while gazin' head-on into the boom box with this buggered glint in his eye and this twisted grimace on his face that almost pleads aloud for some kind of transistor malfunction, tweeter meltdown or any other variety of holy intervention.

Eddie and Jehan prefer rap music. On occasion, Jehan brings in his own battery-powered blaster and engages in this furious battle-of-the-blare with Hogjaw's almighty boom box. The Kings of Rap vs. The Dead Rock Stars vs. The Steady Clang of Industry. It makes for quite the raucous stew—sorta like pluggin' your head into the butt end of a Concorde during acceleration mode.

Management's stance on all of this usually boils down to a simple matter of see no evil, hear no evil. If the guy in the tie can't actually *see* the visible evidence of how you're wastin' millions of corporate dollars, he's most often inclined to let the music flow. It keeps him off the hook. He doesn't have to play killjoy. He can dummy up and pretend that all those guitar solos he hears screechin' through the middle of the night are only happy by-products of a contented work force. His boss will love him, his wife will love him, his men will like him and the Company will somehow stagger on. Industry on the march. Bravo!

But even in victory, there's often a price to pay. Let us not forget that General Motors has already informed the work force that there won't be any profit sharing to spread around this year. Too much waste. Too many buyouts. Too few pennies. And I imagine those damn utility bills are way out of sight too.

Oh well, what can I say? I'm just sitting here waiting for the next chassis to arrive. I'm tapping my toes to the beat of the Dead Rock Stars. Ten feet to my right, I can hear the trickle of untold billions bein' sucked outta the corporate coffers through the base of the water fountain behind Dougie's workbench.

I'm thinking that rock stars, even dead ones, don't come cheap.

RIVETHEAD

 **1**

I WAS SEVEN YEARS OLD THE FIRST TIME I EVER SET FOOT
inside an automobile factory. The occasion was Family Night at
the old Fisher Body plant in Flint where my father worked the
second shift.

General Motors provided this yearly intrusion as an opportunity for the kin of the work force to funnel in and view their
fathers, husbands, uncles and granddads as they toiled away on
the assembly line. If nothing else, this annual peepshow lent a
whole world of credence to our father's daily grumble. The
assembly line did indeed stink. The noise was very close to
intolerable. The heat was one complete bastard. Little wonder
the old man's socks always smelled like liverwurst bleached for
a week in the desert sun.

For my mother, it was at least one night out of the year
when she could verify the old man's whereabouts. One night a
year when she could be reasonably assured that my father
wasn't lurchin' over a pool table at the Patio Lounge or picklin'
his gizzard at any one of a thousand beer joints out of Dort
Highway. My father loved his drink. He wasn't nearly as fond
of labor.

On this night, the old man was present. I remember my mother being relieved. If he hadn't been there, it would have been difficult for her to explain to my little brother and me why we had made this exhaustive trek through Satan's playpen just to ogle a bunch of oily strangers and their grinnin' lineage.

After a hundred wrong turns and dead ends, we found my old man down on the trim line. His job was to install windshields using this goofy apparatus with large suction cups that resembled an octopus being crucified. A car would nuzzle up to the old man's work area and he would be waiting for it, a cigarette dangling from his lip, his arms wrapped around the windshield contraption as if it might suddenly rebel and bolt off for the ocean. Car, windshield. Car, windshield. Car, windshield. No wonder my father preferred playin' hopscotch with barmaids. This kind of repetition didn't look like any fun at all.

And here, all of this time, I had assumed that Dad just built the vehicles all by his lonesome. I always imagined that building adult cars was identical to building cars in model kits. You were given a large box with illustrated directions, a clutter of fenders, wheels and trunk lids, and some hip-high vat of airplane glue. When one was finished, you simply motioned to some boss-type in the aisle: "Hey, bring me another kit and make it a goddamn Corvette this time!"

We stood there for forty minutes or so, a miniature lifetime, and the pattern never changed. Car, windshield. Car, windshield. Drudgery piled atop drudgery. Cigarette to cigarette. Decades rolling through the rafters, bones turning to dust, stubborn clocks gagging down flesh, another windshield, another cigarette, wars blinking on and off, thunderstorms muttering the alphabet, crows on power lines asleep or dead, that mechanical octopus squirming against nothing, nothing, NOTHINGNESS. I wanted to shout at my father "Do something else!" Do something else or come home with us or flee to the nearest watering hole. DO SOMETHING ELSE! Car, windshield. Car, windshield. Christ, no.

Thank God that, even at age seven, I knew what I was going to be when I grew up. There wouldn't be any car/

windshield cha-cha awaiting me. I was going to be an ambulance driver, the most glamorous calling in the world. I would spend my days zooming from one mangled calamity to the next. I would have full license to poke my face into the great American bucket seat bloodfest. The metallic crunch, the spiderweb of cracked glass (no doubt installed by my zombied father), the stupid eyeballs of the ripped and ravaged, the blood and guts of the accordion carnage. Ah, yes. To engage the sweet wail of the sirens. To scoop teeth from out of the dashboard. That would be the life. Everything my mother insisted we avoid when we passed a wreck. "Boys, don't look out the window," she would tremble. I always looked. I had to look.

My mind was set. Someday I'd be an ambulance driver. I would eat at McDonald's every night. I would buy a house right across the street from Tiger Stadium. My old man was nuts. Car, windshield, car, windshield: what kind of idiot occupation was that?

As far as I remember, we never returned for another Family Night. It was just as well, for in all likelihood, we'd never have spotted my father. He had this habitual lean for the nearest exit. As soon as my grandmother lined him up for another job, he'd disappear into an eternal crawl for the coldest mug of beer in town. He took turns being a car salesman, a milkman, a construction worker, a railroad hand, a house painter, a mechanic and a landscaper. Each time the suds would devour his sense of duty, he'd get canned or simply quit, and back he'd come to his lumpy retreat on the living room sofa. My grandmother would be less than pleased.

Frequently mixed in with these dashed occupations were the inevitable sojourns back to the assembly line. It was not the least bit uncommon for a man to be fired at one factory on a Friday and be given the red carpet treatment at another automotive facility across town on Monday. If this is Tuesday, this must be Buick. If this is Thursday, how 'bout AC Spark Plug. During the sixties there were ten or so factories in Flint workin' three shifts per day and in this kind of boomtown climate even the beggars could afford to be choosers. "Sign here, Mr. Beerbreath. So glad to have you collapse on our doorstep."

I can't recall how many times my old man spun through the revolving doors of General Motors. However, around the house, we could always sense when Dad was cleaving through the factory rut. He would enter the house with this bulldog grimace. He'd gobble his meal, arise, put on one of his Arnie Palmer golf sweaters and whisk off for a troll through publand. Often, he wouldn't return for days. Then, suddenly one morning, there he'd be—reekin' of Pabst and pepperoni, passed out in a fetal position on the sofa, wearin' the same cool duds he left home in.

Not surprisingly, this led to a fair amount of friction between my mother and father. I could hear them early in the morning, their ferocious bitching driftin' through the heater vent up and into the bedroom I shared with three of my brothers.

It didn't take a marriage counselor or referee to sift to the bottom of these parental showdowns. Propped up in my bunk, I could easily discern the irrationality of my old man's barbs and the meek desperation of my mother's rebuttals. My father insisted that my mother was yanking the family against him. "You're turnin' the whole bunch of them into goddamn mama's boys!" the old man would rant. "Every one of them acts like I'm some kind of villain."

Meanwhile, my mother would score with a hefty uppercut of fact. "Don't blame me, Bernard. Maybe if you hung around the house more than two nights a month the kids might get to know you." My old man abhorred the truth. It was like some horrible, foreign diction that ripped at his core. The car payment was truth. The telephone bill was truth. The six sleeping children, plus the one sitting bolt upright in his bed, were truth. Worst of all, the cars and windshield were truth.

Cars, windshields. Cars, fenders. Cars, whatever. The ongoing shuffle of the shoprat. It wasn't as if this profession was a plague that appeared out of nowhere to ensnare my old man. Quite the opposite was true. His daddy was a shoprat. His daddy's daddy was a shoprat. Perhaps his daddy's daddy's daddy would have been a shoprat if only Hank Ford would have dreamed this shit up a little sooner.

My old man's mother had been a shoprat. The same with Uncle Jack and Uncle Gene and Uncle Clarence. Ditto dear old Aunt Laura. My mother's dad had been a shoprat. (If you're wondering what happened to my mother's mother and her sense of duty—well, Christ, somebody had to stay home and pack this clan a lunch.)

Right from the outset, when the call went out for shoprats, my ancestors responded in almost Pavlovian compliance. The family tree practically listed right over on its side with eager men and women grasping for that great automotive dream.

My great-grandfather got the wheel rollin'. In 1910, he began his twenty-year tenure down on Industrial Avenue piecing together mobilized buggies. This was a period right after the invention of the gas-powered engine and long before the introduction of freeway sniping. My great-grandfather would have hung in there longer, but he bumped heads in the thirties with something called the Depression.

My grandfather hired on in 1930. He rode out the turbulence of the Depression and worked as a skilled tradesman for thirty-two years at Buick. He had no plans to retire, but the cancer took him down at age fifty-two. He died one week to the day after he cashed his first pension check.

My other grandfather hitched his way from Springfield, Illinois, to the Vehicle City in 1925. He put in forty years, from Babe Ruth to the Beatles, as an inspector at the Chevrolet Engine plant. He always claimed that the only reason he retired was his disdain for the new breed of autoworkers in the sixties. He referred to them as "candy-asses." I assumed he was remarking about some inedible new brand of chocolate bar.

During the war, my grandmother helped build machine guns at the AC Spark Plug factory. She later switched over to working on aircraft out on Dort Highway. To this day, my grandmother still helps me change the oil in my Camaro.

My Aunt Laura and her husband Jack put in a combined sixty-five years at the AC plant and the Buick Foundry. Uncle Jack was well known for his lust for overtime, often volunteering to work double shifts and sixteen-hour days. This may provide a valuable clue as to why they never had any children.

For sheer longevity, my Uncle Clarence outdistanced everyone in the family tree. From 1919 till 1964, an amazing span of
forty-five years, he answered the whistle over at the Buick
Engine plant.

Forty-five years! That's longer than the life expectancy of
over two-thirds of the world's population. Forty-five years!
Shit, just imagine—from a cradle down in Dixie to his hunched-
over demise on the potty—Elvis Presley never even lived that
long. Forty-five years! After all of that, what do they give you
for a retirement gift? A grandfather clock? An iron lung? A
bronzed calendar the size of a Yugo?

With a heritage like that you'd think my old man would
have had enough grit and grind floatin' through his gene pool to
practically assure his pod development as a full-bloomin' arche-
type of the species. A purebred shoprat, begotten from sperms
that jingle, jangle, jingle to the jungle strains of Greaseball
Mecca. The fair-haired boy in the rhinestone coveralls. Spawn
of labor. Self-winding fetus with the umbilical lasso looped
around the blue-collared neckbone of Mr. Goodwrench.

Apparently, the old man wasn't much for heritage. He
tumbled out of the family tree, urinated on it and never looked
back. For him, General Motors was nothing more than a
recurring nuisance, an occasional pit stop where he could tidy
up his bankroll before troopin' out on another aimless binge.

It was unfortunate that my father couldn't combine his
love for beer and his dependence on pocket money into one
workable formula. After all, he wasn't the only palooka in the
family who tipped toward the tapper. The majority of my
ancestors were heavy drinkers. Excluding my grandmother, all
of them imbibed frequently as hard-laborin' shoprats are wont
to do.

My mother's dad was especially skilled at juggling work
and play. Monday morning through Friday afternoon he was
the consummate provider. Straight home from work, dinner,
the evening news and immediately into bed at 7:00 P.M. He
arose each weekday at 3:30 A.M., fixed himself some black
coffee, turned on the kitchen radio, smoked a handful of Lucky
Strikes and waited to leave for work at a quarter to five. This
regimen never varied one iota in the forty years he worked for
GM.

Come the quittin' whistle on Friday afternoon, a colossal metamorphosis took place. So long, shoprat. Hello, hooligan. As my mother tells it, they never caught more than a staggerin' glimpse of my grandfather on any given weekend. He occasionally dropped in for a quick supper whereupon he would substitute the dinner hour for an excuse to denounce my grandma's cooking, castigate the children and generously mutter "goddamn-it-alls" for the benefit of the rest of the defective universe.

My grandfather surely could be an ornery bastard, but it should be thusly noted that he was always there to answer the bell. He had a wife and three kids to house and feed. He turned the trick daily. He may have had a passionate lust for booze, but it never interfered with his job at General Motors. When he retired, he was a very wealthy man. Devotion, responsibility and duty to the Corporation. The bottle was never far away, but it always rode shotgun.

Seeing as how my old man constructed this formula completely ass-backwards, the entire burden of support fell solely into my mother's lap. While the old man was off baby-sitting barstools, it was left up to my mom to raise and provide for eight kids.

Throughout my youth, my mother worked two jobs a day. Nine to five, she was a medical secretary at a doctor's office. She walked the two miles to work each day because we were too broke to afford a car. By night, she worked as a medical records transcriber, pounding the dictaphone machine for Hurley Hospital in the tiny, makeshift office in the corner of the living room.

It was unfortunate for my old man that my mother was such a strict and loyal Catholic. Consequently, my mother wasn't allowed to practice the pill and the baby faucet was allowed to leak on unabated. The final tally showed five boys and three girls of which I was the eldest. Eight was indeed enough. In fact, eight was plainly too goddamn many. Every time the stork paid a visit, he left a new bundle of joy for my mother and a fresh load in the chamber of the gun pointed at my old man's skull.

It seemed with each new addition to our family, my father slid further and further away from accountability. He liked children, he just didn't have the space for a clan of his own. It was like the cars and the windshield. The equation never balanced out. The undertow of all this repetition was a riddle he could never hope to untangle.

By the age of ten, I realized that my old man was not soon to be confused with Ward Cleaver. I was hip to all his ploys and well aware of his flair for bullshit. His boozin' never particularly bothered me. I figured if my father wanted to go get plowed, it was his decision.

What bothered me was my old man's insistence on fabricating dreadful, transparent lies. We both knew what he was up to so why not just 'fess up and admit the obvious.

I surely would have respected him more if he'd only come up to me on those occasions of rabid thirst and said "Look, son. I feel like some kind of suffocatin' beast. The world is knockin' me around something awful and it's only fuckin' proper that I find a bar at once. I want to get smashed. I want to play footsies with the locals. I want to sing like Dean Martin. I want to drink until they start clickin' the lights off and on and then I wanna weave home and collapse into bed with the weight of the world slidin' off the sheets. You may not understand any of this now, but someday you'll have a world of your own to contend with."

My friends were always amused with my old man's approach to the duties of fatherhood. Most of their fathers were dedicated shoprats, shackled to some factory titty like hornets to honey. Their fathers wouldn't miss a day's work if their spinal cords were severed. Obedience to the Corporation. An honest day's pay for an honest day's toil. Car, bumper. Car, door latch. Car, dipstick.

For them, my father was the mold breaker—the curious renegade who dared to scrunch himself up in fetal bliss, smack dab in the middle of the workday, snoozin' off the effects of another nocturnal creepy-crawl.

After school, we would tiptoe past him, snickering back and forth at the behemoth in full slumber. You had to be very cautious. To awaken the old man from his beer coma would earn you an immediate pass to have your head dislodged. Sometimes, just for laughs, I'd get as close as I possibly dared and jut my middle finger right in his face. The poor bastard was like some dormant circus geek and he never even knew it.

Of course, my friends preferred to catch my old man in his

glorious prime. This usually occurred whenever I'd have a friend over for the night. My old man would weave in while we were watchin' some late-night horror flick and immediately take over the entertainment. After a full night of drinkin', there was nothing' my old man enjoyed more than a captive audience for his sloshed bar chatter. Even if he was playin' to a crowd comprised of two sleep-starved ten-year-olds.

There were the stories about how he broke said pool stick over said chiseler's head and how the babes he hung with had chests the size of pony kegs ("They'd be through with you boys before you ever got it unzipped," he'd chuckle) and how he knew Tiger great Denny McLain on a first-name basis and how Denny better watch his shit cuz these mob pricks were no one to try and slip a change-up by and how he was rapin' the local bookies with his expertise at pickin' the over and under.

It went on and on. Typically, he would conclude these drunken seminars with horrible denunciations of the black race. My old man was a master of deflecting his own guilt onto anyone other than himself. The blacks were his favorite dumping ground. He would blame them for everything. He'd make all these demented assertions about how Hitler was stopped too early because once he ditched all the Jews, he was gonna wipe out the niggers. Fine fodder for festerin' ten-year-old minds. We preferred hearin' about large breasts and the woes of Denny McLain.

Despite the racial garbage, my friends all agreed that my old man's beer blather beat the shit out of listenin' to their fathers whine about what was on television and how the lawn needed trimmin'. Their fathers were as robotic in their home life as they were about their factory jobs. It was as if the shop had hollowed them out and replaced their intestines with circuit breakers. Car, tailpipe. Food, pork chop. Car, brake pad. Rent, Friday. Car, hubcap. Life, toothpaste.

Mike Gellately's father was a good example. Almost every evening after dinner I headed over to Mike's house. He would greet me at the side door and we'd trail through the kitchen on our way up to his bedroom.

Without fail, Mr. Gellately would be propped at the kitchen table—a six-pack of Blue Ribbon at his right elbow, an overloaded ashtray at his left. He would be staring straight ahead at the kitchen sink and his faithful radio would be stationed in front of him, forever tuned in to the Detroit Tigers or Red Wings. Sip, puff, belch. Occasionally, he would startle the homestead my muttering a random "shit" or "fuck." That would be the extent of his nightly vocabulary.

Neither Mike nor I understood the first thing about our fathers. They were like the living dead. Their patterns differed—Mike's old man held a job most of the time, my old man was on some kind of less-paying treadmill—but their ruts were terribly predictable. We grew to hate our fathers.

By the time I approached teenhood, I no longer wanted to be an ambulance driver. I didn't know what the hell I wanted to be. Mike always suggested that we become disc jockeys. I never argued. A disc jockey would certainly lead a glamorous life. Anything had to be better than the cadaver shuffle the factories were peddlin' our fathers.

Even the neighborhood we lived in was a by-product of General Motors. During the boom years of the twenties, houses had to be constructed in order to keep up with the influx of factory workers arriving from the South to find jobs. General Motors built their own little suburb on the north side of Flint. In keeping with their repetitive nature, all the houses were duplicates.

Our neighborhood was strictly blue-collar and predominantly Catholic. The men lumbered back and forth to the factories while their wives raised large families, packed lunch buckets and marched the kids off to the nuns.

My family was no exception. From the very beginning, I was raised a good Catholic boy. Catholic church, Catholic school, Catholic home, Catholic drone. I was baptized, confirmed, anointed and tattooed with ashes all in the hope that one day I might have a spot reserved for me on that glorious flotilla up to the heavens.

No matter how tight the budget was at home, my mother always managed to scrape up the necessary funds to provide for our Catholic education. It was never intended that I grow up to be anything other than a good Catholic man—a steady churchgoer with a steady factory income, a station wagon parked under the elms and a wife with an automatic door on her womb.

St. Luke's Elementary provided a very capable boot camp
environment for those who would later deposit themselves in
the rigid bustle of factory life. The education-through-intimida-
tion technique favored there was not unlike the jarhead gang
mentality of the General Motors floorlords. Our fathers' overseers were brutes with clipboards, sideburns and tangled rhetoric. Our overseers, the sisters of St. Luke's, were brutes with
clipboards, sideburns and tangled rosaries.

A pattern was developing. During the seventh and eighth
grades at St. Luke's, the nuns divided the students into groups
according to intelligence and behavior. There were three groups:
the obedient eggheads, the bland robots of mediocrity and, my
group, the who-gives-a-shit-hey-have-you-heard-the-new-Cream-
album-yet-yup-my-daddy's-a-stinkin'-shoprat-too clan.

Being a proud underachiever of the latter grouping, I was
relieved of much of the pressure to succeed in life and was left
with my drowsy peers to clog up the classroom while we
awaited our almost certain fate as future factory nimwits. Not
much was expected of us and we went out of our way to ensure
that was how it would remain. Consequently, the nuns cut us a
great deal of slack figuring that for every Einstein and Aristot-
le flipped out of the cookie cutter there had to be a couple
mental dwarves available to assemble a life's procession of
Buicks and Impalas for those on the road to high places.

Of course this method of reasoning didn't exactly jibe with
our parents' outlook on destiny. At report card time, our folks
would raise all kinds of hell while cringing over our grades. I
suppose it only makes sense that every mom and pop wants
more for their tuition dollar than a series of lazy failures
guaranteed to pave the lane right into the turd dump of the
assembly line. You could achieve that predestination at any
public school and save the family till a lootful.

My folks were no exception. My mother would gaze at my
report card and the color would leave her face. It was like a
slap to the head—a horrible betrayal on my part considering
the long hours of work she had put in to assure her son a fine
Catholic education.

"An E in Math, a D in History and Science, a D– IN
RELIGION?" my mother would howl. "How could any child

who attends mass SIX days a week possibly do so poorly in Religion?"

I would make a pathetic attempt to switch to the highlights. "Look, Mom, I did raise my Self-Conduct mark from a D to a C–. And I did receive passing grades in Music and Gym."

"Music and Gym? MUSIC AND GYM! Just what is that supposed to tell me? That you have a secure future singing the national anthem at basketball games? Just wait until your father takes a look at this mess."

I could wait. If there was one thing I detested, it was my old man preachin' to me about my shortcomings as a model Catholic youth. It was such a bad joke. What the hell qualified him to criticize anything I did? I felt that he should reserve his critiques for matters that more closely coincided with his niche in life. Education? Shit. He should have stuck to advising me on the proper methods of wife cheating and check forging and navigating a car with triple vision. And what about the studied art of smoking an entire Winston without ever removing it from your mouth or the precious knack of impersonating a morgue stiff for forty-eight consecutive hours on the living room sofa. This was the kind of heavy data no nun could ever pass along.

I was my father's seed. Technically, I guess that was reason enough for him to meddle with my grade situation.

"You think you're hot shit, don't you, son?" my father would begin. I would shrug nervously. "You think you've got a pretty soft thing going for yourself. Am I right?" I would shake my head slowly.

"Well, the way I see it, you ain't nothin' but a bad actor. You may be snowin' your mother, but I can smell your game a mile away. You wanna play wiseass with me and I'll knock you down a few pegs. Anytime you feel like you can take the old man, I'll be right here. Anytime you wanna wear the pants in the family, you just let me know. I'll be more than willing to put my foot right up your ass. Understand, son?"

"Yes," I would mumble enraged and full of regrets. If only I were eight inches taller and had a reckless set of balls. I could envision myself springing from the interrogation seat and suckerpunching my old man right in the chops. "Here, sweet father of mine, take this busted lip as a loving token of my esteemed adulation and let this punt to the rib cage serve as a loving reminder that your eldest son worships the ground you piss on."

But back to reality or, at least, my father's version of such. "Now, son, you must realize that your mother and I have worked very hard to see that you receive some proper schooling. All this report card tells me is that you don't give a good goddamn one way or the other. You keep this shit up and you'll be just like half the other morons in this city who end up spinnin' their wheels and suckin' some heavy ass down at Chevrolet or over at Buick. You can clown it up now, but you'll be laughin' out of the other side of your mouth once the blisters appear and some bastard starts leanin' over your shoulder with another bumper to fasten down."

I heard this speech often during my formative years. I came to refer to it as my old man's "State of the Hometown" address. Do as I say, not as I did, kid. My friends received similar pronouncements from their fathers. The factories weren't looking for a few good men. They were dragging the lagoon for optionless bumpkins with brats to feed and livers to bathe. An educated man might hang on for a while, but was apt to flee at any given whistle. That wasn't any good for corporate continuity. GM wanted the salt of the earth, dung-heavers, flunkies and leeches—men who would grunt the day away void of self-betterment, numbed-out cyborgs willing to swap cerebellum loaf for patio furniture, a second jalopy and a tragic carpet ride deboarding curbside in front of some pseudo-Tudor dollhouse on the outskirts of town.

Which is to say that being a factory worker in Flint, Michigan, wasn't something purposely passed on from generation to generation. To grow up believing that you were brought into this world to follow in your daddy's footsteps, just another chip-off-the-old-shoprat, was to engage in the lowest possible form of negativism. Working the line for GM was something fathers did so that their offspring wouldn't have to.

In the case of my ancestry, we had been blessed with this ongoing cycle of martyrs. Men who toiled tirelessly in an effort to provide their sons and daughters with a better way of living. Unfortunately, at the same time, our family was also cursed by a steady flow of uninspired descendants who scoffed at alternative opportunity and merely hung around waitin' for the baton to be passed from crab claw to puppy paw.

By deftly flunking my way through St. Luke's Junior High, I was already exhibiting symptoms of one who was pointing squarely to the loading dock of the nearest General Motors outpost. Even my father was accurate with his diagnosis. Another Hamper banging at the gate of idiot industry with a ten-foot scowl and a forehead fresh for stampin'. I could practically hear my great-grandfather yelpin' from his crypt: "Not another one! Hey, don't any of you pricks wanna become lawyers or somethin'? Huh? HUH?" Silent decades drifted by choking on indecision. "Well, piss on ya, I'm going back to sleep. Car, windshield. Car, fuel pump. Car, ignition switch. Car, zzzzzz..."

•••••2•••••

FLINT, MICHIGAN. THE VEHICLE CITY. GREASEBALL MECCA. The birthplace of thud-rockers Grand Funk Railroad, game show geek Bob Eubanks and a hobby shop called General Motors. A town where every infant twirls a set of channel locks in place of a rattle. A town whose collective bowling average is four times higher than the IQ of its inhabitants. A town that genuflects in front of used-car lots and scratches its butt with the jagged peaks of the automotive sales chart. A town where having a car up on blocks anywhere on your property bestows upon you a privileged sense of royalty. Beer Belly Valhalla. Cog Butcher of the world. Gravy on your french fries.

Flint, Michigan. Detroit as seen backwards through a telescope. The callus on the palm of the state shaped like a welder's mitt. A town where 66.5 percent of the working citizenship are in some way, shape or form linked to the shit-encrusted underbelly of a French buggy racer named Chevrolet and a floppy-eared Scotchman named Buick. A town where 23.5 percent of the population pimp everything from Elvis on velvet to horse tranquilizers to Halo Burgers to NRA bumper stickers. A town where the remaining 10 percent sit

back and watch it all go by—sellin' their blood, rollin' convenience stores, puffin' no-brand cigarettes while cursin' their
wives and kids and neighbors and the flies sneakin' through the
screens and the piss-warm quarts of Red White & Blue and the
Skylark parked out back with the busted tranny.

"Just like half the other morons..." my old man had
warned. He was certainly more wise than most of my friends'
fathers. They questioned nothing. They accepted their birthrights and strode sheep-like into the vast head-fuck of the
factories. My old man was at least honest with himself. He
realized a ball vise when he saw one. It didn't matter that he
was a five-star drunk with the cumulative ambition of an
eggplant. The old man held on to a chunk of his soul, concealing
it from the fangs of lamebrain labor, accomplishing a small
piece of everything while doing absolutely nothing. In Flint,
Michigan, that was an achievement in itself.

My old man was determined to make sure that I, Bernard
Egan Hamper III, his pipsqueak namesake, the eldest of his
five sons, wouldn't follow the feed line into General Motors.
When I was at St. Luke's, he tore at my ass relentlessly. When
it came time for high school, he often threatened to ship me off
to a military academy. My mom furiously opposed this solution.
Her suggestion was that I enter the seminary. Fortunately,
both of these horrid plots were laid to ruin due to lack of
funds.

I entered St. Michael's High School with a more determined outlook on things. I was pretty sure that I didn't want
any part of General Motors and I didn't profess any great
yearning to become a world-class drunkard. Beyond that, I
knew very little. Mike and I still clung loosely to our private
visions of becoming hotshot radio personalities. We had an
ever-escalating fondness for the female breast and in order to
collect heavily on the mammo-meter we had to achieve some
kind of cool notoriety. We figured just about any radio hack
worth his beans was bound to be holdin' fort with big-busted
Donovan mamas and bra-free Beatle booty.

Spurred on by parental badgering and fueled with the
heady octane of boobs galore, I pulled off an amazing stunt my
freshman year at St. Mike's. I wound up making the honor roll!
Apparently, my leftover cronies from St. Luke's found this

development hard to grasp, for on the list saluting the honor students that hung on the bulletin board in the school lobby someone had scrawled the words "How?" and "Why?" next to my name. I didn't have a ready answer. What could I say? "I owe it all to the persistence of my drunken pa and a hormonal yen for watermelon teats?"

Before my sophomore year, they closed down St. Michael's. Shit, I thought, right when I was gatherin' a groove. The diocese decided that the small parish high schools were a thing of the past. In other words, resorting to the norms of Catholicism, they had fond a more lucrative method of bleeding coin out of the flock.

Ground was broken on the northern border of Flint and construction began on this enormous structure that would consolidate all of the area's Catholic high schools. Say good night to St. Mike, St. Matt, St. Agnes, St. John, St. Mary and to those southside swine, Holy Redeemer. What was wrong with them Redeemers, anyway? Couldn't they find a saint to lift a name from? Seein' as how they annually mopped ass on the football field, possibly St. Joseph of Namath would have been appropriate.

The braintrust at the diocese ran into the same predicament when they settled on the name for the new high school we were all about to attend. They called it Luke Powers High. Hmmm, Luke Powers. I must have skipped right past that guy during Bible Study. Surely, there had to be more saints out there without earthly monuments celebrating their good deeds. Luke Powers? It sounded like a cowpoke from an old episode of *The Big Valley* or the name of some pockmarked pump jockey down at the corner Sunoco.

During the tenth grade of Powers, I was able to bluff my way onto the honor roll once more. It wasn't so much attributable to any sense of goal-setting on my part, I just had nothing else to do but hit the books as I baby-sat my younger brothers and sisters night in and night out. My mother was now working the second shift at McLaren Hospital. My father was quickly becoming an endangered species at home. That left me in charge of six kids to cook for, delegate chores for, clean crappy diapers for, officiate rumbles for and to safely stow in bed and bunk. When all grew peaceful, I would flip open the books.

Powers was significantly different from the small parish schools I had attended at St. Luke's and St. Mike's. My classmates weren't middle-class kids. These were not the sons and daughters of the assembly line. Most of the new blood at Powers hailed from wealthy families. Some of them weren't even Catholic. Their parents just deposited them here as a means of avoiding the turbulence of schoolin' down with white trash and blackies and hoodlums and druggies and things that go bump near the water fountain. None of them possessed any shoprat heritage nor were any likely to spend a lifetime affixing trunk lids to the ass ends of Buicks.

Things were definitely on the upswing my sophomore year at Powers. My honor roll status delighted my mother and seemed to soothe my father's doubts regarding my factory-bent tendencies. I was even beginning to think I might defy my shoprat heritage after all. I became interested in poetry and spent long hours up in my bedroom concocting silly little love poems that combined all the worst elements of Rod McKuen and my hippie mentor, Richard Brautigan. I actually penned my own large collection of poems called "Intestines of a Balloon." Ouch.

I did discover that the poetry, as awkward and schmaltzy as it was, drew great favor from the girls of my sophomore class. Suddenly I was no longer just another wiseacre with a pesky libido and murky future. My lovelorn poetics won them over. I grabbed an honorable mention for one of my poems in a contest that ran in the *Detroit News*. Presto, I was like some hippie-dippie Alan Alda twangin' heartstrings in the sap-happy Love Generation. Someone to be trusted. An alternative to the sex-starved jockos and wily potheads and the piranha greasers in their clunky Dingo boots. Everyone had an angle and since I didn't have any money or any terrific athletic prowess and I didn't dance very well, I relied on the muse of the poet to garner whatever female appreciation I could drum up.

We had an English teacher named Miss Kane who took a particular shine to my budding enshrinement as the poet laureate of Powers High. She often mimeographed my poems and passed them around her Creative Writing class. She'd read some of my poems in front of the class and the girls all smiled brightly in my direction. I smiled back, thankful for their innocence and terrible judgment of talent. Meanwhile, the guys all slouched down in their desks, half pissed that they hadn't stumbled onto such an ingenious scam.

By my junior year in high school, strange new vices had risen from out of the murk to pull me under. I exchanged my textbooks for Mothers of Invention albums. I grew my hair down to my ass and attended classes on an infrequent basis. I exchanged my loner personage to join up with a small band of brooding hooligans. I spent most of my time swallowing or inhaling every type of illegal substance they would pass me. Needless to say, my two-year run on the honor roll dissolved in one glorious heap of incompletes and lazy failures.

I was feeling more and more pressure trying to hold the family together while my mother worked. The occasional run-ins with my old man were tense. He'd rip into my ass about the length of my hair, my hoodlum pals, my grades, my wardrobe, anything he could find. I would stand there in silent rage. All I could really dwell on was kicking his drunken ass. My fists would ball up and then recoil.

In the end, I was just too chickenshit to try the old man. I turned to the bonds I had made with my new friends. We ate acid at every opportunity. I sat in the back of the classroom throughout my junior year stoned to the gills on orange barrel mescaline or windowpane acid. Sometimes I laughed so hard at the proceedings taking place around me that the teacher would ask me if I had a problem. Outside of the fact that I hardly knew my name and everything around me had this incredible purple glow, there was no problem at all. Acid replaced lots of things. Most importantly, it took down reality.

By the time my senior year rolled around, things were beginning to get jumbled. My father had mysteriously slid away one autumn night and the only information any of us had was that he was shacking up with some bar floozie somewhere in southern Florida. He'd taken off without so much as an adios or a fresh change of skivvies. This desertion again thrust me into the role of surrogate dad while my mother toiled long hours on the hospital night shift.

My devotion to school matters became a complete joke. I

rarely attended class, preferring to hang out at a friend's
dreary apartment with a bunch of fellow lunks who were most
certainly headed for jail, the morgue or. General Motors. Our
scholastic majors ranged from chemical abuse to hashish ped-
dling. My long-standing reign as love poem ambassador dissolved into a mire of radical blatherings. Quaaludes became the
new curse on campus and I gobbled my fair share, often falling
asleep in various stairwells and auditorium catwalks.

Having arrived this far on the academic route, it was time
for all students to start funneling a vision career-wise. They
had guidance counselors who summoned you into their offices
attempting to find what kind of mold fit you best. Doctor?
Attorney? Accountant? Shoprat? No, no, no—they never
mentioned shoprat. Nor did they mention serial killer, pimp,
poet, ambulance driver or disc jockey.

I went to the guidance counselor's office and stared at the
floor. He rummaged through a thick file cabinet bursting with
worthless, lunatic occupational data while I sat there and
daydreamed about Darlene Ranzik's breasts. The lime green
halter was the best. You got a good sideview of the complete
works. They were as round as cantaloupes and easily twice the
size. Some lucky fucker was gonna tie his nuts around a
wedding band and be nursin' on those miracles for the rest of
his life. It wouldn't be me. I didn't have a game plan in order.

The guidance counselor pulled file after file. Time dragged
on and on and I sensed that he was growing increasingly edgy
with my indifference to latching on to a viable vocational goal. I
felt sorta sorry for him. There just wasn't anything in there for
me. This seemed to upset him far more than it did me.

I began writing love poems again. For the first time, I had
a specific reason why. Her name was Joanie, a hippie maiden
with beautiful red hair. We had attended Catholic school together ever since St. Luke's though we had never really
spoken. We were attracted to each other, but shy. The arrival
of drugs seemed to knock that barrier down. Before long, we
were inseparable—skipping classes, making love in my station
wagon, dropping LSD at football games, trompin' off to every
rotten rock 'n' roll concert within the Saginaw valley.

I enjoyed spending time at Joanie's house. It was like a
replica of what I wished mine could be. Her father was a

wonderful man—always fair, always friendly, always available. Not an easy trick considering Joanie's folks had eleven kids. You would think *her* father would be the ragin' alcoholic nomad. Not so. They all got along just fine and it seemed I would concoct any excuse just to visit there.

By the middle of my senior year things at home were at least beginning to settle into a tolerable routine. With the old man gone there were no more early morning tantrums. No more stolen paperboy loot. No more idiot IOU's wadded up in sock drawers where our allowance money used to hide. No more intimidation and lies and confusion and guilt and surrenders to snockered lunacy. Joanie would come by and together we would cook dinner for the troop. We'd play with my brothers and sisters and once they were put in bed, we'd lie down and make love in the middle of the living room floor. It all seemed to be healing over. Even my stinkin' love poems were improving vastly.

Nothing lasts forever. One Friday night in March, while we were all huddled around wrestling and watching *The Brady Bunch*, my old man reappeared. He had been AWOL for a total of six months. And, as always, he acted like he had merely stepped out to buy a loaf of bread or get a haircut. He was wearing this ugly Hawaiian shirt and reeked of alcohol. "Hi, son," he said. I didn't respond. Within ten minutes, he was snorin' like a bulldozer on the sofa.

The old man was back and as full of shit as ever. The flooze down in Florida had tired of his mooching and sent him packing northward. Everything returned to its horrible norm. What little faith I had in anything soon evaporated. I retreated deep into my own little universe of chemicals and inhalants. The higher I got, the less it hurt. This arrangement didn't preclude me from making a major ass out of myself on a regular basis.

There was the time I flipped out in Journalism class. My job was to provide headlines for all the articles that went into the school newspaper. My fellow classmates started clamoring around me for witty scrawls to peg above their precious columns. I was totally gone. I politely told everyone to fuck off and ran outside to my car. I started it up, drove ten feet and hopped back out. It felt as though I was driving on the rims. I circled the car several times, kicking each tire. They appeared just fine. I got back in the car and goosed it. Unfortunately, during my little stoned escapade to check the tires out, I hadn't noticed that the entire Powers High marching band had paraded out to the parking lot. Some kid with a tuba went rollin' across my hood. The band instructor started screaming. I sped away shivering badly and breathin' funny.

Then there was the time I got caught rolling a mammoth joint on a desk in the school library. Miss Kane, the same teacher who thought so highly of my weepy poems, marched me right to the principal's office. The evidence was presented, a small confab was held and I was immediately expelled. My mother came up to the school to plead for my reinstatement. The principal refused. It killed me to see my mother reduced to begging. I got the principal off to the side and started talking deal. I told him if he would allow me back in school, I would become his own private narc. The idea caught his fancy. Of course what he didn't know was that I was lyin' through my teeth. We shook hands and I was reinstated. As the months went by, I became a very unpopular guy with the principal. Each time he shook me down for information, I turned dumber than a tree stump. He'd been scammed. I rolled my joints in the john from then on.

By graduation time, my old man had once again taken flight to Florida to shack up with who-knows-who. Good riddance, the family concurred. My mother finally had had her fill of the bastard and started divorce proceedings. It was only after the old man had left that my mother discovered she was going to be giving birth to the eighth addition to our clan. A child that my father would never return to see.

There must have been something in the frosty Michigan air that winter that fueled the reproduction cycle. The Catholic-as-rabbit theory was suddenly twirling amuck. Joanie called me over to her place one evening to inform me that she too was bloomin' with child. Joanie's due date was only a couple of weeks from my mother's.

Since Joanie already had accumulated enough credits to graduate, the school let her have her diploma early. She was just beginning to show and there was no way in hell they were gonna allow her to waltz the hallways in her preggy state. The nuns would have spewed pea soup and banged to their knees.

Joanie stayed home while I finished up my senior year. One day I was summoned to the counselor's office. Terrific, I thought, maybe the guy had found a job for me in that fat file cabinet of his. With a baby due, I had a feeling I might need one.

This was not the case. The counselor instructed me to have a seat and as I sat down I could gather that the news was not good. He told me that he had been poring over my transcript and found that I was several credits short of the required number necessary to graduate. All those days skipping class and chucking textbooks had finally caught up to me. The counselor said he would have to see what would need to be done and talk it over with the principal. He said he would let me know in a couple of days.

The counselor never did call me back to his office. All I can assume is that when my name was mentioned, the principal must have told him to rig the paperwork so everything fell into place. He had seen enough of my act. There was no way he was going to flunk me and have me back for another fun-filled year. Here's your fuckin' diploma, get scarce and may the Lord be with you always!

After graduation, I hurriedly planned for the unknown. First up came marriage. Since we'd both been reared as God-fearin' Catholics, the inevitable solution to this teen pregnancy mishap was immediate matrimony. Abortion and adoption were sordid eight-letter words that existed only in made-for-TV movies starring Kay Lenz or Susan Dey. We tied the knot at Sacred Heart Church. My best man was some guy we found cleanin' the pews.

My uncle got me a job painting apartments for a large rental complex. After our marriage, Joanie and I moved into one of the apartments. In August, Joanie had our child, a beautiful little girl with bright red hair we named Sonya. We were poor but happy in our sudden little universe. Back at home, my brother Bob filled my role as teen nanny. Bob was much stronger than I. It worked well.

I enjoyed painting apartments. There were no human beings to contend with and everyone at the complex just left me alone. The closest thing I had to a boss was this senile old man who was the maintenance manager. Once upon a time, he

had been a big-league attorney for Ford Motors. Then he had a
nervous breakdown and began plowing the bottle. His son-in-
law owned the company and the old·man I were just another
pair of his uninspired lackeys.

After months of practice, I got a routine down to where I
could blaze my way through a unit in the morning, be finished
by lunch and spend the rest of the afternoon reading paperbacks and listening to the oldies station on my latex-splattered
transistor radio. I could have easily painted two units per day
but, with the way these pricks were payin' me, I felt it only
justified to give them the lowest accountable output for their
lousy three bucks an hour. Besides, where several of the other
maintenance workers were receiving their apartments rent-
free, I was being charged the full shot just like any other
tenant. What it boiled down to was that I would have to turn
over half of my earnings right back to the company just to keep
a roof over my family's head. They weren't gettin' anything
extra out of me.

I met another guy who worked at the apartments who was
in the identical situation I was. His name was Glen and he was
also newly married with a new baby and was living it dime-to-
dime like Joanie and I were. They lived in the apartment
building next to ours and we all became accomplished at
dodging the rut of constant poverty.

Glen and I received our paychecks on Mondays and we'd
skim seven or eight bucks off the top of our measly pay and buy
a week's worth of this piss-water beer called Columbia. The
local grocer sold this crap for a dollar a six-pack, a real bargain
for fun-starved minimum wagers like Glen and myself. Almost
every night we held court at Glen and Barb's, swigging down
this awful-tastin' beer while Barb cued up scratchy Abba singles and wonderful Lou Christie albums salvaged from the junk
bins of the nearby Goodwill. We laughed and danced and got
very intoxicated.

After the wives dropped off, Glen and I stayed up late
talking. He was hell-bent on landing a job at General Motors
and stressed all the benefits of working for the hometown
team. I sucked on my lousy Columbia and shook my head.

"Have you ever noticed the looks on the faces of those

bastards when they get home from work?" I asked Glen. "Fuck the money, I don't need that monster gaze."

"Well, what the hell are you gonna do when you grow up?" Glen laughed.

"I don't know," I said. And I truly didn't.

"And you ride me for wantin' to get into the shop! Shit, you need another beer."

It was out of our hands anyway. There was a recession going on and the gates to Greaseball Mecca were temporarily padlocked. Job seekers were forced to follow the detour signs to McDonald's or Arby's or Maplebrook Village Apartments, at least until the Arabs let go of our balls and the market began to chug again.

I, for one, could wait.

3

MY MARRIAGE TO JOANIE WAS QUICKLY BEGINNING TO CRUMBLE.
Between my nightly beer-bombing over at Glen's and our
continual teetering on the brink of poverty, my young bride
was getting fed up to her eyebrows with life in the comatose
lane. We were just two confused kids playing house, flailing at
each other with every blunt collision that sudden adulthood
generated. High school sweethearts can make for strange bed
partners once the reality of the rent and the groceries and the
car payments descend on the dollhouse.

As my father-in-law saw it, there was only one antidote to
our marital woes: finding me gainful employment. He kept
suggesting that I pursue a career at General Motors. We
happened to live right in the shadows of the Chevrolet Manu-
facturing plant, the Chevy Engine plant and the enormous GM
Truck & Bus facility. How convenient, he often pointed out. I
paid my father-in-law nothing but lip service. I told him the
shops weren't hiring. I insisted that there were other things on
some invisible horizon awaiting my induction. I spouted and
sputtered brave ignorant lies about how a young man should
pause and blossom into clever vocations that would surely lie in

wait once the haze receded and the clear adult mind began to function.

I was full of shit. I would say anything to turn the subject around from the inevitable. The inevitable being this: I knew in the tenth grade that I would be a shoprat. It was more an understanding of certain truisms found in my hometown than any form of game plan I might have been hatching. In Flint, Michigan, you either balled up your fists and got career motivated the moment the piano quit bangin' the commencement theme or, more likely, you'd still be left leanin' when the ancestors arrived to pass along your birthright. Here, kid, fetch.

There were times I was actually drawn to the shops. Occasionally, I would get drunk and park next to one of the factories just in time to watch the fools pile out at quitting time. I hated the looks on their faces. Miserable cretins, one and all. I would sit there with a can of beer in my lap and try to focus on one alternative career goal. There weren't any. All I ever came back to was the inevitable admission that I didn't really want to do *anything*. And around these parts, in the fat choke hold of Papa GM, that was just chickenshit slang for asking "What time does the line start up on Monday?"

I quit my job at the apartment complex. I decided to go into freelance painting, a job where I could at least name my own hours. After eight or nine months of near starvation, I ditched this stupid stratagem. I was no hustler. I needed someone to tell me what to do. Meanwhile, the recession dragged on.

I caught on with a guy who ran a janitorial service. We worked at night cleaning up business colleges, drugstores and attorneys' offices. I wiped down toilets for the minimum wage. The boss was always hollering at me for missing some wayward pee stain or leaving streaks on some lonesome stretch of linoleum. No wonder I soon gave up this promising career and took to sitting around the apartment drinking beer, playing with my daughter and waiting for my wife to come home from work at her father's bridal store.

The marriage had all but disintegrated by then. Joanie worked and I drank. We rarely even spoke to each other. There wasn't anything to say. She was the breadwinner and I was the louse. The parallel between my behavior and my old man's was something that didn't escape me. Just the thought of it made me want to drive our dilapidated Mustang head-center into the nearest bridge abutment.

Joanie finally kicked me out of our marriage and took custody of our daughter. My life was so screwed-up by then that the idea of working for GM not only lost its repugnance, it took on the frantic allure of a rope tossed to a quicksand victim. I not only surrendered to the inevitable, I began begging for it. General Motors was the only possible panacea to the erosion of my marriage and my own personal bout with suicidal mind fatigue.

It was birthright time, goddamnit. Though the recession was still hovering over the city, I didn't let it detour me. I began getting up at 5:00 A.M. and hustling over to the factories. Right on the entrance gate to the personnel office was a sign that read NO APPLICATIONS. Undaunted, I would stride forward. Don't play games with me, GM. My name is Hamper. Surely you remember that loyal, long-suffering clan. Just show me to my setup and everything will be fine.

The personnel people didn't see it that way. They asked if I had noticed the sign. I said I had. Then they asked if I could read. I said yes. Then they asked me to vacate the plant grounds immediately. It wasn't the type of red carpet treatment I felt entitled to, being the son-of-a-son-of-a-son-of-a-shoprat. So much for ancestral privilege.

My father-in-law started passing me these tips on what office to go to and whose name to mention. He must have been gettin' some bogus info because every time I followed his instructions I received nothing more than blank bewilderment.

I was also following up tips from an old German lady I had done some painting for. She had worked for GM for thirty-some years. She claimed to know everybody. In the end, her information was no better than my father-in-law's. I struck out repeatedly, becoming more embarrassed with every desperate rejection.

The so-called tips dried up. It was just as well. I was beginning to feel ridiculous haunting personnel offices on every goofball's whim. It had gotten to the point that when the white-collars saw me grabbing the door handle to the Personnel office, they would all line up abreast and start shakin' their heads emphatically as if they had infective lice digging at their scalps. *No applications.* Zero. Void. Confute, rebut, deny.

Months went by. Joanie and I separated. I moved into my mother's basement where I slept all day and caroused all night on the biweekly unemployment funds I had earned after my stint as the inept janitor. I still clung to the belief that the marriage could be salvaged if I could only hitch up with the screw train and bring home some of that sweet GM loot. Screw my old man and his forewarnings. Screw the nuns and their lesson plans. Screw the guidance counselor's bulging file cabinet. Screw the ambulance drivers and disc jockeys and midnight janitors. Screw me and screw you. I wanted to be a shoprat, true and blue.

The recession of the mid-seventies began to lift. Car sales were beginning to rise. Truck sales were booming. Relatives were once again able to start funneling those sacred applications out the door to their street-walkin' kin. My good friend Denny got one off a cousin. My buddy Mike picked one up from his father. Half of the idiots I hung out with in high school were layin' claim to General Motors work applications. I was glad for them. Still, I wondered when, if ever, my precious birthright would be forked my way.

Finally, my father-in-law came through. Some distant aunt on my wife's side of the family worked as a nurse in the Truck Plant hospital. I was sent over to her house to fetch the elusive ap. There it was on the dining room table—the paperwork drivel at the end of the rainbow. I jotted all the shit down, fibbing on the section that asked had I ever taken drugs, handed it back to Aunt Nurse and skipped out the door like a man who had just wormed his neck from the noose. Maybe there would be another noose with my name on it on the other side of this application, but I didn't care at all. Suddenly, the sky was full of dollar bills and pay stubs the size of blimps.

Denny got called in for his physical. Paydirt! GM only scheduled you for a physical when they intended to put you right to work. He called me up and we talked about the rapture of capitalism—the bankrolls, the new cars, the best booze, the choicest drugs, new stereos and new digs. This was in April, two months after his application had been filed. Figuring that two months was the standard waiting period, I assumed that I would be getting my phone call any day.

Nope. While Denny was already completing his ninety days service in the Truck Plant (the minimum amount of service required to secure your job at GM), I was still sweating it out in my mom's basement, jumping every time the phone rang. What the hell was it that was making them stall?

Just to make sure that my application hadn't been incinerated or used for butt-wad, I called the Personnel office every Monday morning. The voice on the other end always put me on hold for a lengthy period and then returned to tell me that my application was still treading ink in their paper lagoon. I hadn't even worked a day yet for General Motors and already I didn't trust these shills.

I wasn't home the day they finally did call. It was a Saturday afternoon and I was planted on a barstool up at Jack Gilbert's Wayside Inn. I didn't expect to get called in on a weekend, so I left the house with no instructions to where anyone could reach me. My little brother, a real wiseacre, told them that I could be reached at any number of North Flint area bars. I'm sure this tickled them pink.

Fortunately, I had given GM my in-laws' number as a backup and my sister-in-law came racing into the Wayside where I was in the process of getting shit-faced with her boyfriend Rick.

"Ben. BEN! GM just called you! They want you to come to work."

"Shit," I hollered, "it's about time those bastards rang me. On a weekend, no less. That gives me and the old Ricker here time to do some much-deserved celebrating. Did they mention what time they need me on Monday?"

"No, no, no! They want you to work TODAY! They said to be there at four and to wear some work boots if possible."

"TODAY? Saturday? It is Saturday, isn't it? Four o'clock? WORK BOOTS?"

"Four o'clock," my sister-in-law repeated. "Work boots if possible."

This was some heavy shit. To be called in during the middle of the weekend smelled like an emergency. GM was now in the midst of one of their all-time boom-boom quota years, so

I supposed reinforcements were needed on Saturdays, Sundays, Salad days—any time was the right time. This also marked the first time I ever remembered being asked out on a Saturday night by a corporation.

"I better move out," I told Rick. "Mustn't keep Papa Jimmy waitin'."

"Wear something sexy, ratboy," Rick laughed. "And don't forget to write."

I hustled home. I didn't have any work boots, so I just threw on a pair of old Converse hightops along with a T-shirt and a pair of filthy jeans. My head was reciting all the advice my distant aunt had filled me with: Keep you guard out for troublemakers. Don't be coerced into drinking. Be on time. Do everything you're told, try to do extra, don't engage in horseplay, address your supervisor as "sir." Check, check, check.

Before we were to begin working, the group I was hiring in with was instructed to meet for a physical examination in the plant hospital. We were a sluggish-looking crew. There were about twenty of us all together—each person chainsmoking and staring at the floor, waiting in silence to be pronounced fit for active drudgery. We resembled some awkward casting call for the next Maynard G. Krebs. I had a strong hunch that there wasn't a marketable skill among us.

A doctor came out and directed us into a single-file line. The urine test was up first. We were each handed a small vial and told to line up for the restroom.

The guy standing in front of me kept looking over his shoulder at me. When it was his turn to enter the can, he spun around and asked if it would be all right if I donated a little of my urine for his vial. He seemed to be very stressed. This was long before drug testing was ever common in the workplace. I wondered what the big deal was.

"I just can't get it to flow right now," the guy claimed. Apparently, the fear was that the Company might look down upon any prospective serf who was incapable of bringing forth the pee when it mattered most. No piss, no job, ingrate!

I didn't care much for the idea of passing around my piss with a total stranger. It didn't seem like a solid career move. Besides, for all either of us knew, I might be holding on to a bad batch. I had a long, painful bout with hepatitis when I was twelve. My formative years were spent wolfing down a wide variety of menacing chemicals. I drank like a sieve. I had an ulcer that ate at me like a cordless drill. Hell, who'd wanna take a crapshoot on the chance that any of that might come floating to the surface of their corporate dossier?

Evidently, this guy. He returned from the john and, true to his work, the vial he held before me was completely empty. "C'mon," he said. "Just a squirt. I'll *pay* you for it."

Christ, that did it. "Gimme the thing," I groaned. It probably wasn't the most noble act of giving one had ever made on behalf of a needy Union brother but, somehow, it sure seemed like it at the time.

We were almost through with our urine samples when a member of our group, a late arrival, walked into the hospital and began to speak with our overseer. I sensed that the guy was in deep shit. He kept apologizing over and over—something to do with getting messed up in traffic and being detained. Judging by his performance, I doubted he was lying.

It didn't matter. The man with the clipboard wasn't buying a single word. He stood there shaking his head from one side to the other—just another weasel in a short-sleeve shirt, deputized to protect the status quo. He did his job well.

"You were told to be prompt," he spouted. "There can be NO EXCEPTIONS."

The realization that he'd blown his big audition seemed to overwhelm the late guy. He looked down at the floor, his voice started breaking and, right there in front of everyone, he began to cry. It all came spillin' out—what was he gonna tell his family and who would understand? For the sons and daughters of the assembly line, 1977 wasn't the best of years to go fumblin' the family baton.

We stood there clutching our little vials of piss as they escorted him out. We had been on time. We were going to build trucks for the GM Truck & Bus Division. The man with the bow tie and clipboard had written down all our names. Our friend had been ten minutes late. He had already proven himself undeserving of a hitch on the screw train. There could be no exceptions.

Ten years later, I found myself still thinking about the late guy. On those terribly humid shifts when the parts just weren't going together right and the clock was taking two steps back for every step forward, exhausted and desperate, I'd see him over by the pool table in the bar across the street. He'd have a cold beer in his hand and a grin a mile wide. I would imagine myself walking up to him with my safety glasses, my locker key and my plastic identification badge held out in my hand. "Here, it's all yours, buddy," I'd say. "I need a cold one."

Immediately, the jukebox would stop playing. Everyone in the bar would turn toward me and begin to laugh. The late guy would slip his arm around the waitress and they both would shake their heads. "You were told to be prompt," he would say. "There can be no exceptions."

I was assigned to the Cab Shop, an area more commonly known to its inhabitants as the Jungle. Lifers had told me that on a scale from one to ten—with one representing midtown Pompeii and ten being then GM Chairman Roger Smith's summer home—the Jungle rates about a minus six.

It wasn't difficult to see how they had come up with the name for the place. Ropes, wires and assorted black rubber cables drooped down and entangled everything. Sparks shot out in all directions—bouncing in the aisles, flying into the rafters and even ricocheting off the natives' heads. The noise level was deafening. It was like some hideous unrelenting tape loop of trains having sex. I realized instantly that, as far as new homes go, the Jungle left a lot to be desired. Me Tarzan, you screwed.

I had been forewarned. As our group was being dispatched at various drop points throughout the factory, the guy walking beside me mumbled about our likely destination. "Cab Shop," the prophet said. "We're headed for Cab Shop." Perplexed, I wondered if this meant we would be building taxis.

The group trudged on, leaving a few workers in each new area. We stopped by the Trim Line. The Axle Line. The Frame Line. The Tire Line. The Receding Hairline. When we arrived at the Motor Line, my friend with the bashful bladder hopped off. "Thanks," he told me. It was kind of strange. All we had in common was a small, useless vial of urine. "Have a nice career," I offered.

Soon, all but two rookies had been planted—the prophet

and me. We took a dark elevator upstairs and, when the gate opened, the prophet let out a groan. "Goddamn, I knew it! The bastard's lettin' us off in Cab Shop." I had to agree with the prophet. Our overseer did seem like a bastard. Just the way he had gleefully shot down that late guy made me hate his guts. Not only was he a bastard, he made for one lousy Johnny Appleseed. We stood at the foot of the Jungle. We were doomed. There could be no exceptions.

"Here you are, boys—the Cab Department," our overseer spoke. "In this area you are advised to wear clothing made from a nonflammable fabric. Also, you will need to purchase a pair of steel-toned work boots, available at fair cost in the shoe store next to the workers' cafeteria." He grinned. "Good luck, boys," he said and walked away.

A pudgy, slick-dressed black guy directed us down the line toward our job setups. This was Brown, our foreman. As we tagged along behind him, the workers paused to give us the razz. We were fresh blood, ignorant meat. "Turn around before it's too late," someone shouted. "Hey, Brown, let 'em hang tailgates," another chimed in. Hang tailgates? Christ, that sounded like a ball-buster.

Our foreman stopped next to a big red-haired guy and a man in a filthy welder's cap. He pointed at me and informed me that I would be replacing the guy in the welder's cap. The guy seemed elated. "It's about goddamn time you got me outta here." The guy in the welder's cap looked at me and smiled. He had very few teeth. "My name's Gary and this is Bud," he said, pointing to the big redhead. "You'll love it here, just love it." Both of them laughed.

It turned out that my fellow rookie, the prophet, would be working directly across from me. His name was Roy and he'd come to Flint from Oklahoma to live with his brother and find work in the factory. It seemed like an awfully long haul just to wind up in this dreaded Jungle. Anyway, I felt glad for his presence. Having a greenie like myself across the line could only help during this assimilation process.

For the entire shift, I was asked to do nothing but stand back and examine how Gary performed his job. I was told that I would have three days to learn the job and then it would be all mine. Always the pessimist, I asked Gary what happened if after three days were up I still didn't have a handle on the job. "Then they give you the Van Slyke shuffle." He chuckled. Van Slyke was the street the factory was located on.

"I'll have it down in a day," I told Gary. "I've seen enough of the street."

Gary and Bud worked their jobs together. They combined them so that one of them was working while the other guy sat out and read the paper or did a crossword. I figured the job couldn't be too difficult if one of them had the time to complete both jobs while the other guy lagged around doin' nothin'.

This form of combo workmanship was termed "doubling-up," a time-honored tradition throughout the shop that helped alleviate much of the boredom. Bud assured me that once I got my job down at a steady pace, he would teach me his job and we could survive much easier with a double-up arrangement. I nodded hesitantly, wanting only to conquer one detail at a time.

At the end of my first shift, I walked out of the lot with Roy. His martyr's grumble about bein' stashed in the Cab Shop had quickly vanished.

"Fuckin' A, Ben, do you realize we just grossed about $100 for standin' around doin' absolutely nothin'?"

"A $100 gross?" I repeated.

"Sure, this is Saturday. Saturday means time and a half. You can also include our night shift premium. A hundred dollar gross for watchin' a bunch of dipshits tinkerin' around!"

"Yeah, but don't forget starting next week you and I will be the dipshits."

"Hell, those jobs they gave us are pussy detail. Once we get settled in, we'll be sittin' on our asses half the time while bringin' home three or four bills a week. It's a highway robbery. I'm gonna go get drunk. Care to join me?"

"I'll pass this time," I told Roy. "See you Monday."

Our jobs were identical—to install splash shields, pencil rods and assorted screws with a noisy air gun in the rear ends of Chevy Blazers and Suburbans. To accomplish this, we worked on a portion of the line where the cabs rose up on an elevated track. Once the cabs were about five feet off the ground, Roy and I ducked inside the rear wheel wells and busted ass. Standing across from each other in those cramped wheel wells always reminded me of the two neighbors in the Right Guard commercial who met every morning in their communal medicine cabinet. "Hi, guy! Care for a scoop of sealer on that pencil rod?"

Within a shift and a half, I had already conquered my new job. The foreman turned Gary loose and I was on my own. After I fastened down my required parts with my air gun, Bud jumped into the wheel well with his bulky spot-welder and zapped the truck bed and wheel well together. Sparks flew out in these crazy curvatures and danced to dust. Tiny clicking explosions dash-dotted the atmosphere like some jumpy Morse code. It was sorta like Nam without the Motown soundtracks and mosquito netting.

Bud introduced me to some of the nearby natives. There was Dan-O, the resident prankster, who mig-welded the truck beddings. He constantly chewed cigars while keeping up a running racial tease with the black guy who worked next to Bud and me.

Another was a guy they all called Bob-A-Lou. He had this gleaming crew cut and a belly that hung down halfway to his knees. Bob-A-Lou worked down the line a bit and it was fairly obvious that whatever he did involved some heavy-duty welding. His T-shirt was dotted with a few thousand burn holes and his forearms were a road map of tiny pink scabs. Bob-A-Lou had a voice like Andy Devine and it was funny to hear him gripe about something. The guy never cursed. "By golly, men, it's a steamer in here today. I wish these goldarn fans would kick out a little more air." I liked Bob-A-Lou right off.

Then there was Robert, the black guy who worked next to Bud and me. He was the sullen type and I had a hunch he didn't warm up to rookies quickly. I shook his hand and he muttered something to me. "Okay," I said. Turning away, I asked Bud what the hell Robert had said. "He told you to make sure you keep the fuck out of his area. He doesn't like getting pushed into the hole." The hole? Bud explained the hole was a term used to describe falling behind. I waved at Robert. Hard work, hold the hole.

By the end of my first week on the job, Bud was already pestering me to double-up jobs with him. I was uneasy about the offer. Doubling-up with Bud meant that I would have to learn how to navigate his fire-breathing spot-welder. I had my reservations about coming within ten feet of that flaming albatross. Besides, I was quite content with my jerky little air gun. The screws and the J-clips shot right in and all you had to do was stand there and hoist the thing like some bad-ass cop pointin' his piece.

Another consideration was that I was a new hire. I worried about the foreman's reaction to seeing me sitting on my ass half of the day. They liked to refer to this place as Generous Motors, but I had my doubts whether this pet phrase extended itself to greenhorns like myself who lacked the necessary seniority to operate their own scams.

"You're worried about *Brown?*" Bud whined. "Fuck Brown. He don't give a shit what goes on around here as long as the quota's met and the general foreman isn't gnawin' his nuts."

And I suppose it was true. One night Brown was hanging around the back of our workbench, scrunched up on a palletful of #202 screws. I was convinced he was here to eyeball me for possible infractions against the rule manual. I moved swiftly from job to job all the while attempting to affix this professional square-jawed look to my face. After about fifteen minutes of this nervous setup, I whispered to Bud asking what Brown was up to.

"By the looks of it, he's giving me the once-over," I told Bud.

"Is that what you think? Listen, you've got that silly-assed job whipped. Brown doesn't even know you exist."

"Then WHAT THE HELL IS HE DOING BACK THERE?" I demanded.

"He's drinking beer," Bud said.

"DRINKING BEER? Brown? Our foreman? Where'd he get it?"

"I brought him in a six of Miller's at lunchtime. It's hidden in an empty J-clip box under our bench."

I looked over at Brown. He had a big dumb smile on his face. Every thirty seconds or so, he'd pivot his head around toward the aisle and then dive-bomb out of view behind our workbench. It was hot in the Cab Shop and I couldn't help but envy his access to a cold beer.

"And I bet there's a payoff for you, right?" I asked Bud.

"Now you're catching on. See, I have information that the

Suburban tailgate buildup job will be open in a week or so. I asked Brown about it and he told me he'd seen what he could do when the time comes. I figure some cold beer here and there might help give me a leg up when the job comes open. Brown's a fuckin' alkie."

"In other words, you're greasin' the foreman's liver."

"Something like that." Bud grinned.

Here I had been told to be on my most saintly behavior. What a lousy joke. My very own supervisor was suckin' down the brew three nights a week twelve feet behind my back. Once he'd finish, Brown untangled himself from his makeshift hooch cellar, punctuated the occasion with a large belch, gave Bud a nod and walked on down the line to check up on the rest of the department.

It was apparent, in the wake of my own supervisor's misconduct, that Bud's double-up urgings couldn't be as jeopardizing to my career as I had originally believed. If the foreman could squat around chuggin' beers during line time, most everything else would have to be tolerated. I already had enough on Brown to assure his silence.

"About time we started combining these pussy jobs," I told Bud.

"Now you're comin' around." Bud gleamed.

He showed me how to operate his spot-welder. It wasn't an easy task. First you had to yank the machine down a large pulley and position the two tips of the welder in between the truck bed and the wheel well. Once you had it situated, you dragged it over to the right corner of the wheel well and began firing the trigger. Every inch or two you smacked out a weld—ideally, twenty-four welds per truck. All the while, sparks would be sprayin' all over the place. When a job was completed, you jerked the spot-welder free, stood back and let it bounce back up the pulley.

I gave it a try. I tugged. I groped. I strained in anger. I couldn't get the damn thing to budge more than a half inch every cycle. I ended up putting about fifty-five welds in the wheel well. Someone out there was gonna have a right rear wheel well toasted to the crisp. The sparks were gobbling me. They came pouring down on my head, sizzling what was left of my sparse crop of hair. Finally, I had dragged the welder down so far out of the normal path that I was halfway into Robert's area. He stood there waiting to weld on his splash shield. He didn't look pleased at all. Just before I was convinced he was gonna jab me with the red tip of his mig-welder, Bud bailed me out.

"Relax," he said. "You're trying to outmuscle the thing. The welder will do all the work if you just hold it lightly and go for the ride. The more you fight the damn thing, the more grief it's gonna give you."

It took some doing, but within two or three days I was an accomplished spot-welder. I found out how to tilt the machine so that the sparks flew out sideways and not straight down on my head. There was something very hale and manly about husking that mean hunk of hell once you got the hang of it. It gave me a sense of complete reign—King Rat, Ball-Buster Goliath, the hysteric bombardier makin' flame-broiled waffle mince out of the rib cage of BAD TRUCK POWER. This crunchin' dinosaur was my bitch. A flame-snortin', black goose Magnum. In comparison, my air gun was strictly Hasbro. A snifflin' little insect flittin' around the buttocks of the bull.

Bud had certainly been right. Doubling-up jobs, whenever and wherever possible, made the utmost sense. This arrangement totally destroyed the monotony of waiting for that next cab to arrive. When it was my turn to handle the two jobs, I'd be so busy with my work that I wouldn't have time to agonize over the crawl of the clock. I patterned myself a brisk routine and the minute hand whirled by.

When it was Bud's turn at the grind, I would hop the line and read paperbacks next to Roy at the workers' picnic bench. It was like being paid to attend the library. Roy was extremely jealous of my sweet setup. He was locked into the old up and down and the clock was already beatin' him senseless. He nagged and nagged at Dan-O, his neighbor, to work out a similar setup. Dan-O always turned him down. He was too busy concocting practical jokes to mess with a new routine.

The more shortcuts I learned, the more Bud and I would lengthen our tours of duty. We went from doubling-up for an hour at a time to two hours. The longer the layover between times up at work, the more time we had to sprawl out and investigate methods of passing time. I read two newspapers, a magazine and a good chunk of novel every evening. Bud spent most of his time off horsing around with Dan-O or doing homework for college classes he was taking during the day.

At times, I got bored and restless sittin' on my ass in the middle of the Jungle. With my job securely covered, I occasionally set out wandering throughout the factory. I was completely overwhelmed by the size of the plant. It was the largest truck-producing facility in the entire world. I could only compare it to some huge, metallic ant farm, doomed and domed-over, a clamorous burg with a tall tin roof.

I walked for miles down the various aisleways and corridors with no idea of where I was headed or where I might end up. One night I might end up in the Tire Bay watchin' the beer bellies wobble as they hustled tire after tire off the conveyor line. The men down there were in constant motion. They looked very depressed. I could recall that look from the visit to my own father's job. Car, windshield. Truck, radial. Repetition as strangulation. Shit, how'd I get so lucky?

The next night I might end up on the Final Line checkin' out the finished product as they raced the engines and spanked life into those gleaming, overpriced Suburban and Blazer newborns. Way the hell down at the end of the Final Line you could see the sun setting. I would follow the rays and dip outside the door of this giant womb to lean against the wall and smoke cigarettes. No one knew who I was. I didn't know them either. That was part of the beauty. There were so many of us shoprats that we were all just part of some faceless herd. I could have been an inspector or a rookie or a guard or Roger Smith Jr. No one gave a shit.

As a summer progressed and the weeks slid slowly by, my pal Roy was beginning to unravel in a real rush. His enthusiasm about all the money we were makin' had dissipated and he was having major difficulty coping with the drudgery of factory labor. Unable to arrange a double-up system with Dan-O, he wallowed in the slow-motion injustice of the time clock. His job, like mine, wasn't difficult, it was just plain monotonous. We hadn't even put in our ninety days yet (the minimum amount of service required for a worker to apply for sick leave) and Roy was already fast on the track to wiggin' out.

We had been able to conquer the other annoyances. We

adjusted to the heat and grew accustomed to the noise. After a while, we even got used to the claustrophobia of the wheel wells. The idea that we were being paid handsome wages to mimic a bunch of overachieving simians suited us just dandy. We had no lofty career goals. In America, or at least in Flint, as long as the numbers on your pay stub justified your daily bread, there was nothing more to accomplish.

The one thing that was impossible to escape was the monotony of our new jobs. Every minute, every hour, every truck and every movement was a plodding replica of the one that had gone before. The monotony gnawed away at Roy. His behavior began to verge on the desperate. The only way he saw to deal with the monotony was to numb himself to it. When the lunch horn sounded, we'd race out to his pickup and Roy would pull these enormous joints from the glove box. "Take one," he'd offer. Pot made me nervous so I would stick to the beer from his well-stocked cooler or slug a little of the whiskey that was always on hand.

The numbing process seemed to demand more every night. We'd go out to the truck and Roy would burn two joints at a time. He'd snort coke whenever he could find it. "I don't know if I'm gonna make my ninety days," he'd tell me. It was all part of Roy's master plan. Once he reached his ninety days' seniority, he would round up a reliable quack, feign some mystery injury (spinal aggravations were the most popular malady) and, with all the paperwork, semiretire to an orbit of singles bars, dope dens and sick pay benefits. The old invisible Ozzie Nelson work ethic festering deep into the wounded psyches of the young.

But Roy never did make his ninety days. To those who were on hand during his last days of service, it came as no real surprise. We all realized that Roy was cracking up.

There was the classic evening Roy took a hit of some powerful acid and ended up barfin' his guts out all over the floor next to his job. Tune in, turn on and build trucks. At first, I thought Roy was actually gonna make it. There was much merriment radiating from his side of the wheel well. Everything was a hoot or a holler. It was a shame it couldn't last.

I returned from one of my aimless jaunts around the

factory and Bud pulled me aside. "What the fuck is wrong with Roy?" he asked.

"Why, is there a problem?"

"Well, for one thing, he's speakin' total gibberish. His face looks like a ghost and he's sweatin' like a butcher. I swear the dumbshit's on some crazy drug trip."

I jumped into the next wheel well and looked over at Roy. The merriment was certainly gone. He looked horrible. The goblins of psychedelic had parked their paranoia machine smack dab in the center of Roy's cranium.

For the next hour, I tried mightily to keep him together. I told him if he could just make it to the lunch horn, we'd get him out of here and settle everything with Brown. We'd concoct some story about how Roy got terribly ill and had to be raced home to bed.

We both tried our damndest—Roy forging on while I counted down the minutes. It was all in vain. Just five minutes to go before the hour, Roy let loose. The puke shot every-where. Dan-O bravely stepped in to handle Roy's job as he went tearing off for the exit. Jesus, did it reek.

Brown came down to check on the commotion. I told him that Roy had been sick right from the beginning of the shift but, not wanting to abandon his post, tried desperately to make it to the lunch break.

"That's what I call dedication," Brown declared.

At that, I could have puked myself. "I'll say," I said.

A few nights later came the infamous incident involving the sacrificial rodent. Roy had managed to capture this tiny mouse that had been sneaking around one of the stock bins. He fashioned an elaborate cardboard house for the creature and set it on his workbench. He fed the mouse. He gave it water. He built windows in the house so his pet could watch him doin' his job. Any worker who passed through the area was given a personal introduction to the mouse. For all the world, it seemed like a glorious love affair.

I never figured out whether it was due to the dope or the drudgery or some unseen domestic quarrel, but things sure switched around in a hurry after the lunch break. Roy would rush through each job, run back to his workbench, and start screaming at the mouse through the tiny cardboard windows.

When asked what the problem was, Roy insisted that the mouse was mocking the way he performed the job. He ranted and raved. He stomped and cursed. He put his arms around the mouse condo and shook it violently.

Finally it was over. Before any of us could react or shout him down, Roy grabbed the mouse by the tail and stalked up the welder's platform. He took a brazing torch, gassed up a long, blue flame and, right there in the middle of Jungleland, incinerated his little buddy at arm's length. Then he went right back to work as if nothing had happened.

Then, the day before he quit, Roy approached me with a box-cutter knife sticking out of his glove and requested that I give him a slice across the back of the hand. He felt sure this ploy would land him a few days off.

Since slicing Roy didn't seem like a solid career move, I refused. Roy went down the line to the other workers where he received a couple charitable offers to cut his throat, but no dice on the hand. He wound up sulking back to his job.

After a half dozen attempts on his own, Roy finally got himself a gash. He waited until the blood had a chance to spread out a bit and then went dashing off to see the boss. The damage was minimal. A hunk of gauze, an elastic bandage and a slow, defeated shuffle back to the wheel wells.

After that night, I never saw Roy again. Personnel sent up a young Puerto Rican guy to help me do the Right Guard commercial and the two of us put in our ninety days without much of a squawk.

The money was right, even if we weren't.

4

DURING THE SUMMER AND FALL OF 1977, THE TRUCK PLANT was hummin' six days a week, nine hours per shift. All of this overtime added up to one gorgeous stream of income. There was the time-and-a-half money. There was the second-shift premium bonus and there were frequent cost-of-living adjustments. It seemed like every time I turned around, the paymaster was stuffin' another wad of currency into my waistband.

Any dumb hireling was bound to adopt a sweet craving for this kind of repetitive generosity. I was certainly no exception. I had been poor all my life, then suddenly I couldn't turn my head without bumping into another financial windfall. I'd get up in the afternoon, start rummaging through my drawer for a fresh set of skivvies, and there would be a couple of $100 bills I'd forgotten about. Howdy, Mr. Franklin. By chance, you haven't seen a pair of sweat socks in there minus a hole in the toe?

These were truly prosperous times at our plant and they were enriching us all. Roger Smith was browsing for yachts, my General Foreman was looking at property in the Upper

Peninsula, several of my linemates were seen swapping Kessler's
for Crown Royal, and I was devoting a miniature fortune to
punk records, girlfriends and bar tabs.

It seemed no matter how many we pushed out the door, we
just couldn't assemble those fad-happy recreational vehicles
fast enough to suit a slobberin' public who'd gone cold turkey
throughout the recession of the embargo years. Here they
came: pent-up, petrol-guzzlin' Americans with their waverin'
hard-ons barging through showrooms on lurkin' prowl for a
chrome-laden beastie to bulldoze down the boulevard. Suburbans and Blazers, the elixir of the hog masses.

We built and we built. Demand was so high that the
Corporation would have surely had us working on Sundays if
our local union agreement hadn't prohibited it. Besides, six
days was plenty. A seven-day workweek would have guaranteed a work force that was subhuman at best—a slaughterhut
full of foul-smellin' mutants who couldn't tell dusk from dawn
nor harmony from homicide.

It was during this boom period that I attended my first of
the annual "State of the Factory" addresses. The presentation
was to keep us informed on just where our plant stood in
relation to efficiency, quality rating, cost procedure, worker
attendance and overall sales. We were also to be apprised on
the condition of our dreaded dogfight with the Japanese and,
our main source of competition, the bullies at Ford with their
sleek fleets of pickups and sub-snuff Ford Broncos.

We were herded next door to this mammoth hangar called
the Research Building. I have no idea what kind of research
went on there, but it's a fair bet that the place was at least a
partial foil for all the legions of smock-clad highbrows who
weaved around the assembly line each evening trying their
damndest to look brilliant and concerned about who knows
what. I stuck by Bob-A-Lou, who was an old pro at these
corporate hoedowns. He told me to settle in for an hour's worth
of propaganda, cheerleading and high-tech gibberish that would
gladly float right over my head. We made a quick beeline for
the free doughnuts and Pepsi. Whatever was on the agenda, it
sure beat working.

"There's the Plant Manager now," Bob-A-Lou mumbled
through his forth or fifth jelly doughnut. He was pointing

toward the stage which, by this time, was completely overrun with about two dozen clones in drab neckties.

"Which one is the chief?" I asked Bob-A-Lou, hopelessly confused.

"The John Wayne look-alike," he said.

"Oh, yeah." I laughed. "All that's missin' is the pistol and spurs."

"I can positively assure you of one thing," Bob-A-Lou said while assaulting a new doughnut. "Sometime during his spiel, he's gonna tell us that he will be regularly touring the plant, pausing to listen to any of our gripes or suggestions. He will pledge to be visible and accessible. Just remember I told you so."

"Bullshit, I presume."

"You better know it. In all my years here, I've yet to see his face in the factory. He's probably afraid that he'll scuff one of his cuff links or something."

The pep rally began. The Plant Manager started by back-patting everybody in the galaxy. Up with us, down with them! He introduced a steady parade of weasels who dutifully took their bows. The Plant Manager was a very happy man. Outside the back of the building, I could envision a Brinks truck carting away his company bonus. We received jelly doughnuts and warm pop. Up with us, down with them!

He started talking about the enormous popularity of our best-seller, the Chevy Suburban. "We can't even meet the demand for this product," he bellowed. "Do you realize that there are people in New England who have never even SEEN a Suburban!" I took a gulp of Pepsi and wondered to myself. Is there no limit to the human suffering some people must endure?

The Plant Manager's Knute-Rockne-reborn-as-poorboy's-Leo-Buscaglia-on-the-threshold-of-industrial-Guyana rah-rah speech continued for another half hour or so. As Bob-A-Lou had predicted, the boss started playin' footsie with the workers: "I plan to make every effort to visit with as many of you as I can. Your input is invaluable to the future of our operations. It is essential that each and every one of us join together in unifying our..."

"Shut the fuck up," a guy behind me groaned.

The Plant Manager introduced the man in charge of overseeing worker attendance. In contrast, he didn't seem happy at all. The attendance man unveiled a large chart illustrating the trends in absenteeism. With a long pointer, he traced the roller-coaster tendencies of the unexcused absence. He pointed to Monday, which slung low to the bottom of the chart. Monday was an unpopular day attendance-wise. He moved the pointer over to Tuesday and Wednesday which showed a significant gain in attendance. The chart peaked way up high on Thursday. Thursday was pay night. Everybody showed up on Thursday.

"Then we arrive at Friday," the attendance man announced. A guilty wave of laughter spread though the workers. None of the bossmen appeared at all amused. Friday was an unspoken Sabbath for many of the workers. Paychecks in their pockets, the leash was temporarily loosened. To get a jump on the weekend was often a temptation too difficult to resist. The Corporation saw it quite differently.

The attendance man took his pointer, which was resting triumphantly on the snow-capped peak of Thursday evening, and, following the graph, plunged the pointer straight down through Friday, a motion that resembled falling off a cliff. Again, there was much snickering.

"Unfortunately, this is not a subject that lends itself to any amount of humor," the attendance man bristled. "Absenteeism is the single largest factor in poor quality. No replacement, no utility worker can perform your job as well as you. Each time you take an unexcused absence, you damage the company along with the security of your own job!" With that said, he packed up his graphs and charts and stalked off stage to make way for the techno-cretins. The veins in his neck were visible all the way back to the doughnut table.

Hardly anyone tuned in for the technical presentation. It was one long lullaby of foreign terminology, slides, numerology and assorted high-tech masturbation. Why would any of us give a shit about the specifics of the great master plan? We knew what holes our screws went in. That was truth enough. Point us toward our air guns and welders and drill presses and save all the particulars for the antheads in the smocks and bifocals.

"Be sure to help yourselves to the doughnuts and soft drinks on your way out," the Plant Manager shouted as the pow-wow broke up. It was time to pour ourselves back into the mold and attend to our well-paying jobs. Up with us, down with them.

I met all kinds of bizarre individuals during my first year at GM Truck & Bus, characters who would prove to be constants throughout my factory tenure. Dementia and derangement were rampant traits. Most of these guys were not unlike myself—urped forth from the birthrights of their kin, drowsy with destiny, uninspired, keen for drink, unamused with the arms race or God or the Middle East, underpaid and overpaid, desperate, goofy, bored and trapped. It was the rare one who would come out and fib in the middle of a card game about how he didn't really belong here. We belonged. There were really no other options—just tricky lies and self-soothing bullshit about "how my *real* talent lies in carpentry" or "within five years I'm opening a bait shop in Tawas." We weren't going anywhere. That pay stub was like a concrete pair of loafers. Sit down, shut up and ante.

Our linemate Dan-O was an irreplaceable native up in our neck of the Jungle. He was the master of diversions. His relentless pranks kept us entertained and loose. More importantly, he had a terrific knack for keepin' our minds off that wretched clock.

Each night Dan-O would have a new trick. I recall the time he took a long cardboard tube used to hold brazing rods, painted it all psychedelic, and passed it off to the unsuspecting as a porno kaleidoscope. He told all the guys that if they held it directly into the overhead lights and looked through the hole, they would get a gorgeous glimpse of *Hustler*'s Miss August. There was never any shortage of volunteers.

There was never any Miss August either. The victim grabbed the peep tube, tilted it straight up to the lights, only to get doused with a generous flow of water right in the eyeball. Dan-O also made sure to line the peephole with black paint. Not only did the victim wind up drenched, he'd also slink away sportin' a shiner the size of a tennis ball.

Another Dan-O favorite was his "crucified wallet" trick. He would nail down an old wallet into the woodblock floor in the aisleway, flip the wallet closed to conceal the nail, and insert the torn corner off a $20 bill. Invariably, some guy would stroll by and notice the apparent gold mine. As we pretended to look the other way, the victim casually glanced around and, feeling unnoticed, swooped down for the wallet only to wind up tumbling on his face or developing an instant hernia. The Jungle would explode in laughter as the victim retreated sheepishly.

The most entertaining of Dan-O's pranks, from a spectator's view, was the "charging tarantula" trap. Dan-O would take fishing line, attach it to a very realistic-looking rubber tarantula, and rig the fish line so that at the flick of his wrist the tarantula would come scampering out from beneath a stock crate near the aisleway. For bait, Dan-O would crumple up a dollar bill and place it in the aisle. The innocent pedestrian would come along, start to reach for the dollar, and... SHIT GOD ALMIGHTY... the bug-eyed terror you would see in the faces of these victims was enough to send you howling to your knees. After the victim had fled, Dan-O would leisurely reset the trap and we'd await the next pigeon. Man, the time just flew.

The absolute craziest co-worker I met during my first year was my relief man, Jack. He was a doper, the pied piper of dumbdom, always banged to the gills on some queer mix of speed, mescaline, hash or cocaine. As my relief man, his duties were to come around twice per night and spell me for my break period. I would often hang around as Jack ran through my job. Though there was something plainly dangerous about him, it could never be denied that Jack was always a great source for laughter. His rantings were legend.

Jack also presented me with one of my first confrontations with an enigma that had been bothering me since I had hired in. He was so resolute in his hatred toward General Motors that it completely baffled me as to why he hung around. He had this persecution complex that ate at him like a bellyful of red ants. I didn't really understand it. I was still relatively raw, but I assumed a deal was a deal. GM paid us a tidy income and we did the shitwork. No one was holding a gun to anyone's head. I didn't harbor any hatred toward GM. My war was with that suffocating minute hand. With Jack, General Motors was the taproot for all that was miserable and repellent in his life. To hear him tell it, GM was out to bury him. He was obsessed with vengeance and anarchy.

For instance, one night Jack arrived to send me on break. Before doing so, he raced around the corner to buy a pack of smokes. A moment later, he reappeared screechin' his lungs out. Apparently, the cigarette machine had eaten his money. An unfortunate break? Not the way Jack saw it. This was just another GM conspiracy designed to crank up the animosity level. The war was on. Jack reached into my workbench and grabbed my sledgehammer. I had a very uneasy feeling about the look on his face.

Moments after Jack charged off with my sledgehammer, I heard the sound of glass being shattered. The pounding continued. He was obviously destroying the vending machine. GM had absolutely nothing to do with these machines. They were serviced by private vendors. Still, Jack bashed away at the machine as if he were poundin' the very last breath out of Roger Smith himself.

Finally, Jack returned. He had about two dozen packs of cigarettes bunched to his chest. Blood trickled from his forearms. His smile was one demented line stretching from ear to ear. The war had been won. From that day on, Jack always referred to my sledgehammer as the Better Business Bureau. He was convinced that he had delivered a furious blow against the infernal GM empire. All he really did was deprive the department of access to cigarettes for the next several months.

Whenever I asked Jack why he just didn't quit and move on to something that was less aggravating, he would jump all over me. "Goddamnit, that's *precisely* what they're banking on. That I'll weaken and bow to their endless tyranny. NO WAY! They'll have to drag me out of here."

Besides the crazies, there was also the occasional violent type. We had one guy up in the Jungle, a black dude named Franklin, who kept our department on constant edge. He was forever picking fights with co-workers. It wasn't any kind of racial thing, Franklin had it in for everyone. When something set him off, he just went to whalin' on people.

One night, he got Henry, our Quality man. Henry had refused to give Franklin an extra pair of work gloves. Franklin became enraged. Later in the shift, he snuck up on Henry and smashed him over the head with a door latch. Henry received a dozen stitches in the back of his skull and Franklin got thirty days on the street.

Franklin worked as a utility man, floating daily from job to job depending on where he was needed. At the beginning of every shift you could hear him throwin' his customary shitfit about what job the foreman had assigned him to cover. It didn't matter what type of job it was, easy or difficult. He'd scream and holler and demand to see his union rep.

I felt a certain amount of pity for our boss. No matter how he tried to soothe the situation, it only made it worse. For example, I firmly believe that if our foreman were to have come up to Franklin one sunny afternoon and told him his only duty for the shift would be to fornicate with Miss America on some sandy beach with a dozen bottles of chilled Dom Perignon at hand, he would have thrown himself into a blind rage and accused the boss of denying him the right to sweat it out all night on the door hang job.

Franklin didn't pull any of his crap with the veterans or guys who outbulked him. He preyed mainly on the timid, the brittle and the rookies. The rookies were at a severe disadvantage. Without having served the first ninety days of their probation period, there was no way they could risk swinging at anybody. To do so would mean instant termination. GM didn't have time to sort out who was to blame in these skirmishes. You could get sucker-punched while saying a rosary and still receive the same punishment as your attacker. It was professional suicide for any rookie to fight back. Franklin exploited this situation and made a career out of intimidating rookies.

Besides his violent streak, there was something else about Franklin that had me very intrigued. He was forever writing stuff down on little notepads, scraps of cardboard, napkins—anything he could find. Several co-workers I talked to joked that he was probably just scrawling down ransom notes or bomb threats. One thing was for certain. Franklin wouldn't allow a soul to see what he was writing. If you came anywhere near him while he was jotting, he'd quickly cram the paper away.

My curiosity was getting the best of me. Jerome Franklin. Bully. Terrorist. Cutthroat. Man of letters? I had to find out

what was behind his mysterious sideline. One evening, while
Franklin was covering Roy's old job across the line from me, I
went over to the picnic bench and began thumbing through the
sports section. In between jobs, Franklin was furiously hammering out something on a piece of paper towel. I decided to
make my move.

"Shit, Franks, you rewritin' the Bible over here?"

"Just some bullshit to pass the time," he muttered.

"Mind if I took a look?" A big pause. A brutal pause. A
pause with a vanity plate that read U EAT ME. Finally, Franklin
gave me a nervous grin. "Go ahead," he said. "But I don't want
one word of this shit bein' spread through the department or
it's your ass."

I laid out the paper towel on the picnic bench. The printing
was barely legible. Grease spots and sealer smudges covered
the page. I began reading and was quickly amazed. Franklin
was writing *poetry* of all things. The poetry was not only a
surprise, the damn shit was red-hot. He had some great lines
in there, plenty of imagery and anger and this passionate raw
beauty that welded together in a furious glide. The guy wasn't
writing as much as he was attacking the beast. The poetry
leapt at your spine and shook you down.

"Jesus, Franks, this stuff really kicks ass."

Franklin shrugged and dumped another load of pencil rods
into his bin. He said nothing. He was obviously uncomfortable
about being exposed as someone who could actually accomplish
something more than pounding skulls and bustin' out teeth.

I read on. Who'd have ever believe it? The resident high
priest of mayhem was a poet of enormous talent. No whiny
art-fag lip service here. No candy-ass dime-a-rhyme. Franklin
got in and got out. No excess baggage, no gristle. It was all
red meat and arteries burstin' wide open and gray matter
boiling in flame. He had the goods, the bads and plenty of the
uglies. I put down the paper towel and was about to say
something. Franklin cut me off.

"Not a word. Let's just fuckin' drop it."

In the nights to come I hounded Franklin to let me check
out his writings, but he always blew me off. I knew better than
to press the matter too far and run the risk of having my face
flattened, so I just gave up. It was sad that he couldn't funnel

his hostility into something more worthwhile than brawling with co-workers and behaving like the campus bully.

Franklin never did change his stance. Within a couple of months, GM had him by the balls. His constant fighting combined with his atrocious attendance record had finally dug him a hole so deep that even the union couldn't bail him out. He was fired and they had to bring up three guards to haul him away.

There's probably no tellin' what he's whalin' on today, nine years removed from the Jungle. Apartment walls. Cell bars. The skulls of the bewildered. Possibly, there's a typewriter mixed in there somewhere. I hope so. I would hate to think that all of that rattlesnake scrawl died along with the job. What a waste.

After a few weeks I managed to develop a good rapport with another black dude, Robert, the mig-welder who worked right down from me. Having been sequestered in Catholic schools my entire youth and adolescence, I didn't have much of an opportunity to meet many black folk until I hired on with GM. You just didn't find too many bro's hangin' around the communion rail hummin' verses of "Holy, Holy, Holy" while awaiting their tongue's worth of Mr. Christ. Just your basic bunch of white hypocrites sheenin' their souls for another week's worth of fetch and wretch.

While Robert was from Alabama, our stories were much the same. His forefathers, like mine, had drifted into this moron dragnet lookin' for steady work and a pocketful of beer change.

And like my father and me, Robert liked to drink. Once he'd had a few, he'd start in with hilarious stories of his childhood in the backwoods. He talked about the perverse sexual practices of his cousins and their clumsy endeavors with farm critters, the white trash hookers who'd lay it all out on a haymow while charging the bystanders a buck a pop to watch it go down. It was all very funny and that prick minute hand would buzz by in circles.

We'd often end up discussing our fates as proud American truck builders. We both shared the contention that neither one of us should've ever been forced to attend even one miserable day's worth of formal education. What good was schooling to someone who was just gonna turn screws and shoot sparks the rest of his life? Robert suggested that this time could have been better spent gettin' high and chasin' females. I would heartily agree, insisting that *anything*—masturbating, bowling, fishing, blowing up banks—would've been better than the crap all those nuns had crammed down my throat.

If Robert tended to be a pissed-off sulk at times, he had every right to be. He'd been divorced a couple of times and the Friend of the Court was slicin' him to pieces. They took the child support right out of his check and, on Thursday nights, while everybody would be gettin' all giddy over the big numbers starin' back at them from their pay stubs, Robert would be slouched over his workbench tryin' his damndest to formulate a budget from the remains of his week's earnings.

It was a shame that guys like Robert had to drag their asses through the Jungle nine hours a night, inhaling fire and growing deaf from the din, only to wind up taking home a paycheck that was more in line with what your average zithead from Taco Bell was making. But, like so many shoprats, Robert had mortgaged his soul to the bitch goddesses of whiskey and women, and he paid for it every Thursday night.

Robert introduced me to an old guy known only as Louie who worked at the end of our line in the repair station. Louie had a great little racket goin' for himself. He peddled half pints of Canadian Club and Black Velvet up and down the line in the Cab Shop area. He charged three bucks a bottle, almost double the store rate, but who was gonna argue. The booze was in the door, you didn't have to wait for it, and Louie delivered right to your bench.

When ordering from Louie, all one had to do was slip the word down the line through a network of fellow workers. You passed on your selection and detailed your location by using the numbers stenciled onto the big iron pillar nearest your job. It was like conjuring up a genie. You'd lay out your money on top of your bench and Louie would come stragglin' down the aisle just like Mr. Green Jeans with the booze stashed somewhere in his floppy coveralls. What a wonderful little microcosm of American capitalism Louie had goin' for himself. Just goes to show that there's an endless array of clever ventures one can concoct to assure that one's grandkids are able to afford the sissy college of their choice. All by ourselves, Robert and I probably paid off a couple semesters.

Shoprat alcohol consumption was always a hot debate with those who just didn't understand the way things worked inside a General Motors plant. While not everyone boozed on a daily basis, alcohol was a central part of many of our lives. It was a crutch not unlike the twenty cups of coffee millions of other Americans depend on to whisk them through their workday. We drank our fair share of coffee, but the factory environment seemed to lend itself toward something that was a great deal more potent and rejuvenating.

I frequently found myself defending this custom with nonfactory acquaintances. They conveniently put the blame for everything square in the laps of those who drank on the job: "NO WONDER the Japanese are moppin' up the market floor with your asses! NO WONDER my new vehicle farts like a moose full of chickpeas! NO WONDER the rear end of my Chevy Suburban rattles like a Hari Krishna in a cement mixer! NO WONDER they want to phase out all you juicers and replace you with robotics!"

The criticisms came from all sources—friends, neighbors, retirees, relatives, the local media. It was a popular bandwagon full of self-righteous dickheads and know-nothings. The yappin' hypocrisy that never ceased to amuse: "IT'S THOSE OVERPAID, SPINELESS FACTORY HACKS AND THEIR DEMONIC CRAVING FOR FIREWATER! THEY REPRESENT TOTAL HUMILIATION TO THE GREAT AMERICAN WORK ETHIC! THOSE INGRATES CAN'T BE SATISFIED WITH THEIR GARGANTUAN PAYCHECKS OR THE FACT THAT THEY POSSESS MORE MEDICAL COVERAGE THEN EVEL KNIEVEL COULD PISS AWAY IN A MILLION UNSUCCESSFUL BUS HURDLES! TO TOP IT OFF, THEY'RE ALL CODDLED AND PROTECTED BY A UNION THAT WOULD PROBABLY EMBRACE RICHARD SPECK AS JUST A MISUNDERSTOOD DRIFTER WITH A HARMLESS YEN FOR VODKA AND ROPE TRICKS!"

Oftentimes, the *Flint Journal*, the unofficial GM gazette, would devote large portions of their editorial page to the miserable whines of these blowhards. "I worked in the plant for thirty-six years and never once needed to rely on alcohol..." "I think that it is an outrage that my neighbor, a GM employee, spends half of his shift sitting in a bar..." "The autoworker of today is weak and corrupt and..." Blah, blah, blah.

It's one thing to be harangued by those who have gone before—the forebears, the sit-down strikers, the providers of the torch, my very own grandfather—but to be put through the verbal shredder by townsfolk who've never even *seen* the innards of an auto factory, well, that was a different matter. Their pious deductions always made me squirm.

The total farce of it all is that given our jobs, these same moany denizens would be lined up right next to us at the barstools and beer coolers if they could somehow weasel in the gate. They'd lose that sacred work ethic baloney and clasp on to Louie's coveralls faster than you can say "the mercury reads 118 in the Paint Department tonight." Keep in mind, the grass is always greener on the other side until it's your turn to jump the fence and chop the shit down.

There is simply no need for apologies. Hell, when you get right down to it, General Motors management doesn't even pay much heed to the drinking habits of its own work force. They realize it would be a massive and futile effort on their part to attempt to stymie a widespread tradition. And moreover, they really don't give a good goddamn who's tippin' and who isn't just as long as the parts keep flowing by in their assigned locations. Start sending down inferior product and then drinking would become an issue.

Drinking right on the line wasn't something everyone cared for. But plenty did, and the most popular time to go snagging for gusto was the lunch break. As soon as that lunch horn blew, half of the plant put it in gear, sprinting out the door in packs of three or four, each pointed squarely for one of those chilly coolers up at one of the nearby beer emporiums. Talk about havoc. It was like some nightly cross between the start of the Indy 500 and chute-surfin' out of the fuselage of a burning jet. Engines racing. Tires squealing. Pedestrians somersaulting over car hoods.

I half expected one night to find Marlon Perkins propped in a jeep near the gate narrating this frantic migration: "Notice, friends, the fleet mobility of our subjects. The wide eyes and gaping mouths are timeless clues that another pilgrimage to the watering hole is well under way."

A half hour is all most workers had. Make no mistake, this small opportunity to bust open the monotony of shop grind helped many guys avoid cracking up, cracking skulls, missing work or mutating into supervisional bullies. A jumbo of beer certainly wasn't gonna save anyone's life, but the odds were it would certainly enhance it. John DeLorean himself proved that factory critters can't triumph above the ordinary on black coffee and Twinkies alone. Hell no. On a clear day you *can* see General Motors and, if you squint a little harder, you can also see a frosty quart of Budweiser just as plain as the cocaine attaché case at the end of the motel bed.

It was during these early years that my old friend Denny and I spent our lunch breaks together. With a double-up arrangement not much different from mine, Denny was able to tag along as we indulged in every shoprat's dream scam: the Double Lunch. With our jobs securely covered by co-workers, we could slide out and overlap the two lunch periods designated for the two separate truck lines. Instead of a half hour for lunch, we now had a sprawling hour and twelve minutes to get lost. It was wonderful what you could avoid accomplishing with that extra forty-two minutes off.

One particular double lunch from that period has always stood out. The plant was really roasting that night with the kind of corraled heat that often rendered the overhead fans useless and forced a horde of dehydrated reeking shoprats to line up at the drinking fountain and gulp down salt tablets.

On that night, Denny came to my job with an invitation to slug down a few at lunch. Though nothing in the world sounded better than cold beer, I knew we would have to be careful. The beer was always a godsend goin' down, but you had to watch out for the fatigue factor it brought on when the heat was high. If you overdid it you ran the risk of drowsing out during the second half of the shift. By night's end you'd be totally gassed and ornery enough to punch out your own grandmother.

But the offer was just too appealing. "I like beer," I said. "Beer tastes good."

At the convenience store we stood in line behind three attractive young ladies. They were purchasing diet pop and wine coolers. I remember thinking that they must be part of some very special breed, a sorority of angels who simply forbade themselves to perspire. They giggled and fussed with their perfect hair—all the while glaring at us with their terrible animal eyes.

We smiled back at them. It was all so hopeless. We couldn't help our appearance. We didn't normally smell this way. It was the $12.82 an hour and the benefits package and the opportunity to swill a cold one in between breaks in the madness that doomed us to trudge into convenience stores lookin' like Spam patties in wet suits. Our grandfathers had taken this route. Our fathers were right behind them. Now it was our turn to be thirsty, rank and every bit as unlucky.

We took our quarts of Mickey's Malt Liquor and headed for the back of the employees' lot. It was always wise to park in a section far, far removed from the roving eye of the surveillance cameras. Otherwise, the guards might scope you down as you tipped that cold chalice to your lips and decide to wheel out and give you some shit. This rarely happened, but it was a nuisance all the same. There would be ID requests. There would be boring lectures. Sometimes there might even be a slow shuffle down to the Labor Relations office.

Denny and I drank, mostly in silence, while a Lesley Gore Greatest Hits tape poured out of the dash of my Camaro. We were beginning to feel human, the beer workin' its magic, the edge dissolving, the shoprat's humble version of the multiple martini lunch. We sat there staring off into the smokestacks with the weight of the world gradually sliding through the floorboard. The guards and the bossmen were absolute madmen. How could anything that felt so good be a punishable offense? Our screws were all in place. Our welds were shining brightly. It was all working out. What could be the problem?

We both loved Lesley Gore and, on this most humid of nights, Les was really lettin' us have it: "California Nights," "I Don't Wanna Be a Loser," "That's the Way Boys Are"—her complete arsenal. We slurped faster and faster on our malt liquor jumbos. At that precise moment, there was very little doubt that we had everyone in the galaxy squarely beaten.

We were on a roll. We raced back to the convenience store, this time purchasing two forty-ouncers of Mickey's Malt. We hit on the beer and sang along with Lesley and laughed at our great fortune. We looked like trash, we smelled like death, we had no idea who was winning the wars or the rat race or the relentless struggle to get on top. It was all so very meaningless. Someone would be declared the victor and the rest of the world would roll over and begin to plot tomorrow's lousy comeback.

"I've gotta admit," Denny laughed, "it doesn't get much better than this. The whole world is on fire and here we are parked in the shadow of this mausoleum drinkin' the coldest beer on the planet. With Lesley Fucking Gore! No one else on the face of this earth is doing this! NO ONE!"

"I wonder what Lesley Gore is doin' right this minute," I mused. "I wonder what Al Kaline and Roger Smith and Sister Edward Irene are up to—right NOW! Right this very second. I feel sorry for their asses!" We laughed until our sides ached.

Nine fifty-four returned to the assembly line. Denny and I hustled back in to relieve our partners. In the nights to come we were never really able to recapture whatever it was that led to that precious double lunch we spent with Lesley Gore. After a while, we simply quit tryin'. Perhaps we were just crazy from the heat. It was known to happen. Whatever the cause, we always remembered the night we had you and you and the rest of the world thoroughly dicked for seventy-two minutes.

Bud had grown weary of the spot-welder's shuffle. In a way, he wasn't anything like the rest of us spark-eaters. He always had his nose buried in some college textbook. He had big plans that spread far beyond the walls of the GM Truck & Bus plant. Bud's master plan was to own and operate his own grocery store. He was only using GM as a temporary means to support his family and pay his tuition.

As the days neared for Bud's departure, I was struck with an immediate fear. What if they were to replace him with a woman? This was known to happen in cases where two guys were observed crunching their jobs together and outfoxing the braintrust who were responsible for splitting up the chores. It wasn't that a woman would be incapable of doing either of the two jobs. It was more that most any given woman would be hard-pressed to combine *both* of the jobs, especially when one of the jobs would require her to navigate a bulky spot-welder that spit fire like the bastard son of Mount Vesuvius. A man was needed. Either that or some steroid-gulpin' she-goat from the women's Bulgarian gym team.

I pleaded with our foreman to send down a rugged sort. The last thing I needed was a wimp, regardless of sex. I was far too spoiled with the lazy benefits of doubling-up to return to the old nightly up and down. For sanity's sake, the gimmick had to keep rollin'.

The foreman brought down a new hire named Dale. As they came stridin' down the aisle, I could tell that this guy was the answer to all my prayers. I was about to receive 225 pounds of solid, gullible rookie girth. I immediately took Dale under my wing. Within a week we were glidin' through our paces. An hour on, an hour off. The gods had been smiling on me.

As for Dale, I had never run up against a more curious journey than the one that had brought him to the hub of Jungleland. He lived way the hell up in Twining, Michigan, a tiny farming village located 115 miles north of Flint. This meant he had to commute 230 miles per day, six days a week, to toil for General Motors. It seemed ridiculous. I didn't put on 230 miles to get to work over an entire summer.

I had only one question for Dale. *"WHY?"*

"Well," Dale said. "Do you have any idea how much a new John Deere with fully synchronized 24-speed PowerSync transmission and built in Hi-Lo will run you nowadays?"

"Um, a bundle?" I suggested.

"You ain't shittin' it's a bundle. That's what brings me here."

Dale went on to list all kinds of other mechanical nightmares needed to keep his farm updated. The price tags were astounding. It was all giving me a headache. At this rate, Dale was going to have to pull sixty years of moonlighting at the truck plant in order to pay off his fleet of farmyard bloodsuckers.

Dale also raised pigs. Now there was a combination you didn't run into every day—pig farmer/autoworker. He told me he had to get up at 6:30 in the morning to mess with his pigs. This allowed him about three hours of sleep per night. How in the hell did he do it? Why in the hell did he do it? I asked Dale

why he didn't just give up the farm and pig biz, move down-
state, and carve out a sweet living as just another rat in the
pack. Flint wasn't Oz, but it had to pull rank over a town called
Twining.

"Move... HERE?" he groaned. "Move to Flint?"

"Why not," I answered. "Lots of bars, plenty of women,
cable TV, a semipro hockey team, large shopping malls, superb
Coney Islands, movie theaters, record stores... um, did I
mention lots of bars?"

Dale was more interested in fishing holes and deer trails.
He also chided me about the murder rate and whether people
had to lock their doors at night.

"Now that's hittin' below the belt, Dale."

"I'll stick to Twining," he said.

Despite our different lifestyles, Dale and I clicked well
together. He was much more experimental than Bud had been.
Dale shared the same commitment I had to tryin' anything that
would budge that minute hand in our favor. We quickly scrapped
the hour on, hour off arrangement and went straight for the
summit of the double-up system—a half day on, a half day off.
This meant you could actually spend as little as four or five
hours in the plant, get paid for the full time, and escape out of
the chaos by sunset. What a setup.

This is how it worked: Dale and I would both report to
work before the 4:30 horn. We'd spend a half hour preparing all
the stock we would need for the evening. At 5:00, I would take
over the two jobs while Dale went to sleep in a makeshift
cardboard bed behind our bench. Having been up since sunrise,
Dale was a very eager candidate for some shuteye. He'd stuff
some plugs into his ears, crawl into his bed, and often be sound
asleep before I had even finished my first truck.

I'd work the jobs from 5:00 until 9:24, the official Suburban/
Blazer Line lunch period. When the line stopped, I'd give
Dale's cardboard coffin a good kick and rouse him from his
sweaty dreams of compression ratios and pork products. It was
time for the handoff. I would give my ID badge to Dale so that
he could punch me out at quitting time. This was the riskiest
part of the operation. If a supervisor or security guard managed to spot a worker punchin' out two badges, his ass was
dead. Next to stealing and sabotage, this act was the most

severe crime you could pull. Immediate dismissal was the result. I had seen it happen to a couple of careless workers and they were promptly put to the curb. No, this was not a solid career move; however, it had to be done to assure that the early escapee would get paid a full shift's worth.

As risky as it was, you really had to be a complete idiot to get caught ringin' out two badges. All it took was common sense to do the job proper. The first rule was that you *never* used the same time clock for both badges. Since there were a dozen time clocks to choose from this wasn't difficult. You moved up to the first time clock, took a look around, always making sure you punched out your partner's badge first. This done, you quickly stashed his badge down the front of your pants. Then you moved on to another clock and punched yourself out. This way even if a guard caught you ringin' out a second badge, at least that badge would be your own. If questioned as to why you were seen punching out twice, you became very upset, insisting that the first clock had malfunctioned, a frequent aggravation. If the guard persisted and asked to see what you slid down your pants, you really became livid, accusing him of a shameless come-on. Then, you hauled ass.

I have some wonderful memories of sittin' on a barstool on a Friday night at the Limberlost Bar in Houghton Lake, Michigan—130 miles north of the truck plant—nursin' on my third beer while lookin' up between the antlers at the clock as it turned over to 2:00 A.M. At that precise moment—130 miles to the south—Dale would slide my General Motors ID badge through one of the twelve time clocks.

Perfecting this kind of immaculate trickery called for complete reliability in one's partner. You had to be sure that the quality of the jobs remained faultless. You had to make extra certain to avoid any type of injury. You had to refrain from all drinking. With your partner not around to intervene, you couldn't risk having to piss out a load of beer.

Over the weeks and months to come, Dale and I accelerated our routine. We got the operation down so well that we could actually do both jobs and still have time to stand around. Unfortunately, this didn't escape the eye of our General Foreman, who was already having a difficult time swallowing our system. Doubling-up was one thing. But to double-up while working and still have time to browse the paper or kibitz with fellow linemates just didn't wash. We were being watched. We knew it and we should have slowed it down to make it appear more difficult than it really was. But we didn't. We'd simply become too damn cocky.

Not surprisingly, Dale and I arrived at our jobs one afternoon to find a swarm of bossmen grouped around our bench. There was our supervisor, the General Foreman, the Repair Foreman and a couple other big players milling about. They had a large box of some kind of stock piece I didn't recognize. They also had a strange, tiny air gun that they were passin' around.

The picture was dreadfully clear. The bastards were adding work to our jobs. The Repair Foreman grabbed the tiny air gun and a piece of the foreign stock and bent way beneath the belly of the truck cab. Zzzzzzz-zing! He reached for another. Zzzzzzz-zing! Then another. Then another. Then one more. With every squeal of that runt gun, I felt a bit more nauseous.

Dale and I slouched down at the picnic table. Bob-A-Lou came to express his condolences. "They've been over there for a half hour fiddling with those new parts," he said. "Tough luck, guys."

"What *are* those goddamn things, anyway?" I groaned.

Robert shrugged. "Hey, you had to see it comin'. They've been hawkin' you like naked pussy for the past month."

Dale finally spoke up. "Screw 'em. We'll get around it somehow. We'll just have to crank it up a gear."

The bossmen motioned for Dale and me to come over. They explained how it would be. We would read the schedule taped to the front of each cab and this would inform us as to whether a certain truck called for air-conditioning clamps. There would be no set pattern that we could rely on. Sometimes the clamps would be required on three consecutive trucks. Other times they might fall on every fourth truck. This kind of suspense was just what the bossmen were hoping would break up our system.

Attaching the air-conditioning clamps was a pain in the ass. It wasn't a strenuous chore, it was more of an exasperation. You couldn't see the holes you were supposed to be screwing into. You had to feel around and, once you found them, you had to balance the air gun perfectly still so that the screw and clamp didn't vibrate off the miniature tip of the gun. If you missed your mark, everything would fly apart and you would be forced to start all over.

After a couple of days of this new arrangement, I was ready to surrender. Just when I thought I'd drilled in all five clamps securely, one of them would go clanking off and land on the ramp track. I'd start cussin' my brains out and stompin' around like a madman.

Thankfully, Dale was there to calm me down. Mechanical plights and misbehaving gizmos were hobbies for him. He began teaching me a new stance that would give me much better accuracy with the air gun. I practiced and practiced. Dale wouldn't allow me to give up, assuring me that we'd be right back in business within a week.

And that unconcerned, soothsayin' pig farmer was right. Through determination, perspiration, acceleration and pure spite, we swallowed up the air-conditioning clamps into our routine and were back doubling-up within a week. We made for a helluva team. The neurotic, scam-happy city kid and the bullheaded, work-junkie farm boy.

Our return to glory didn't escape the notice of our supervisors. They'd pause while passing our jobs and ogle us a while. They had been so convinced that the additional work would halt our schemin' ways. They'd called our bluff and been beaten.

As exasperated as they probably felt, they knew there was nothing they could really do to stop us. We showed up for work each and every day. We ran nothing but 100 percent defect-free quality. We kept our workplace spotless, provided you overlooked Dale's ugly slick of chewing tobacco juice. GM was very big on bottom lines and the bottom line as it pertained to Dale and me was that we were exemplary shoprats.

The months sailed by. The bossmen left us to our own devices. The opportunity to cleave through the monotony of assembly line labor by combining our two jobs was something neither Dale nor I ever took for granted. We were dumbshit-lucky and we knew it. If the Plant Manager himself had shown up with a contract binding the two of us to stick to our Jungle ruts for the duration of our thirty years, we'd probably have

scrawled our names, dates of birth and Social Security numbers on it in warm blood.

With two years down and twenty-eight to go, Dale and I
were more than satisfied with our lot in the corporate web. We
reasoned that we would grow old together on our job combo.
We envisioned ourselves becoming potbellied old farts, docile
and harmless, staying our course toward that gold watch and
wonderful pension plan. Proud old bucks stompin' on Father
Time Clock.

We wanted nothing more than to follow in the footsteps of
Cab Shop legends like Lightnin' and Same-O. Here were two
old-timers who'd been around so long that they probably could
remember when there was no GM Truck & Bus plant on Van
Slyke Road—only an Indian settlement or a trading post.
When a worker had reached this amount of seniority, not much
was expected of him performance-wise. They just shuffled
through the motions and GM stuck a paycheck in their pocket
every Thursday night.

Lightnin' was a real study. No one had the faintest clue as
to what his job assignment might be. The popular theory was
that it had something to do with the men's room located in the
stairwell leading up to the Cab Shop. That was the only place
you ever caught a glimpse of Lightnin'. He'd be leanin' up
against a wall near the last urinal, sound asleep on his feet.

It didn't make any sense. There were a million hideaways a
man could find to lie down and take a snooze—the cushion
room, the tool crib, the locker room, the cafeterias, the picnic
tables, the stock pallets, the back seat of a defective Blazer.
Why Lightnin' chose to sleep leanin' against the men's room
wall remained one of the great mysteries of Cab Shop. He
wasn't an old queer or anything like that. Hell, he wasn't even
conscious.

Bob-A-Lou was the resident speculator when it came to
the topic of Lightnin'. It was his theory that Lightnin' was a
custodian assigned to clean this specific men's room way back
when. Bob-A-Lou believed that through the ugly crawl of
years, Lightnin' had slowly dissolved all memory of his actual
calling, perhaps his entire identity. However, he never forgot
for a moment his assigned battle station. Bob-A-Lou theorized
that Lightnin' was like one of those confused old Japanese

soldiers you occasionally heard about still holed-up on the Kiribati Islands thinkin' the war was still wagin'.

Who really knew? When the horn blew to begin each shift, Lightnin' took up his silent vigil as the fossilized overseer of the LL-16 stairwell men's room. When it got crowded in there on break, you sometimes had to give old Lightnin' a little nudge in order to find some elbow room at the pisser. It was neither funny nor sad. It was something that went on and on and, after a while, he was another piece of the milieu.

Then there was my old pal Same-O. What a character. Same-O was a living landmark up in the Cab Shop area. He was very old and very tired. I could never understand why he stayed on at the plant. Surely, he had more than enough time in to retire. He was like so many of the old guys—lurchin' around the aisleways, givin' an occasional swipe of the broom to some ancient pile of dust, molded to the scenery like trolls to the shadows. It was as if they had nowhere else to go.

There wasn't any mystery as to why everyone called him Same-O. No matter what was said to my old friend, whether it be a simple hello or a request for the correct time, he invariably replied "same old thing." I'd finish up welding down a wheel well and turn around to find him leanin' on his broom behind my workbench. His face looked like leather. Before I'd be able to speak, he'd smile at me and mutter "same old thing." I might comment on the heat or the Detroit Tigers or ask him if he had another Viceroy. No matter. "Same old thing," he'd offer. I could already make out the script on his gravestone. There would be no mention of birth or death or surname. Only: SAME OLD THING. Same-O had it sussed. I often believe he was the only genius I ever encountered at GM Truck & Bus.

Lightnin' and Same-O. They were our role models. Survivors, lackeys, barons. Real victors. They had trampled the Jungle into mulch. It was all Dale and I really hoped for. To develop a niche, flip down the blinders, and pulverize our job assignments into a meaningless ghost walk through the necessary quarter century and change. No surprises. No speed bumps. No tampering with the existing terms. Obscurity and triumph.

It didn't happen. It turned out that we were just a couple of wistful lunks. From our blurry vision inside the foxhole, we couldn't catch a glimpse of all the shit that was piling up on the corporate horizon. The market downturns, the consumer swoons, the untimely return of another recession. We were as naive as they came. With only two years' seniority, we hung to this belief that we were glued to our placements for eternity—or thirty years, whichever came first. We wanted to hold on together like some shrewd tag team spiraling through the useless decades. Like Lightnin' and Same-O and our very own granddaddies.

It didn't happen. Somebody forgot to buy their gleamin' Suburban. Someone else left their marvelous Blazer to rot away on the showroom floor. The overtime evaporated. The rumors began to fly. The ranks began to thin. What had happened to all those desperate people in New England? Had they finally *seen* a Suburban? Was that all they wanted . . . a look-see?

Oh, that crazy auto industry. Here today, Twining tomorrow. Hi there, bye now! They handed over my spot-welder to a guy who held higher rank. Dale was gone before I was. They ushered him out on a Thursday night after drumming on the side of his cardboard crypt. I told Dale we would meet up again. I was a very good liar.

It's been over nine years since we danced with a spot-welder or cursed at a clamp. And, right now, we're neither young nor old. Just another couple of middle-aged shoprats, ex or otherwise, clawin' for coins.

Right now it's a very chilly afternoon in November. It's almost 4:30 P.M.—the old start time. I'm pecking away on a typewriter inside a pool shed that's been hastily converted into a writer's retreat. I keep fiddlin' with this jerkoff space heater that's very near death. I have no idea what Dale is up to. Boots full of pigshit, he's probably messin' with a deadline of his own.

5

1979 WASN'T THE BEST OF YEARS FOR FLINT. MY BELEAGUERED
hometown was like some banged-up middleweight resting its
rump on the ropes, covering up its soft belly, hoping only to
last out the round. The big paydays, the cool precision, the
bully mystique—all of it was being soundly trounced.

Prosperity was no longer the same happy tune. Nineteen
eighty was more like a funeral dirge. The nation's highest
unemployment rate affixed itself to the home turf and relative
newcomers like myself and half of the crew up in Cab Shop
became instant driftwood. The rookies of '77, those fair-haired
recruits of the last real boom era, suddenly looked like a
mighty confused bunch spilling out of the doors of the local
Michigan Employment Security Commission office. For once
Papa GM started to wheeze, every little sib was bound to catch
that bug.

However, being laid off from General Motors wasn't the
worst thing a shoprat could run up against. On the plus side,
you obviously weren't required to work. That in itself was a
remarkable new pleasure. No longer did you have to bend or
lift or stoop or strain or pick at the burn scabs on your skull.

No more clipboard kaisers playin' rent-a-God. No more smoke and soot and fumes and sonic puree. No more minute hands circling like vultures over dead prey. No more propaganda and cafeteria poison and post-shift demolition derbies.

As for the downside, you no longer had real job security. That was not good. No longer could you just nuzzle up to your birthright. No more hefty wages for idiot labor. No more... um... let me think a minute. There must have been *something* else. Hmmmm. Oh yeah, no more stupid shit to commit to memory just in case some curious publishing firm decided to risk handing you a book contract. I guess that about covers it.

So, as you can see, being laid off wasn't such a terrible dilemma. The good far outweighed the bad. There was no reason to get... hey... HOLD IT! Jesus, where's my brain? I totally blanked on the biggest, baddest, meanest minus of 'em all: THE UNEMPLOYMENT LINE! Just the sound of that phrase makes me wanna fling lunch.

A little history of my life's main phobia is in order here. I'm prone to being the nervous sort when required to stand in line. For me, the ultimate tension in life is to be stuck in a supermarket jampile waiting to buy my goods while surrounded by throngs of housewives sifting through the *Midnight Star* for grainy pics of Tom Selleck's buttocks. Help!

Many is the time I felt I was going to go stark raving shit-brained wacko. I wince at this vision of a twitching lunatic someday pole-vaulting the counter, smashing through the store-front glass, and streaking off into the horizon with a horde of suburbanite ghouls nipping at his Air Hampers with ferocious demands to "HAVE A NICE DAY!" Make it stop! No more dimwit skull sessions about Sparky Anderson and the weather. No more lilting mutilations of Jim Croce's "Time in a Bottle." No more insanity, grief, terror, disgrace and coward's luck.

I've heard that in some states the unemployed simply receive their checks via the mail. Not so in Michigan. Never mind all the time and money they could save with this solution. Never mind all the mayhem and chaos they could prevent with just a stamp and an envelope. Nope, that would make too much sense. It would also deprive them of their sick fascination of seeing you shake, quake and quiver as they dragged their dead asses around in circles.

Realizing this, my old advice to all you panicky types out there is to do EVERYTHING within your power to hang on to your job. Heap your employer with phony plaudits, offer to baby-sit his kids, gulp amphetamines and perform the work load of ten mules. If you have to, get down and smooch his dusty wingtips anew with sheen. In your spare time go to church, pray to Allah, pray to Buddha, plead with Zeus, beg of Jah, implore the graces of whatever deity landed the '69 Mets a pennant to keep your nervous butt in the fold and out of places like the Michigan Employment Security Commission (MESC) logjam of human languish. No, this is not the spot to be if you get clammy in a crowd.

First off, the MESC has no windows. Once you pop through the doors, it's like entering a holding tank for sodden sumo wrestlers. You're required to check in at the front desk where a little old lady will put a red check next to your appointment time and ask you if you have any paperwork to turn in. Always, absolutely *always*, answer no or you will be detained for a period long enough to qualify for having your face reprinted on the side of a milk carton. Paperwork makes these people freeze on contact. If you have paperwork to hand in, wait until you've got your check passed on to you and then broach the subject as if it were some dumb, accidental oversight. Don't worry if they get upset. These tyrants were born pissed off.

After your card has been checked at the front desk, you will be instructed to fall in line. Being a shoprat, the most popular of jobless hacks, I always had my choice of lines 6 through 12. Without fail I always managed to select the wrong one. My method of choosing a line hardly bordered on the scientific. I would simply give a deep glance into the eyes of the assorted claims people and somehow try to determine which one felt like drivin' herd. Sometimes I'd try the stiff old man. Sometimes the pretty young woman. Sometimes the evil lady who looked like Agnes Moorehead ripped from the grave. The strategy, if one could call it that, never worked. I always ended up in a linoleum tar pit.

A friend of mine always insisted that the MESC had made a widespread effort to stock its ranks full of people with fetishes for dominance. He may have been right. So many of their employees seemed to delight in having you grovel, squirm and plead total ignorance to their cascade of bureaucratic muddle. They acted as if you had laid yourself off, that you had no intention of ever lifting another finger, that you were in a frantic rush to get back poolside to your bevy of naked stewardesses, that you hated this country and wanted to use their money to buy explosives to lob at the governor's motorcade.

Wading through their standard, hypnotic probes, I was always tempted to liven things up:

MESC: "Have you received any income during the past two weeks?"

Answer: "Yes, I was paid $10,000 to carry out a hit on a United States senator."

MESC: "Are you receiving any other benefits from any other state?"

Answer: "Yes, I am currently on a retainer fee from the State of Maryland as a procurer of young male prostitutes."

MESC: "Have you been able and available for work the past two weeks?"

Answer: "No, I've been too busy selling PCP to third graders up at the corner arcade."

Occasionally, you'd see people get really irked over a development with their claim. On one memorable visit I recall the desk people dropping this big, ugly bombshell stating that due to some new hitch in the law, the extended benefits program was being cut and that many of these jobless folks had run the old money meter dry. Believe me, this message was not received with much jubilation, as proven by one enraged castoff who—being of sound strength, if not entirely sound mind—saw fit to retreat to the MESC Personnel parking lot and play Zorro on the office workers' radials with his switchblade. He was eventually captured and thrown in jail where I guess he pretty much accomplished his objective—the State was still gonna be footin' his meal ticket.

Above all, the thing you wanted to avoid when visiting the unemployment office was to be detained in the section of seats over by the side wall. This is where they would send you if you developed a complication with your claim, if you needed to file for a new claim, if you acted unappreciative or if you had gone to the bathroom in your pants. If you were instructed to have a seat in this dreadful limbo it was advisable that you have your mail delivery halted and prepare to wait, wait, wait. I was very fortunate, having been able to avoid this section. What they did with these people was not apparent. Sporadically, some figurehead would poke his head out from beyond the partition and summon one of the waiting multitudes to follow him.

Never, but never, did I ever witness people reappear once they'd been ushered into the back chambers of the MESC. At first I thought these folks were merely ducking out a side exit, but casual research into this possibility showed me that THERE WAS NO SIDE EXIT.

I assumed that this was how it must end. A silent trudge down a narrow hall, led by a cranky claims executioner with cold eyes and blue lips. Finally having your benefits exhausted, you were a total nonentity. No one missed you. No one could see you. You disappeared from the unemployment statistics. You no longer existed.

A miniature Auschwitz had been assembled far behind the clicking of the cashier's keys, far removed from the lazy shuffle of the fresh claimant's feet, off in back where you now only waited for the pellets to drop and the air to get red.

Oh, I guess it could have been worse. You could have been burned to death in a Pinto. You could have been snagged in a plane prop. You could have been fatally trampled at a Paul Anka concert. You could have had to go out and find a job.

That was the funny part. A job? Most of us already had jobs. We worked for the goddamn General Motors Corporation. We were shoprats stuck in a holding pattern. This was all temporary, a fluke of the trade. Soon enough those showrooms would start bustling. Phones would begin to ring and we'd all straggle back to our callings. It was just one of the quirky fates that went along with being just another cog in such a mammoth flywheel.

With this understood, it was such a joke when the folks over at the MESC announced that you were now expected to make the rounds looking for an alternative occupation. Instead of just pickin' up your biweekly check, the claims people insisted that you must take along four sets of job applications to be filled out and returned upon your next visit. It was ignorant, but you had to play along in order to keep receiving your money.

This new requirement was a real grin. For instance, on the day before I was to go pick up my check at the MESC, I would reach for the yellow pages and randomly select some of the most bizarre places of business I could find. On a given week I may have "applied" for work at a taxidermy shop, a porno theater, a limousine service and a funeral home. They had a spot on the job form where you were required to write in the name of the individual you had spoken with. I'd call up the business and ask whoever answered the owner's name. I'd jot it down and hang up. The form also had a line asking "Outcome of Job Interview." I put down phrases like "enormously unqualified," "lacking sufficient training" and "a stalemate of mutual disgust."

I assume the MESC never followed up on any of it. It was just another way for them to make you feel pressured. They had to know that any shoprat with half a brain wasn't likely to sacrifice his hefty unemployment benefits by accepting a job flippin' burgers or scrubbin' toilets. We may have been crazy, but we weren't fuckin' dumb.

It was fairly ridiculous how much money we were being awarded for *not* going to work. Unemployment paid you $377 biweekly. Add to this the $80 a week courtesy of the GM-UAW Supplemental Unemployment Benefits and you were takin' in a comfortable $268 a week, hardly anyone's definition of chump change when measured against the fact that you weren't required to do anything but survive the snail plod over at the MESC every other week.

It didn't end there. This being the tail end of the Jimmy Carter era, we were presented another bonus. It seemed Jim had a powerful soft spot in his lust-leechin' heart for unemployed factory goomers. Before he was booted out of office, he shoved through some bill called the Trade Readjustment Act (TRA) and, yipes, it was feedtime all over again for the old hip pocket.

TRA was designed to provide financial assistance for autoworkers whose plants were closed due to the influx of foreign competition. I gladly took their money, though the pretense seemed rather misguided. I still maintain that blaming it all on the Japanese was a rather cowardly way of admitting "Aw, shit, who was the asshole in charge of mass-producing RHINOS when the public can only afford GERBILS."

I remember the day I received my lump-sum TRA payment. I had never seen such mirth and hysteria inside the GM-UAW Benefits office. Men were actually smiling and talking to one another. They would go sprinting out the door plantin' high fives

and wavin' their odd-colored checks above their heads. It was all
so contrary to the usual dull isolation of the cattle clog.

When it was my turn, I stepped forward and presented my
card. The claims lady handed me a receipt and directed me to
the cashier's desk. The cashier handed me my SUB pay and
then began typing up my TRA check. Judging from the reaction of my fellow workers, I was soon to be a very exuberant
heir. Who'd have guessed that gettin' canned from your job
could be such a bull market? Who cared? Praise the Lord and
pass the allocation.

I waited until I got back to my Camaro to look over my
TRA check. The greed factor was already consuming me. I felt
like a kid on Christmas morning. I held my breath as I glanced
over to the amount line. My eyes immediately popped out.
Flashing back at me was a check in Bernard Hamper's name
for TWENTY-SEVEN HUNDRED AND 00 DOLLARS. Jesus,
was I ever glad I had voted for Mr. Carter.

I sped home to the house I shared with my brother Bob. I
proudly unveiled my TRA check. Bob looked at it and shook his
head. "Generous Motors strikes again." He chuckled. "What
are you gonna do with all that money? Or need I ask."

"Ask not! As your eldest brother, it is my considered
opinion that we call up the crew and convene the next several
evenings in one overindulgent cesspool of liquor, drugs and rock
'n' roll trash. It's the very least we can do to show appreciation
to that peanut-shuckin' commander in chief and the fierce
Japanese who, in emergency tandem, saw fit to impregnate my
coffer twenty-sevenfold."

What other route was there for a young, unemployed
party buffoon who didn't give a rip about his bank balance but
to squander such a silly gift of generosity on crud that would
help dissolve his nightly ennui? It was like free money. Like
hittin' up the Lotto. When all was burned and buried, I had
managed to hold back just enough to pay off the loan on my car.

The most silly irony in being laid off during this period was
that I was now actually making *more* money by not going to
work. When you sat down and averaged in the TRA windfall, I
was coming out about twenty bucks per week to the better. It
really dampened your enthusiasm for any rapid return to the

ranks of the employed. Hell, being rehired would effectively mean taking a cut in pay.

During my layoff I paid a visit to my aunt's house for her annual family reunion cookout. My grandfather was there, holding court, drinkin' beer with my uncles, and discussing the world at large. I attempted to stay on the fringe, fully aware that my grandfather was bound to switch the subject over to General Motors once he spotted me. He had put in so many years at GM that, though he'd been retired for more than a decade, the shop remained his favorite oratorical topic. He could talk factory until your ears turned blue. I anticipated these conversations with a most definite lack of zeal.

My grandfather saw me and approached. "Y'know, I've been readin' in the newspaper about all of that TRA money you guys are receivin'." Uh-oh, prepare to enter the time tunnel. "Pretty good money for not havin' to work at all."

"You won't hear me complaining," I replied.

"I should say not. Christ, you boys today are gettin' a free ride. In my early years at GM, you were left high and dry when they pulled a cutback. There wasn't no unemployment check or SUB pay and there sure as hell wasn't any of this TRA junk. You scraped up work anywhere you could—tendin' bar, moppin' floors, sellin' apples. You didn't have no pamperin' union wipin' your ass at every turn. Shit, no. Back then a foreman could run you right out the door for no reason at all. The next day his brother-in-law would be doin' your job."

My grandfather went on and on. I couldn't help but get a little pissed-off. He took it too far, making it sound like I should feel a terrible guilt over all the benefits I was getting. Christ, I couldn't help it if I was born too late to scrounge and suffer. What the hell was I supposed to do? Refuse unemployment insurance? Turn down pay hikes? Demand the removal of my fan? Insist that GM stop paying me such bloated wages and return me to the damn stone age?

It was an uncomfortable stalemate. Two generations of shoprats who simply couldn't relate to each other's era. Indeed, I owed a tremendous debt to my grandfathers and uncles and to all those who bravely took part in the historic sitdown strikes of 1937. They were truly working class heroes who bettered the path for all factory men and women to come. But, hold on, we worked damn hard also. We sweated and humped and hammered it out just as they had. What did they want from us? Our left nuts?

Things had improved immensely due to the efforts of our forefathers. We would always remain grateful to them. However, some things never did change. The factory was still a shithole, comparisons be damned. One large shithole and you'd better believe that that unbearable clock on the wall never moved one iota faster for us than it did them.

GM phoned me. It was bound to happen sooner or later. The big callback. Actually, the timing couldn't have been better. Since I had been laid off nearly nine months, my benefits were in danger of skidding to a halt. I only had two more visits to the MESC before my last extension was exhausted. After that, who knew? My résumé was sorta blank.

I was instructed to rendezvous back up to my old department in Cab Shop. This suited me fine. I hated surprises. As I arrived upstairs, it was as if a day had never passed. The old gang was sitting around—Bob-A-Lou, Robert, Dan-O, Tim, Bigfoot, Ronny, Larry, Armando, Ty, Jimmy. Of course, there was Same-O leanin' on his broom. The only one missing was Dale. He had opted to quit GM and stay up in Twining with his pigs and combines.

We had a new foreman, rather, foreperson. A beautiful young black woman named Lydia. She asked that we all group around the picnic table. I wedged in next to Ronny. Lydia paused and looked down at her clipboard. Damn, she was pretty.

Lydia began. "Most of you workers are familiar with the Cab Shop. This will make the start-up procedure much easier. I will now read a list of what jobs are still open. If I mention a job you are interested in, please raise your hand."

She began reading off the job descriptions. Looking across the line, I could see that my old job was already filled. Some older guy was busy fillin' up the screw bins and stackin' the pencil rods and clamps. I wanted to kill the bastard. Didn't he realize he was trespassing?

I wasn't even listening to Lydia's job auction when I suddenly felt someone jerk my arm into the air. It was Ronny.

"We'll take 'em," he yelled.

"We'll take WHAT?" I demanded.

"The Suburban and Blazer tailgate buildup jobs."

"Oh."

Ronny already knew both of the buildup jobs. Hell, he knew practically every job in the entire Jungle. Ronny also knew me well enough to know that I'd work my ass off in order to set up a scheme. He knew that if the two of us worked the tailgates as a partnership, we could fancy out a little system that would allow us plenty of free time. I thanked Ronny for volunteering me. It wasn't the marvelous setup I'd had with Dale, but it was probably the next best thing in the department. Had he not grabbed my arm, I might've wound up boltin' down cargo beds or fittin' doors.

We attacked our new jobs. The hitch was to bust ass and built up the tailgates faster than they were pulling them off the end of our feeder line. We each drilled our separate tailgates, leaned them aside, and once we had enough built, it was time to converge and arrange the tailgates on the conveyor line. When the bottom layer was finished, we began double-stacking. When all was completed, the conveyor line was this trudging, two-tiered mountain of gleaming silver slowly creeping toward the buttocks of the nation's finest-built recreational vehicles.

Being twenty-four jobs ahead of the line amounted roughly to forty-five minutes of free time. Not bad, not bad at all. It wasn't nearly enough time to reach last call up at Houghton Lake or hibernate in a cardboard tomb, but it was time enough to play some three-handed euchre with Gary, the door-build guy, or, more frequently, to go wandering down to the cafeteria with Ronny on one of his massive feeding frenzies.

The GM Truck & Bus cafeteria—Dachau for the average stomach lining, a linoleum nightmare, Guyana soup kitchen for the famished and foolhardy. The place always looked yellow to me as if the air itself had contracted hepatitis. The inedibles were provided by an outside catering service who when asked the proverbial probe "How do you handle a hungry man?" must have replied "Botulism, just say ahhh." The astonishing part of it all was that so many workers partook in this bow-wow chow on a daily basis. I guess that's what happens when you're subject to a monopoly. There was nowhere else to eat. Your only alternatives were a few vending machines stocked with tantalizing entrees like canned chili, vinegar-flavored potato chips, pork rinds and stale Zagnut bars. Fasting was both a popular and intelligent option.

On one side of the cafeteria they served what they called "Full Course Meals." For about five bucks you would receive a slim gray slab of cow-thing, a side of artificial tater goop, a washed-out rainbow of veggies, a rectangle of lime Jell-o and a carton of warm milk.

The other side of the cafeteria featured "The Grill." This is where Ronny always did his serious chowin'. He had a soft spot in his hardened arteries for their cheeseburger deluxe with extra bacon. Watching Ronny consume two or three of his favorite monster burgers was both hilarious and hideous. All you could hear was this incredible suction noise punctuated by various slurps and burps. He wasn't eatin' the damn cheeseburgers as much as he seemed to be having oral sex with them.

I often had to warn Ronny to slow down. "Watch it, Jethro. You're gonna gnaw off a fingertip if you're not careful."

"Grrrrabll-aggaga-mooshrrrr," Ronny would respond, his mustache gloomed with mayo, his eyes glaring back at me like some fevered boar. What could be said. A boy and his burger. It was as inherently American as Washington crossing the Delaware or Billy Carter pissing on an airport runway.

THE SHOP FOOD MATCH GAME

Hey, just for kicks. Here's the directions: simply match the food listings in the numbered column with the corresponding taste sensations in the lettered column. No fair approaching a shoprat for assistance. Scoring: 9 or 10 correct—ready to dine on the set of a snuff movie. 7 or 8 correct—consider moving to the Republic of Mylanta. 5 or 6 correct—too wimpy to have a beer gut. Less than 5—pray that you never become blue-collar.

1. Mashed Potatoes
2. Beans & Franks
3. Reuben Sandwich
4. Chicken Soup
5. Tater Tots

A. Construction Paper
B. Alan Trammel's Sweat Socks Immediately After a Doubleheader
C. Sunoco High Octane 260

6. Turkey	D. Airplane Glue
7. Coney Dogs	E. Embalming Fluid
8. Patty Melt	F. Sam Kinison's Shower
9. Cole Slaw	Mat
10. Salisbury Steak	G. Squirrel Death
	H. Golfball Skins
	I. Collie Dung
	J. Grated Crickets

ANSWERS: 1-D, 2-C, 3-B, 4-E, 5-H, 6-F, 7-G, 8-A, 9-J, 10-I

Bob-A-Lou developed a total, heart-stompin' crush on one of the cashiers down in the cafeteria. She was this sassy, glam-babe blonde whose sole mission on earth seemed to be nothing more than providing herself as groin-swell for the hungry droves who wove through the slop lines. She'd lean there on her cashier's stool with her cleavage tumblin' out of her shrunken smock, her legs all stacked up for maximum eyeballin', a Doral forever dangling from the corner of her mouth. It was all just a game of show & tell.

Not for Bob-A-Lou. He was in love with the cashier queen. It all amounted to one terrible mismatch—the brutal cock-teaser and the hopeless romantic. Bob-A-Lou had never even had a girlfriend before. He was thirty-one years old and still lived with his mother. He was a complete innocent with a heart as big as a house. It all spelled trouble.

For the next couple months, Bob-A-Lou asked the cashier out repeatedly only to be given some lame excuse. Bob-A-Lou remained undeterred. Sooner or later, his cashier queen would agree to a date. I couldn't bring myself to tell Bob-A-Lou he was in for a terrible letdown. What I wanted to do was approach the cashier and ask her why she just didn't tell Bob-A-Lou she was engaged or something. C'mon, mercy kill the poor bastard. Let him down, bitch. Let him down before he proceeds with the wedding invitations.

The inevitable finally took place. One Monday afternoon after Ronny and I had filled up our conveyor line, I went over to chat with Bob-A-Lou at his welder's job. He just sorta nodded at me and flipped down his welder's visor. After he'd shot his welds, he took off his visor and sat down next to me. He was completely silent. Something had to be wrong.

"Everything all right?" I asked.

"You know Karen, the gal I'm always talkin' to down in the cafeteria?"

"Sure, the pretty one," I replied. "Something wrong with her?"

Bob-A-Lou shook his head. "No, she's feeling fine. In fact, she's feeling so fine that she was able to go bowling last Saturday night out at North Lanes after she told me she'd be out of town over the weekend for her aunt's funeral."

Bob-A-Lou went on to relate this long story about how he and his cousin had decided to go bowl a few frames the previous Saturday evening. While heading up to buy another Pepsi, pure Bob-A-Lou, he was shocked to spot the cashier queen a few lanes over smoochin' and gropin' all over this Surfer Joe look-alike. She even waved at Bob-A-Lou. His heart had been ripped apart ever since.

Then Bob-A-Lou paused. I was sure I could see it building up in his face. A cuss word! It was as if after years and years of polite constipation he was gonna finally let it loose. A limo-length volley of vulgarity along the lines of "goddamn whore-face shitball!" or "useless lyin' skag bait cunt." He was way overdue. There would be no better occasion. Let it rip!

"The dumb trollop," Bob-A-Lou hissed. Huh?

I stood there wanting to say it for him: BITCH! I wanted to say a lot of things. I wanted to tell him that there was much more to getting yourself laid than being an honest Joe. That crap rarely counted for anything when it came pork time. I wanted to tell him about all the bar scum right across the street who were having their peckers nibbled nightly and that the only jump they had on him was that they were complete selfish assholes who didn't give a shit about anything other than biceps and booze and tattoos and emptyin' their testes into the first shallow flooze who stumbled into their double vision.

There was hope, I wanted to tell him. There was always hope, but he was just gonna have to quit actin' like such a swell fuckin' pilgrim. He needed to ditch the crew cut. Act like a jerk. Develop a substance abuse problem. The girlies would come fallin' out of the trees.

Cynical or not, it was true. The shoprats I knew who did the most business with the ladies were utter cretins. Drunks, druggies, bullies and ten-time losers. Bob-A-Lou had more class than any roomful of them put together. But class rarely won the ass. The majority of these women wanted reclamation projects. Lost souls that they could clamp on to like precious martyrs. A guy void of defects mustered no challenge. Send in the cruds.

After the debacle with the cashier queen, Bob-A-Lou vowed to take his pursuit overseas. I thought he was shittin' me. He wasn't. He developed this hot pen pal relationship with some woman over in the Philippines. He flew over to marry her over our Christmas break. When he returned, he proudly displayed his wedding band to the entire Jungle. I felt happy for Bob-A-Lou. He was his old self again. Maybe now he could move out of his mother's house.

Meanwhile, my own personal marriage to the General Motors Corporation wasn't faring as well. Just like some wishy-washy broad who couldn't make up her mind, I was about to be sent packing on another indefinite layoff. Hello Reaganomics, goodbye occupation.

It was rather upsetting. Not so much the layoff part—I'd danced that dance and found it very compatible with my underachiever lifestyle. What rankled me about being laid off again was the knowledge that another pussy job was about to go slidin' through my fingers. My gravy setup with Ronny would be irretrievable just like my original scam with Dale had been. There was no way of knowing where I might end up and what kind of horrid rat maze would await me once everything settled back into place and the consumers started gettin' horny again.

During my second extended layoff, I spent most of my time drinking. My usual hangout was the Rusty Nail—a large, dimly lit tavern nestled downtown among the vacant store-fronts, and plywood palaces that effectively defined the flagging overall condition of Flint in general, and GM in particular. My brother's girlfriend, Jackie, managed the bar and we had full run of the place.

Looking back, I think the Rusty Nail days were some of the best times of my life. I was surrounded by my best friends, most of them shoprats in limbo. I was once again getting paid to do absolutely nothing. I felt detached and secure in this cocoon of nightly buffoonery. There was no reason to feel guilty. I had a job, they just didn't need me at the moment. I'd be back whenever the signal was given. Until then, I had found a handy place of refuge, possibly the last little fortress I'd ever be able to reside in before such puerile forays would be branded as stupefied adolescence or repeating the path of my father.

Jackie allowed me to take over complete control of the Rusty Nail jukebox. A well-stocked jukebox was essential to the atmosphere of any decent bar. I ditched all the top-forty flotsam and hackneyed standards. I loaded up on spazz-out masterpieces by the likes of Arthur Conley, the Troggs, the Mutants, Aretha, Black Flag and the Bobby Fuller Four. For us, the marvelous segue from Dino, Desi & Billy's "I'm a Fool" plowin' headlong into the spite and rancor of the Sex Pistols' "Holidays in the Sun" was beer-drenched ecstasy. Even the geezers and bag ladies got up and pranced.

It didn't take long before the twerps at the local college leeched on to our Shindig Mecca. The local art fag community soon followed. The bar was quickly overrun with the kind of clientele we most wanted to avoid. Before long, the Rusty Nail was doomed. Jackie started booking these prissy New Wave bands to come in and play almost nightly. God, it was putrid. These cheezy bastards wore these skinny little ties and spewed out lousy cover versions of the hitmakers of the day. It was more than we could bear. The place was now nothing more than a preppie playpen for the terminally dull.

We surrendered and moved our nightly reveling back to the house I shared with Bob. We danced, we drank, we threw up, we threw down, we broke up every piece of furniture and basically behaved like a bunch of raving lunatics. Women would drop by and scoot right back out the door. We didn't care. All of us were too loaded to get it up anyway. The Flint police got in the habit of dropping by. Occasionally, they'd take a few of us with them. Every cent we had went toward alcohol, cocaine and new records.

Drinking all night was fine, but I needed something to fill up the afternoons. That was one of the problems with unemployment. So often it wove itself into unenjoyment, sentencing you to a vague sprawl where the days all lumped together in one faceless herd. Working was almost preferable. Almost.

It was truly difficult to understand. I had hired in during such a boom era that the overtime alone would have provided enough income to survive on. Yet here I was four short years later assembling nothing but a crop of serious sloth and one mighty pickled liver. I guess it was that old inverse spiral motion where I had peaked in my rookie season and was now hurtling through the galaxy toward that warm plate of mystery stew on some lonesome mission room floor. At times I felt like standing out front of GM Headquarters and hollerin' through a bullhorn: "Attention! Enough with the fickle bullshit! Are we gonna build trucks or keep playin' hide-the-birthright? Hello! HELLO!"

Layin' back is a fine reward when you're employed. However, layin' back tends to wear thin when it itself becomes your job. Gettin' loaded, readin' magazines, staring at the television becomes a rut rather than any form of relaxation. It's like a kid nearing the end of summer. He might really hate school, but he begins to get awful antsy after three months of tossin' a ball back and forth and ridin' his bicycle halfway to hell and back. When every day is Saturday, Saturday is suddenly no big deal.

In an effort to find something to do while waiting out GM's dawdling, I decided to take up my old writing hobby. Each afternoon I'd plunk myself down in front of my mom's old Underwood typewriter and stare out the kitchen window ready to hatch some enormous tome that never came calling. I pecked away at everything from love poems to hate mail to haikus about spring. It all reeked and I knew it, but I banged away for lack of anything else to do.

This went on for a while until I stumbled onto an underground newspaper floating around town called the *Flint Voice*. I used to pick up a copy now and then up at the local liquor store. It was obvious that this rag was just some hippie relic patched together by a bunch of moaners desperately tryin' to reinvent the sixties. They took themselves way too serious and none of them had any real flair for knockin' out the printed word.

"In Times Such as These, We Need a Voice," their cover motto hurrumphed. This statement wasn't totally unfounded. Flint was falling apart at the seams—economically, politically, racially. The major's office was a bunch of liars and cheats, the city's prosecuting attorney was up on charges of embezzlement and the police force were in the·midst of their thunderous off-Broadway production of *Danny Get Your Gun*. In the late seventies and early eighties more people per capita were killed by police officers in Flint than in any other city in the country. Twenty-five percent of all gun-related deaths were done by cops. The boys were shootin' from the hip, askin' questions later and your odds were lookin' especially lousy if you happened to be sportin' an Afro. In times such as these we not only needed a "Voice," we could have used a few thousand bulletproof vests.

The *Flint Voice* was the brainchild and squawkin' brat of a long-haired live wire named Michael Moore. I was familiar with the guy. So was anyone in Flint who had one eye half open. Moore was constantly hurling himself into the midst of some trenchant uproar. You would see him on television, hear him raisin' hell on the radio, read about him causin' a ruckus down at a meeting of the City Council.

The underground paper biz was not the easiest boat to float, especially when half the town looked upon you as nothing more than a communist blowhard. In order to get his paper off the ground, Moor went delving for funds. Rather than appealing to the listless townsfolk, he attempted a crazier stunt. He latched on to an international recording artist and persuaded him to headline a steady stream of *Flint Voice* benefit concerts.

The recording star was the late Harry Chapin whose string of hits included "Taxi" and "Cat's in the Cradle." Moore managed to weasel himself backstage at the Chapin concert in nearby Lansing. After the show was over, Moore went to Chapin's dressing room and knocked on the door. No response. Moore kept a knockin'. Finally, a security guard began hauling Moore away. The resulting fracas caused Chapin to open the door to check things out. That's when Michael Moore put his silver tongue into gear. Intrigued by his notions, Chapin invited the persistent hippie into his dressing room.

Moore must have delivered some kind of impassioned oracle for, soon enough, Chapin became a regular fixture around Flint. He performed no less than eleven benefit concerts for the *Flint Voice*. The total take from these concerts was in the half-million-dollar range. Moore took the money and bought a big old house in the neighboring community of Burton. He bought a typesetting computer, layout equipment, telephones, copy machines. He hired ad men, secretaries and found himself a printer. Michael Moore and *Flint Voice* were on their way.

Meanwhile, it was Harry at the auditorium. Harry at the luncheon club. Harry at the union hall. Harry in your living room. Harry runnin' upstairs to use your can. Everyone was wild about Harry and so on and so forth. Chapin's appearances never failed to turn out the natives. He adopted Flint as his second home. If there was ever such a thing as a godsend, the *Flint Voice* had Harry Chapin as the living definition.

Anyways, one afternoon after the game shows had faded and the beer was kickin' in nicely, I decided to write up a record review and send it off to the *Voice*. They had a music section in the paper that was as bland and retro as a faded Nehru. I typed up a review of an album by a band called Shoes and tossed it in the mail.

A couple days later, Moore called me and asked if I would come out to the *Voice* to meet with him. Apparently, he had enjoyed the record review. Either that or he just wanted to know whether my basement would be available over the week- end to host one of Harry's gigs. No matter, just the prospect of gettin' off my sofa for a few hours, for any damn reason, had me feelin' mighty chipper. It was July 15, 1981.

The next afternoon I drained a couple beers and headed off for the *Flint Voice* office. I kept thinking maybe I was on to something. Something that might provide a buffer against the increasing humdrum of unemployment. Something that might distract me from the terrible lagoons in Richard Dawson's eyes. Something. Any damn thing.

I was about two miles away from the *Flint Voice* when the guy on the radio let it fly: "Popular musician and songwriter Harry Chapin was killed today when his small car collided with..." I pulled into the first convenience store I saw, bought a twelve-pack, and drove back home.

Eventually, I had my meeting with Michael Moore. We hit it off well. He was in no way the jaded hippie leftover I had come to envision. Moore shared my twisted sense of humor and, underneath his cocky veneer, he was just as mixed-up and insecure as I was. The only major difference between us was that he was loaded with drive, where I was just prone to bein' loaded. Moore put me on the staff as a music critic. It was the only thing I knew much about besides shoprats.

Without the generous benefit money raised by Harry Chapin, the *Flint Voice* soon began tilting toward debt. It was a strange period. Moore would insist that the *Voice* staff have a meeting once a month. Rarely would much be accomplished. Moore would stand up in the middle of someone's living room, plead for financing schemes, outline a new subscription drive and collapse on the couch while everyone turned their attention to their bawlin' infants or some pukish-lookin' asparagus dip one of the veggies was passin' around.

I could never figure out why I showed up for these briefings. There were never any ashtrays, no one smoked. There was never any beer or liquor, no one drank. I couldn't chime in on their heated discussions about El Salvador, I didn't even know where the damn place was. Everyone seemed to know everything about something and nothing about anything. Polyester rebels with fine homes and pretty wives and economical Japanese cars parked in the drive. I imagined their idea of revolution might be to refrain from mowing their lawns on consecutive Saturdays or cranking their goddamn Fleetwood Mac albums so loud that the mailman would frown.

Michael Moore would frequently approach me after these meetings, asking whether I would be interested in writing features for his paper. I would remind him that I knew very little about the struggles of mankind and all the other atrocities that seemed to rankle these people so. Never mind that shit, he'd tell me.

One night we were standing on the porch watching the others drive off. With El Salvador packed neatly away on the shelf, they needed nothin' but prompt shuteye. "You work in the shop," Moore mentioned. "Why not write about that kind of experience?"

"Write about working in the factory? Who'd wanna know anything about *that* kind of shit? Besides, half the time GM keeps my ass out on the street. Where's the appeal in that?"

"You'd be surprised," Moore said.

A few weeks after our little discussion, I received a phone call from General Motors. It was time to rejoin the ranks of the employed. I was told to once again report to the Personnel office.

I stood around with the other recalls awaiting placement. I assumed that I would be briskly escorted back to the Jungle. The thought didn't discomfort me. It would be nice to see the old gang again. Perhaps I could even land one of my old jobs.

After an hour or so, a big black guy in snazzy threads came into the room and pointed his finger at me and a couple of the other recalls. He looked like a post-forty version of Muhammad Ali. He told us to follow. I had never seen this man before. Obviously, this didn't bode well. An unfamiliar face would likely assure an unfamiliar place. As fucked-up and filthy as Cab Shop was, I still considered it my home.

We were not heading for the Cab Shop. I began feeling nervous and betrayed. We walked on and on, finally coming to an abrupt halt downstairs on the Rivet Line. I had heard various condemnations of this area—hard work, hard bosses, hard hours. You could only get lucky just so often. My luck was up.

The Ali clone had us huddle together. He introduced himself as Henry Jackson. I didn't care for the way he was smiling at us. Whenever a member of supervision slapped you with that kind of grin, it was like an unspoken broadcast that you were about to be dealt a shitload of misery and flung on the rack.

Henry Jackson spoke. "You men are now property of the Rivet Line. You will find that like any other department the Rivet Line has its share of good jobs and difficult jobs. I will confess, mostly the latter." He paused as if waiting for a chuckle that never came. "If there is only one thing that I want to stress to you men today, it is this. Follow me, please."

At this point, Jackson walked over to one of the dangling rivet guns. He stooped over and picked up a nearby board. He stuck the board in between the pinch space of the rivet gun and squeezed the trigger. The board immediately crumbled to the floor, splintered in half.

"Men, that could have just as easily been your finger," Henry Jackson stated. "Never, but never, for any reason put your hand anywhere near this section of the rivet gun."

Having demonstrated the danger that lurked within the jaws of the rivet gun, Jackson announced that he would now show us to our supervisor. I looked over at the guys I was with. We all seemed to be thinking the same thing: thank God, I thought *this* prick was gonna be our boss! Jackson introduced us to some horn-rimmed fella who had ASS SUCKER stamped all over his giant forehead. He was probably one of those textbook Einsteins from the General Motors Institute who'd never spent one lousy hour workin' the line and couldn't tell a callus from a collarbone. It didn't seem fair to have to take orders from someone who'd never gotten dirty or put a screw in its required locale. These guys were often marked for torment and mutiny.

Our foreman began dispersing us onto open jobs within the department. The Rivet Line was the starting point for all that went on during the three-day snake trail needed to assemble a truck. The complete birth procedure began right here. It started with a couple of long black rails. As the rails were hoisted onto crawling pedestals, the workers began riveting them together and affixing them with various attachments. There weren't any screws or bolts to be been. Just rivets. Thousands upon thousands of dull gray rivets. They resembled mushrooms.

Stanley, our foreman, stuck me on a job right near the beginning of the process. He introduced me to the guy who would be breaking me in. The lucky bastard was going back to his old job on sanitation. This realization caused the guy to start whoopin' and hollerin' and jumpin' around like a man who'd just wriggled out of a noose. I took this as a bad omen. I waited as the ex-riveter finished his celebration dance.

Exhausted, he shook my hand. "I'm gonna give it to you straight," he said. "This job fucking sucks. There's no sense in lyin' to you. Until you get it down, your hands will ache, your feet will throb and your back will feel like it's been steamrolled. If you're not jerkin' the rivet gun around, you'll be wrestlin' to get the next frame into position. On top of that, you have to build up your own stock and there's plenty of it."

"Are there any advantages to working down here?" I asked pitifully.

The guy scratched at his beard. "Well, the exit to the time clocks and the parking lot is just down those stairs. Come lunchtime or quittin' time, you can usually get a good jump on the rest of the pack."

That was it? A head start to the parking lot? A shot at bein' the first guy in line at the beer and wine store? Shit, maybe I should've gone to college or attended Bartender's School.

For the next couple hours I stood back and studied the routine. You were given three days to learn your assignment. I didn't plan on jumpin' in until absolutely necessary. I looked around at those who would soon be my neighbors. I'd seen happier faces on burn victims.

When our first break arrived, I snuck across the train cove and sped up the stairwell to the Cab Shop. I was in desperate search of Lydia, my previous supervisor. I was hoping she might be able to pull some strings and get me the hell off the Rivet Line. I was a Jungle boy. Rivets and rails weren't in my blood. I needed a transfusion of screws, sparks and sheet metal.

I caught up with Lydia as she was heading down to the supervisor's cafeteria. She stopped and smiled brightly. Damn, she was pretty.

"Ben, it's great to see you back to work," she said. She looked down at my belly and giggled. "It looks like the layoff didn't hurt your appetite any!"

"I'm pretty good with the beer," I replied.

"So, where are you workin' now? Are you still upstairs?"

"Unfortunately, no. They stuck my ass down on the Rivet Line. That's what brings me to you. Is there any possible way you can twist things around and get me back up to Cab Shop? I'll take any job you have open."

Lydia thought for a moment. "The person you would really have to talk to is Art." Art was our old General Foreman. "We've got a couple of openings, but you would have to go through him."

"Do me a favor, Lydia. The next time you see Art, tell him I have to speak to him. Remind him of what a great worker I've been. I hate to ask you to lie, but I don't think I can hack it on the Rivet Line."

"I'll pass it along, Ben. Hopefully, something can be worked out."

I hustled back down the stairwell and, once again, cut across on one of the boxcars. Taking a shortcut through the trains was strictly forbidden by management. It was a definite safety hazard, one that everybody ignored. If you happened to be caught cutting through the train, there would be a firm lecture and a reprimand waiting on the other side.

This part about having trains moseyin' in and out only twenty yards away from my new job struck me as odd. It was just an example of how large the Rivet Line area really was. One gigantic, barn-like cavern where the trains pulled up, unloaded and departed again. It was all somehow spooky. Trains belonged in train yards. Trains belonged on hillsides. Trains belonged on bridges. Above all, trains belonged outdoors. It made me nervous to be in the same room with a train.

The whistle blew and the Rivet Line began to crawl. I took a seat up on the workbench and watched the guy I was replacing tackle his duties. He'd grab one end of a long rail and, with the help of the worker up the line from him, flip it over on its back. CLAAAANNNNNNGGGG! He then raced back to the bench and grabbed a four-wheel-drive spring casting and a muffler hanger. He would rivet the pieces onto the rail. With that completed, he'd jostle the rail back into an upright position and grab a cross member off the overhanging feeder line that curled above the bench. Reaching up with his spare arm, he'd grab a different rivet gun while fidgeting to get the cross member firmly planted so that it aligned with the proper set of holes. He then inserted the rivets and began squashing the cross member into place. Just watching this guy go at it made my head hurt.

"How about takin' a stab at it?" the guy asked me after a while. "You're not gonna get the feel of the job sittin' up there on the bench."

I politely declined. I didn't want to learn any portion of this monster maze before it was absolutely necessary. Once the bossman thought you had a reasonable grasp of the setup, he was likely to step in and turn you loose on your own. I needed to keep delaying in order to give Art some time to reel me back up to Cab Shop.

"Well, you've got three days," the guy replied. "After that, this baby's all yours."

I puttered around the rest of the day tryin' my best to look like I was in deep rumination regarding the task at hand. It wasn't until the middle of the next day that I was able to track down Art. When I caught him, I practically started yanking off his shirt sleeve. Lydia had already informed him of my urgent appeal. I asked Art what he could do.

He exhaled slowly. "It's simply not that easy," he began. "Once you've been assigned to an area it's damn near impossible to get you transferred out. Especially when that area is the Rivet Line. Not many people want to work down there so they tend to clutch on to their workers. However, I'll see what I can do about working out a trade. They won't surrender one of their bodies without a replacement in return."

Trade? Surrender? Bodies? This was beginning to stink like some insuperable hostage shakedown. Trade positions? In that case, my trade value had to be nil. Who in their right mind would be willing to swap places with a doomed goomer from the River Line? It would be like having a guy in the drunk tank asking to switch spots with a loser on death row.

By the start of my third day on the Rivet Line, it was evident that a trade was not in the offing. Art started payin' me all this lip service about "someday in the future" and "guttin' it out" when all he was really sayin' was "you silly asshole, I could search from now until retirement and never run across a dupe so ignorant that he'd trade spots with you."

I gave up hope and surrendered to my new placement. I was to be a riveter. It was now my sworn duty to learn my job as quickly and professionally as possible. I only had one day left to perfect what they referred to as "the pinup job." If I couldn't answer the bell after the allotted three-day break-in period, GM had every right to usher me down that nearby stairwell, past the time clocks, out the exit and point me in the general direction of nowhere. Nowhere seemed fine in a way, but it was highly doubtful that nowhere paid $12.82 an hour and fixed your rotten teeth for free.

6

MOST CALAMITIES IN LIFE EVENTUALLY FADE AWAY AND LEAVE you scratchin' your skull as to why you allowed yourself to get so tensed in the first place. My River Line anxiety was one such calamity. I soon conquered the toilsome pinup job and burrowed myself a pliable little rut. Along with the assistance of the day shift operator, I squawked and raised enough hell about the stock-building portion of the job to have it taken away and assigned elsewhere. This allowed me a little free time in between jobs—just enough to surface for air and give a quick wink to the madness.

There were several differences between my station on the Rivet Line and my old home in the Cab Shop. Most notable was the fact that I was now ball-and-chained to a job that kept me forever in motion. That merciless minute hand relented somewhat due to the fact that there just wasn't as much time to stand around clock-gazin'. Oftentimes I would get so scoped-in on my duties, so chiseled to the waltz of the rails, that I wouldn't even notice it was break time until I saw the rest of the crew peelin' off their gloves. I'd lock into the mission and stow my mind away so as not to have it interfere with the

absurdity of the regimen. Entire shifts would sail by during
which I hardly developed a tangible current of thought. The
last thing I wanted to do was lacerate my brain with the
nude truth lurking behind this mulish treadmill. A whore was
always better off if he or she avoided the ugly gaze of the
trick.

There were other differences. As opposed to Cab Shop,
the River Line was a place of relative solitude. Conversation
was rare and assembly line hijinks were extinct. This met with
my favor since most of the guys surrounding me were seasoned
rednecks. They wore the telltale garb: bib overalls, flannel
shirts, hunting caps and jackets displaying the logo of our local
union. They carried lunch buckets with their precious Chiquita
banana stickers plastered all over 'em. The banana stickers
were a dead giveaway. The true redneck treated these decals
as if they were Congressional Medals of Honor. If one were to
begin peeling off, the owner would scramble about looking for
some industrial adhesive to secure the sticker back into place. I
hadn't the slightest clue as to what those banana stickers
represented. Perfect attendance? Intelligence quotient? Ani-
mals slaughtered? They were like the helmets of college football players adorned with team decals awarded for outstanding
plays. It seemed silly and useless, but I wasn't gonna chuckle. I
was fond of the notion that my teeth stay rooted to my gums.

The only guy I ever spoke with was my line neighbor,
Hank. He was an old coot whose voice sounded like gravel
being churned against broken glass. He smoked two packs of
Chesterfields each shift. It made me uncomfortable to hear him
speak. Everything was punctuated with a hack or coughin'
spasm or a lung cookie flung toward the aisle. He'd apologize
and light up another.

Hank was a strange one. He kept vacillating between two
very dissimilar personalities. One week he'd be the perverted
old man. He'd start pesterin' me about the size of my girlfriend's
breasts, croakin' on and on about the young female anatomy,
droolin' about his own niece, mesmerized in his lecher's roll call
of "sweetmeat" and "baby cakes." If Hank would have left it at
that, he'd have hardly qualified as bein' remotely oddball. Tits
and tight cheeks and the relentless pursuit of such were
perennial assembly line themes.

What separated Hank was that the very next week he'd transform into this Bible-clutchin' Jesus comrade. He'd spend all of his idle time extolling the virtues of celibacy and the cleansed soul. He'd approach my work area and ask me in that horrible rasp of his whether I "knew Christ." I would reply that Christ and I had been cellmates together for several years in Catholic school systems. This seemed to please Hank. He would look around at our co-workers and tell me that the entire bunch of them were headed to hell. On the other hand, I was to be spared. I feigned delight as Hank returned to his bench for another Chesterfield.

Working beside a full-blown schizoid seemed preferable to jawin' it over with the rednecks. At least Hank wasn't given to the curious worship of banana stickers. I figured Hank's bi-weekly shuffle between perversity and righteousness was just his wacky formula for covering both sides of the tracks. For all I knew, he may have had a crawlspace lined with "sweetmeat" and a shrine to Jesus in his living room. It hardly mattered. I liked Hank, but I will admit that the day they transferred him back to his old booth-cleaner's job I was just as elated about the switch as he was.

After about four months down on the Rivet Line, I had truly perfected the mental and physical strain of the pinup job. The blisters of the hand and the mind had hardened over, leaving me the absolute master of the puppet show. I developed shortcuts at every turn. I became so proficient at twirlin' my rivet gun to and fro that the damn thing felt as comfortable as a third arm. I mashed my duties into pitiful redundancy.

The truth was loose: I was the son of a son of a bitch, an ancestral prodigy born to clobber my way through loathsome dungheaps of idiot labor. My genes were cocked and loaded. I was a meteor, a gunslinger, a switchblade boomerang hurled from the pecker driblets of my forefathers' untainted jalopy seed. I was Al Kaline peggin' home a beebee from the right field corner. I was Picasso applyin' the final masterstroke to his frenzied *Guernica*. I was Wilson Pickett stompin' up the stairway of the Midnight Hour. I was one blazin' tomahawk of m-fuggin' eel snot. Graceful and indomitable. Methodical and brain-dead. The quintessential shoprat. The Rivethead.

However, my ascension into this new sense of dominance

didn't rid me of the age-old plight that came to haunt every screw jockey: what the fuck do you do to kill the clock? There were ways of handling nimwit supervisors and banana sticker rednecks and lopsided rails. But the clock was a whole different mammal altogether. It sucked on you as you awaited the next job. It ridiculed you each time you'd take a peek. The more irritated you became, the slower it moved. The slower it moved, the more you thought. Thinking was a very slow death at times.

Desperation led me to all the usual dreary tactics used to fight back the clock. Boring excursions like racing to the water fountain and back, chain-smoking, feeding Chee-tos to mice, skeet shooting Milk Duds with rubber bands, punting washers into the rafters high above the train depot, spitting contests. Any method was viable just as long as it was able to evaporate one more stubborn minute.

I did have one favorite method of beatin' the clock. What I would do was to pretend my job was an Olympic event. I would become both television narrator and participant. It would go something like this:

"We've come to the end of another long day for the American squad. So far, the Japanese have totally dominated each event, sweeping the gold and silver in every category. Any final hopes the Americans might have of winning a gold medal rest solely on the shoulders of Ben Hamper, an assembler out of the GM Truck & Bus facility in Flint, Michigan.

"Hamper will be competing in the Freestyle Rivet Squash. Though he's considered a long shot at best, you will see in this recent interview that Hamper believes he's capable of pulling off the upset.

"Ben, the word around camp is that you lack experience. Sources point to the fact that you've only been riveting a short while. How do you respond to this line of criticism?"

"[Bleep] 'em! Maybe I don't know apples from oranges, but I can assure you I know my way around a rivet gun. You can toss that inexperience tag right in the crapper."

"In light of their domination in these games, would it be fair to assume that you harbor a personal vendetta against the Japanese contingent?"

"Strictly pride, Mr. McKay. I represent the United States of America. I stand for all that is sacred among Americans: The automobile. Hot dogs. Baseball. Disneyland. Trash bag murders. As for the Japanese, I own their butts. I'm Nagasaki and Godzilla and the *Enola Gay* all wrapped into one powder keg. I'm gonna send them all back to fritterin' with transistor radios and toaster ovens."

At this point in my fantasy, I would stalk around my job psyching myself. I'd begin flexing my arms and jogging in place. I'd hiss and growl. I'd slowly pull on my gloves while staring down my imaginary foe. The crowd would be in absolute pandemonium—Yankee Doodle banshees sensing the kill. I would return to the narration:

"The time Hamper will have to beat is 24.46 seconds, the new world's record set only moments ago by Koy Dung of Japan. Hamper certainly appears undaunted. He's even taking time out to taunt his Japanese rival. It remains to be seen whether this confident young riveter from Michigan can back up such cocky behavior.

"The American signals that he is ready. We now await the whistle. It sounds and Hamper is off. Immediately, he's got the rail flipped and is attaching the muffler hangers. He grabs for his rivet gun and... OH MY... would you take a look at this! All we can see is one frantic blur. Hamper swings in the second rivet gun and begins his attack on the final leg. He twists, he pivots, he unleashes the gun. This very well might be... YES... YES! 22.19 seconds! Hamper has done it! A new world's record. AMERICA WINS THE GOLD! AMERICA WINS THE GOLD!

"Total bedlam has broken loose. Throngs of Americans have broken through the barriers and are now lifting Hamper high upon their shoulders. We can see an exuberant Roger Smith, the Chairman of General Motors, attempting to squeeze his way through the mass of celebrants. Smith has now reached the gold medalist and is extending his hand. This had to be a very special moment for Hamper. In a span of mere seconds, he has sprung from absolute obscurity to a position of corporate eminence. Roger Smith is now embracing Hamper. What an emotional moment! Smith is openly weeping as the jubilant riveter pats him on the head. This outpouring of mirth shall last forever in the annals of Olympic glory."

Actually, it only lasted until the next set of rails arrived.

The roar of the crowd was quickly replaced by the roar of the machines. Jim McKay scurried back into my wealthy imagination. Roger Smith was nowhere to be seen. The cheering faded away and, with it, a few more minutes off the clock. That, in itself, was victory enough.

After nearly a year on the Rivet Line, a period of almost total isolation, I finally met someone who was neither a redneck, a pervert, an ass-sucker or a religious fanatic. His name was David Steel and he worked the gas tank bracket job across the line and three jobs down. Little did I know then how closely entwined our destinies would become within the digestive tract of our General Motors tenure.

It started with a feature article I had written for the *Flint Voice*. I was especially excited about this piece because it was the first thing I'd written to be displayed on the *Voice* cover. Usually I got buried toward the back in between some dyke manifesto and an ad for a new health food eatery.

The article was entitled "Rock is Dead," a personal tirade I had written condemning the state of the airwaves over at the local FM radio crotch-rock mothership. I was still resisting my editor's constant plea to write something regarding my braindead enshrinement as a shoprat. The entire concept made me yawn. I stuck to rambling on about obscure rock music.

I decided to use my cover story as a means of introducing myself to David Steel. One night during a breakdown on the line, I hopped over the track and handed Dave a copy of the *Voice* to examine. He glanced at the headline and seemed enthused by the topic. The line began to roll again and I hopped back over the track to return to my pinup duties.

Though we had never spoken, Steel had always intrigued me. Like myself, he was a total loner. He kept to himself and shuffled back and forth every night with this glum-lookin' scowl. What impressed me most about him was that, for reasons unknown, he appeared to be the personal whipping boy of Henry Jackson, the supervisional brute of the entire Frame Line. Jackson was forever storming down the line and jumping into his shit about something I could never quite overhear. Steel just ignored him. Occasionally, he'd flip Jackson the bird and all hell would break loose. I figured any enemy of Henry Jackson should be a friend of mine.

At the end of the shift that night, Dave motioned to me as we fled for the time clocks. He said he agreed with my assessment on the horrible condition of modern radio, comparing it to the monotonous humdrum of the assembly line. Then, he paused.

"Do you like to drink?" he asked.

"More than most," I said.

"Perhaps we should go get drunk."

"That seems like a sensible idea."

In the weeks and months to come, Dave and I formed our own two-man clique. It was strange how many things we had in common. We both had experienced bumpy childhoods. We both had been drughead outcasts in high school. We both had gotten married far too young. We both held a serious contempt for the majority of the human race. We hated our jobs and our bosses and our union reps. We hated Miss America and sunlight and Christmas. We were discontented and bored.

Like me, Dave came from a fertile background of shoprats. His grandfolks and parents had been lifers at GM. We joked about this constantly—how factory servitude was something so predestined within our genes that we had probably both lain in our mother's wombs practicing assembly maneuvers. ("Bernard, I can feel the baby kicking. No, wait—he's RIVETING!") We referred to ourselves as thoroughbreds.

It did come as a surprise when Dave told me he had gone to college. He had spent five years at Michigan State majoring in telecommunications. This didn't jibe at all with the usual route of a GM thoroughbred. Dave explained that he was just biding time, takin' a few years off to fool around before scrounging back home for that old familiar birthright.

"I always knew I'd end up here," Dave confessed. "I wanted to be a nobody."

"Well, you sure chose the right place." I laughed.

"Exactly," Dave continued. "I figure if you have to work, you may as well do something so lame and uneventful that you're not even required to think. I hate this job, but I hate it less than anything that would require daily human contact."

And herein lay my real attraction to David Steel. I had finally met someone who was ultimately more cynical and sulky than I was. This was not an easy order. There seemed to be no end to Dave's miserable yen for pessimism and self-pity. He was the total opposite of my old friend Bob-A-Lou. For instance, if you were to ask Bob whether a glass of water on the counter was half full or half empty, he would most certainly reply with the former. If you were to pose the same question to Dave, he'd probably reply "bone dry and covered with leeches."

Dave became my vicarious martyr. His rampant gloom and constant self-abasement made me feel comparatively blessed. Anytime I needed a quick fix of cheer, all I had to do was hook up with Dave for a while. It was like being cellmates on death row with Woody Allen.

We spent our lunch breaks together out in Dave's old Vega. We'd share a little whiskey, peering straight ahead at the barbed wire and the moonlight and the gulls pecking away on discarded chicken bones. I remember one night something occurred to me that I'd always been curious about. It was time to approach Dave for an answer.

"What is it with you and Henry Jackson? Why is he always reamin' your ass?"

Dave took a slug off the bottle. "That fuckin' gorilla hates me."

"What'd you do? Spill tranny fluid all over one of his Italian suits?"

"Worse than that. I was born."

"Knowing Henry, I suppose that would be grounds enough."

"I used to work for him when I hired in. From day one, we've been at it. He hates me because he realizes I'm far more intelligent than him. But, then again, so is a lug wrench."

"He reminds me of Muhammad Ali."

Dave shook his head. "You're way off. Henry Jackson is the Idi Amin of the Western Hemisphere. God, I hate that prick. He's always whinin' that I have an attitude problem."

"Dave Steel...an attitude problem?" I laughed.

"Hey, fuck you. My supposed attitude problem could be quickly remedied if only a stock crate fell over and flattened his fat ass. That would improve my attitude immensely."

We got in a few more weeks before the layoffs came calling again. Having spent a year on the pinup job, I was never so grateful to be handed another pink slip. My team spirit was lacking. I needed a seat on the curb to shove the stuffing back under my scalp. Dave was even more elated than I was. He was like some kind of foamin' mongrel strangling to get off the leash.

However, a curious thing happened on our path to the curb. On the last night before we were to be released, Henry Jackson came stridin' through our department and pulled Dave aside. Dave was told that he wouldn't be a part of the layoff. Instead, Henry Jackson had personally arranged it so that Dave would be shipped over to the Pickup Line to work. What made this especially cruel was the fact that there were several workers who didn't *want* to be laid off. Family men who could have used the monetary security of a firm forty-hour work-week. Henry Jackson wasn't interested in such sensible arrangements. He was too entangled in his personal vendettas.

Dave was seething. He wanted out the door with the rest of us. It wasn't to be. David had an attitude problem. It seemed odd that GM would want someone like that to remain behind and tend to business. Then again, Idi Amin was never really known for his rational logic.

On my way out, I stopped to wish Dave the best. He was hardly in a talkative mood. I told him that someday we would both laugh at this ill turn. It seemed strange that I was trying to soothe the rage of a man who was doomed to *keep* his job while all around me there were scores of dejected workers shuffling for the exit bemoaning the loss of theirs.

There was so much that I just didn't understand. Less each day, in fact.

Meanwhile, I was becoming somewhat of a favorite read in the pages of the *Flint Voice*. I was being prodded on by my editor who saw me as some kind of Chuckie Kuralt from Septicland. He was obviously using me as a loony wedge to pry between all the weighty prattle regarding police atrocities, chemical dump sites, women's rights and the ongoing conflicts in Central America and the Middle East. I knew nothing of this shit. That suited Mike Moore just fine. He even temporarily stopped pestering me about writing shoprat chronicles. I was grateful.

As the official *Voice* buffoon, I was enlisted to cover a series of oddball events. I wrote about gettin' drunk and bounced from an Osmond Family concert. I was assigned to undergo the head-whackin' miracle cure at an Ernest Angley revival hoedown. I did an interview with Buddy Holly, who, curiously enough, had been dead for over twenty fuckin' years. I wrote about having intercourse with a woman who damn near dejeweled me after lathering through an Elvis impersonator show. In short, serious goddamn journalism that the nuns had never taught me.

Then came the "Toughman Contest" assignment. Nothing on the face of this planet could have been more representative of the Flint Experience than this human cockfight. An old-fashioned, city-sanctioned bloodletting. Total lunkhead theater. (For the unfamiliar, a "Toughman Contest" is an event where people pay money to watch any asshole off the street try to pulverize any other asshole off the street in hopes of winning a thousand-dollar grand prize.) Several states had outlawed these contests for their sheer primitivism. But this was Michigan. Better yet, this was Flint. Let the pummeling begin.

I remember insisting that I not have to attend this carnage by myself. I surely wasn't going to invite my girlfriend along and no one else I knew was this hard up for kicks. My companions for this ugly venture turned out to be Molly, the world's most sorely underpaid office manager, and Mike Moore, her camera-totin' boss.

We took our seats just as two heavyweights entered the ring. The fighter in the blue corner was introduced as "representing GM Truck & Bus." I immediately stood and applauded. Opposing my gallant union brother was a two-legged mobile home with a Pancho Villa mustache who appeared ready to gnaw through the breastplate of the next thing that moved. The odds looked bad for the good guys.

The bell sounded and the two hulks came out charging. It didn't take long to realize that defense was a worthless priority to these toughmen. They attacked in a continual forward lurch, arms flailing like crazed pistons, legs spread wide and wobbly, their careless chins poking straight ahead like heat-seeking greeting cards. It was total global warfare with nothing held in reserve. A kamikaze rage that had about as much to do with the true art of pugilism as slam-dancing had with classical ballet.

By the third and final round, neither of the boys had much left. Both fighters looked as if they were sleepwalkin' back to the boneyard. Bloodied and swollen, they staggered to and fro in each other's arms, occasionally separating to launch one last feeble attempt at a haymaker. At the same time, the crowd was screeching for a kill. "Hit him with your purse, you pussy!" shouted one fine American down below us. Nothing short of decapitation was gonna soothe the bloodlust of these patriots.

I remember glancing over at Molly. She had her hands over her eyes. I turned my attention to the crowd and looked at them dispassionately. They roared like hyenas in a feeding frenzy, insatiable in their need for pain and turmoil. Malt liquor eye sockets bulging behind shrunken leisure suits. A night on the town for the dead and dying.

Flint, glorious Flint. I think I understood their grief and what it was that attracted them so to this ridiculous mayhem. They certainly weren't here as spectators of sport, for this "Toughman Contest" could hardly qualify as anything more than organized barbarism. I believed they were all here to commit some kind of weird personal exorcism. The toughmen were just convenient foils for the true meat-grinders of the world: the landlords, the foremen, the cops, the judges, the nagging spouse, the fools in charge. Violence as one glorious teething ring for the benumbed and trampled masses.

Flint, with all of its automotive start-ups and shutdowns. All the uncertainty and paranoia and idle tension. It wasn't so strange. It was a real wonder we weren't *all* being fitted for loincloths and nose bones. Where have you gone Joe DiMaggio, our lonely ratpack wants to KICK YOUR SAGGIN', COFFEE-BREWIN' ASS!

We sat through several more bouts. I began to warm to the commotion and repeated calls for blood. Mike rejoined us. For the past hour he had been snapping photos at ringside. "It smells like piss and vomit down there," he offered. Molly put her hands back over her eyes.

Curiously, my editor thought that it would be a great idea if I accompanied him back down and interviewed some of the crowd near the action. Naturally, I refused.

"Ben, a good reporter sticks his nose right into the story."

"In piss and vomit?" I moaned.

"Just come down and talk to some of these people," he pleaded. "A journalist has to move around."

"Listen. I'm not a journalist, I'm not a reporter—I'M A SHOPRAT! Just like 90 percent of these losers. When will you get this through your head?"

The answer, of course, was never. Moore continued to spur me on toward the next deadline. He began to swap and sell my pieces to other underground rags. I knew nothing of this network of left-leanin' publications other than the fact that they paid rather poorly—if at all. Moore assured me that this was fine. The important thing was that I was gaining recognition. I assured him that beer money was a higher priority.

Not everyone was taking a shine to my writing hobby. I became aware of this one morning as I scanned through the *Flint Journal*. Under a headline that read "Fluent Settlement Sought" was the announcement that the *Flint Voice*, Michael Moore and Ben Hamper were being sued for libel in Genesee Circuit Court by an establishment called the Good Times Lounge.

The article I had written regarding the Good Times Lounge was almost a year old. In it, I had noted that the Good Times Lounge was without a doubt the rowdiest launch pad in town. A real thug palace full of biker scum and dopeheads and heavy metal retards who, for the sheer heck of it, would pounce on the clientele and proceed to change a chump's face from gorgeous to goulash. "What this place lacks in ambience it makes up in ambulance," I observed at the time. For such findings, I was being shook down for ten thousand dollars. Ditto Michael Moore and the *Voice*.

On the day of our hearing, I waited for Moore in the court lobby. Fifteen minutes late, he came bustlin' through the big glass doors wearin' these horribly faded jeans and a worn-out flannel shirt that appeared to have been heisted from the bedroom clutter of Eb, the kindly farmhand on *Green Acres*. So much for dazzling the court with dapper threads.

I shook my head and groaned. "Who's the judge in this case, Junior Samples?"

"Oh, sorry, I couldn't find anything clean," Moore understated.

The courtroom seemed to be a busy place this day. A parade of legal dogs flowed back and forth through the hallway as we sat waiting and wondering when it would be our turn to fidget before the robe. Moore seemed to enjoy the atmosphere, engaging in small talk with a few of the assembled litigants. I slouched next to him fumbling for cigarettes, a complete basket case. I yearned to be back on the old pinup job, engulfed up to my elbows in muffler hangers and rivets and total nothingness. There were never any surprises awaiting the pinup man.

At last, our lawyer motioned us into the courtroom. It seemed as though we were sitting in pews. No one smiled. I could smell foul lies and old tears. The court typist stared blankly ahead as if she had just been sentenced to hang for omitting a comma.

The judge weaved his way through the hopelessly legal introduction to the case. When he finished, our lawyer stood and prepared to begin his opening remarks. All at once, the judge stopped him—leaning back with a huge grin, fixing his eyes directly on Moore and me.

Holy shit, I shuddered. He's laughing at us! We're guilty as sin. We reek of guilt and ooze with fault. Oh, sweet Jesus, I'll probably wind up in a cell with some droolin' psychopath who ain't had any rump since LBJ croaked. This couldn't be happening. The court typist looked up at us with dead floating porpoise eyes. She'd probably been a fuckin' nun! I felt like swan-divin' right out the third-story window. Whatever happened to justice for all?

The judge finally spoke: "Gentlemen, I feel it is only fair to both parties that I disqualify myself from this case immediately." Huh? The judge went on to explain that he'd once rented office space from my editor's grandfather, that he was good friends with my editor's parents, that his wife had served on some stupid committee with my editor, and that he had once purchased ad space for his reelection in the *Flint Voice*. Why couldn't this guy just have kept his yap shut? Here we had a judge in our hip pocket and he was bailin' out on us. Forget the damn photo album, let's gavel this libel bullshit right out through the metal detectors. The bottom line was that we were INNOCENT MEN. Who cared about these untidy incidentals? Just because so-and-so knows so-and-so doesn't mean the Good Times Lounge was suddenly the Vatican.

Urrrgh. The case was rescheduled for the next month, supposedly with a judge who hadn't been Mike Moore's Cub Scout leader, poker buddy or gay lover.

While awaiting the next hearing, we were pleasantly shocked

to learn that the Good Times Lounge had suddenly dropped the whole lawsuit. Apparently, the owner had shut the place down and moved away to Alaska. It seemed like a terrific relocation to me. This whole business of attorneys and plaintiffs and motions was making me one goddamn nervous wreck.

My editor realized this and, with it, an opening. He asked if I would meet him at his office. I drove out and he put it to me: "Instead of dealin' with all of this other nonsense, how about writing a factory column each issue?"

I didn't hesitate. "Sounds like a solid career move," I agreed.

I was eventually reeled back into the GM nest. However, this time, a big curveball was awaiting me. I was told to report for duty at 6:00 A.M. the following morning. Something had to be terribly wrong. Six A.M. was the start-up time for the first shift. First shift was always reserved for the old-timers—guys who enjoyed wakin' with the roosters and rollin' into the plant with industrial-sized buckets of convenience store coffee splashin' all over their floorboards.

Considering my comparatively low seniority, how did I figure in with this pack? I was a relative youngster. I didn't have fake choppers or war tattoos or Benny Goodman on eight-track. I hated fuckin' coffee. I hated birds tweetin' and alarm clocks and disc jockeys reciting the wind chill factor. There was just no figurin' General Motors. When it came time to make a move, I think they just threw darts at a board or yanked on straws.

To compound my misery, I was told to report to the Axle Line. The Axle Line was only a short distance from the Rivet Line; however it may as well have been a thousand miles away. The Axle Line area was eerie. The lighting was a very dingy yellow. The workers looked like ghouls dippin' between fog banks. Just as disturbing was the awkward silence. Instead of the normal bashing and crashing, all you could hear was this annoying clicking sound like a far-off game of marbles.

My new foreman, a Mr. Hurley, scribbled down my name and number. He told me to follow him to my new placement. "Have you ever operated a hoist before, Hamper?" he asked.

"No, sir," I answered. "My specialty is riveting."

"Sorry, no rivets down here, pal."

I followed the boss as we weaved our way through countless piles of axles. Each one appeared to be a different shape or
design. They lay there atop each other like missiles ready for
launch.

"Hamper, this is Mark Garrison," Hurley said. "You will be
replacing Mark on the rear axle hoist job."

This Garrison fella was bustin' it so hard that he didn't
have time to turn around for any formal greetings. He flung his
right hand over his shoulder and I gave it a slap. It was only
forty-five minutes into the shift and the poor bastard's shirt
was already soaked through.

Hurley left us alone. In order to talk with Garrison, I had
to race back and forth while he dragged his hoist around
searching for the next axle that coincided with his schedule
sheet. Once located, he hoisted the axle into the air and hustled
back to the outstretched arms of the axle carrier. With one
mighty heave, he slid the axle into place. Immediately, he
pivoted and glanced at his schedule. It was time to fly off in the
direction of another brand of axle. I could only shake my head.
This job made thumping rivets look like a day at the Playboy
Mansion.

First break arrived and I accompanied Garrison down to
the cafeteria. I had many questions I wanted to ask—foremost,
what were a couple of young guys like us doing on the first
shift? Garrison explained that the plant was bringing back
several rehires to plug up some of the shit jobs that the
old-timers wanted no part of. "They figure that a worker fresh
off the streets is basically optionless," Mark relayed. "He has to
take whatever's thrown his way."

"Come on." I laughed. "There has to be plenty of family
men on second shift willing to take these jobs over. They'd take
anything to get off nights. I believe we're gettin' shafted."

"It wouldn't be the first time," Garrison replied.

The rest of the week unwound as one unholy nightmare.
Try as I might, I just couldn't get the hang of the rear axle
hoist job. I continually misread my schedule. I ran several
wrong pieces. I dropped axles on the floor. I busted the hoist
cable. I got shit so out of sequence that they had to shut down
the entire line to straighten things out.

Something was missing. I couldn't put my finger on it, but

I knew it revolved around the unloading of the axle onto the carrier arms. I asked Garrison to handle the job while I stood back in the aisle and observed. From this vantage point, the problem was apparent. It had nothing to do with brawn or style or technique. I WAS TOO FUCKING SHORT FOR THIS JOB! Where Garrison was long and lanky and could get eyeball-to-eyeball with the insertion process of the carrier arms, I was dwarfin' in at five feet six and a half and constantly depending on blind chance when sliding in the axle.

I approached the boss to tell him of my discovery. He was gabbin' to someone on the phone, so I slouched at the picnic bench and lit up a smoke. I felt better than I had in days. Wrong man, wrong job. It was that simple.

Hurley slammed down the phone and ran toward me. "Hamper, that was the General Foreman on the line. According to him, you've run three wrong axles in the past hour. God-damnit, I'm writin' your ass up NOW!"

Now I was hot. "I don't give a shit how many times you try to write me up. The whole problem is that I am too fucking short to see what the hell I'm doin' on that job. How can I hit the carrier arms when I can't even SEE the bastards?"

"Don't try to peddle me that line of bullshit. I've had short people run that job before."

This was getting us nowhere. A different mode of attack was necessary. I had another trump card that I'd been saving and it was time to use it. "I want my committee man down here—NOW!" Hurley raced back to the phone and called down to the union office. He really was convinced that he had me. He didn't know shit.

The committee man arrived. We conferred while Hurley glared at us and stewed at his desk. The issue we were talking over had nothing to do with my height or lack thereof. I was informing my committee man about the propaganda Hurley had been passing me about my request to be transferred onto the night shift. According to Hurley, a transfer was impossible due to my low seniority. In truth, he was lyin' out his ass just so that he could cover an unwanted job.

My committee man motioned for Hurley to join us. Oh, this was gonna be sweet. "Is it true that you have told this worker that he would be unable to transfer to the second shift because he lacked the proper amount of seniority to do so?"

Hurley was caught totally off guard. He was expecting an argument dealing with the height issue. He swallowed and attempted to smile. "Um, I suppose I did. The bottom line is that I have jobs down here that need to be filled."

"I'll give you the bottom line," my committee man growled. "There are a hundred workers with more seniority than Mr. Hamper who are struggling to be transferred onto the day shift. He has no business down here other than the fact that you have purposely deceived him into believing that he has no other recourse. I am prepared to write up a grievance on behalf of Mr. Hamper regarding this matter."

"Let him slide," I said. "All I want is to get the hell outta here."

"He's free to go at the end of today's shift," Hurley replied. Then he glared at me. "However, until then, he better not even think about walkin' out on me."

It was funny. I hadn't even entertained the thought of sneakin' out early until Hurley had brought it up. As soon as first break arrived, I grabbed my coat and hit the door. I went back home and hit the bed just about the time most sane people were fallin' out of theirs.

The next day I headed into the plant and wandered over to the Rivet Line. I had decided to see if there were any openings available on the night shift for a short, homesick ex-riveter. Through phone conversations I'd had with David Steel, I'd learned that Gino Donlan was now the supervisor in charge of the Rivet Line. Dave and I had both worked briefly under Gino the last time around and found him to be extremely fair and honest with his workers.

I waited for Gino in his office. He seemed surprised to see me hangin' around. "Steel told me that you were workin' the day shift back on the Axle Line."

"Ancient history," I replied. "Listen, Gino, you wouldn't happen to have any open jobs available by chance?"

"Are you shittin' me? I've got a whole list of 'em. In fact, your old pinup job is open. I can't find anyone who wants to cover that bitch."

"You have now," I smiled.

Gino laughed and extended his hand. "Welcome aboard, my dear friend."

Gino Donlan probably thought I was completely mad. Perhaps I was. All I knew was that there was something about those rivets that had gotten into my blood. I loved the way they looked jammed into those old rusty bins. I loved the way they felt rollin' around my palm like dice. I loved to see their little round heads squashed beneath the incredible force of the rivet guns. I loved everything about those gray metal mushrooms. I was quite possibly a very sick man.

Things once again returned to a tolerable norm. Once again, I employed my pitiful collection of fantasies to help move the minute hand forward. I also began to take notes, scrawling down some of the more peculiar aspects of assembly life on napkins, stock tags, envelopes, anything I could find. When I returned home after the shift, I would try to decipher the resultant mess and work them into pieces for my new *Flint Voice* column "Revenge of the Rivethead."

Dave Steel was once again across the line from me, this time down to my left on the rail-pull job. We fell back into our old routine of gripin' and groanin' about every vestige of assembly labor. It really amounted to nothing more than moany protectionism. We belonged here, we knew it. We just couldn't confide that deep inside we were comfortable within the dim-sighted womb of a voyage so dull. We would sit in Dave's car at break and curse the entire maze, all the while conveniently dodging the fact that we were humble mercenaries like all the rest.

We also had difficulty conceiving the fact that we still had almost twenty-five years to go before we qualified for full retirement. It made us uncomfortable watching all those drowsy-lookin' goats roamin' around the plant thirstin' for that thirty-year mark. They looked hopelessly drained. Beer-bellied and gored-out, driftin' along like yesterday's news, floatin' along to the finish line where so many would inevitably check out of the shop and croak. It happened too frequently. Some old-timer would retire on a Tuesday clutching his gold watch and, two weeks from the day, you'd hear about how he keeled over in a radish patch before he could cash his first pension check just like it was part of the national agreement.

There were other things that gnawed at us. For instance, I remember one night they stuck this old woman down on the Rivet Line. It was ridiculous, just another example of GM's total aimless approach in evaluating the capabilities and limitations of a given worker. The Rivet Line was simply no place for such an old gal. The guns were heavy and very temperamental. The ₁sensible thing to do would have been to place the old woman up in Trim or the Final Line.

On her second day down on the chain-hitch job, the old woman walloped her head on a rivet gun, knocking herself senseless and straight to the floor. She lay there sprawled beneath the crawl of the carriages like a rag doll. Immediately, one of the guys ran over and pushed the stop button and shut down the line.

Uh-oh. The red alert. If for whatever reason you wanted to mobilize a frantic bunch of white-collar power thugs in the direction of your area, nothing worked as well as pushing that sacred stop button. They'd come swoopin' outta the rafters like hawks on a bunny. Within thirty seconds, every tie within a 300-yard radius was on the scene—demanding answers, squawkin' into walkie-talkies, huffin' and puffin' like the universe had flipped over on their windpipes.

What a pathetic display of compassion this turned out to be. While this little old woman lay crumpled beneath the crawling frame carriers, all these nervous pricks wanted to know was WHO IN THE HELL TURNED THIS LINE OFF! The General Foreman, a real Nazi who we called Penguin, reached up and pulled out the stop button. The line jerked back into motion.

"Goddamnit," I yelled. "What about the old lady?"

"Don't worry," some bosshead offered, "we'll pull her out of there. Everybody else just get back to work and KEEP THIS LINE RUNNING!"

Meanwhile, the old woman was coming to. With the assistance of a couple supervisors, they got her up on her feet and sat her down at her bench. She began to cry—partly terrorized, partly humiliated. Jesus Christ, this was probably somebody's grandmother. It was awful. I thought about my own grandmother slumped on that oily woodblock floor. I thought about all the banners and coffee cups urging SAFETY FIRST and similar lies.

More than anything, I thought of how much I hated some of these dispassionate bastards in the white shirts. Here an old woman had come dangerously close to bein' crushed and all they cared about was their precious production quota. I could see Henry Jackson huddling on the fringe jackin' and jivin' like it was all a joke. I wondered what approach he might have taken had it been his own grandmother konked silly and heaped on the Rivet Line floor.

It was all so typical of General Motors. Their priorities were often scary. It was perfectly fine for a foreman to stop the line and chew on your ass about some minor detail, but it was practically an act of treason for a worker to stop the line in order to extricate an unconscious old lady out of harm's way. Safety and Production—sometimes the two just didn't mesh.

It was around this time that we began hearing a strange new entry into the GM vocabulary. The word was "Quality." The term itself was like some new intoxicating utterance that General Motors had pried outta the ass end of a golden goose. Quality, quality, quality. Suddenly, you couldn't raise your head without having your lobes pummeled with slogans and exhortations hailing this new buzzword. Up until this time, the maxim had always been Quantity. Quantity and Quota. Herd them trucks out the door. Quick, quick...QUICKER!

Evidently, GM was finally sniffin' the wind. Americans didn't give a shit about how fast and how many units you could zoom out the back door. They just wanted a vehicle that didn't begin to disintegrate the moment it rolled off the showroom floor. If they couldn't find something that held together here, there was always the option of purchasing one of those generic-lookin' imports that got about 500 miles per gallon and stuck together as firm as Stonehenge.

Quality represented buyers. Buyers meant sales. Sales meant fat tummies and a fat solid bonus. Quality would loosen those bony fingers off the purse strings. Quality could change the tune and serenade a buyer out of a buck. For living proof, all one had to do was glimpse over at Lee Iacocca, the born-again pom-pom boy of Quality High who was currently splattering himself all over medialand with galvanic jabber along the lines

of "WE BUILD THEM RIGHT OR WE ALL EAT DOGFOOD!"
We gotcha, Lee. Quality was the answer to the illin'.

The GM Truck & Bus plant began fiddling with various
Quality-minded plots as a means to enthuse the work force.
These concepts ranged from the "Build It Like You Owned It"
guilt trip to the voodoo scare tactics of "Here Come the Japs to
Foreclose Your Mortgage" to the gimmicky "Reward the Good
Rodent With a Key Chain" theory. Some of these game plans
were so utterly farcical, one would have been tempted to
guffaw if it weren't for the fact that it was *your brain* that
these follies were bein' foisted upon.

Case in point: the management at the Truck Plant decided
what the Quality concept really needed was a mascot. Con-
ceived in a moment of sheer visionary enlightenment, the plan
was to dress up the mascot as a large cat. Fittingly, this
rat-in-cat's clothing was to be called Quality Cat. Somewhere
along the line, an even more brilliant mind upstairs decided
that Quality Cat was sort of a dull title. Therefore, a contest
was organized in an attempt to give the Quality Cat a more
vital name.

Hundreds of crafty welders, screw jockeys and assorted
shoprats immediately began clunking their heads in an effort to
christen the hallowed cat. Management announced that they
would reward the most creative of these entries with a week's
use of a company truck. Hot damn! The eventual winner of the
contest was a worker who stumbled upon the inspired moniker
Howie Makem. Sadly, my intriguing entry, Wanda Kwit, finished way the hell down the list somewhere right between
Roger's Pussy and Tuna Meowt.

Howie Makem was to become the messianic embodiment of
the Company's new Quality drive. A livin', breathin' propaganda vessel assigned to spur on the troops. Go ahead and laugh, I
know I did. Just for a moment, imagine the probing skull
session that took place in some high-level think tank the day
Howie was first brought to mention.

"You know, slogans on coffee cups just ain't gettin' it, Bill."

"You're absolutely right, Ted. We need something more
dynamic. More upbeat."

"Hey, why don't we give the men their own kitty cat!"

"Kitty cat? Hmmm, I like it! A large kitty cat! Ted, you're a genius!"

Howie Makem stood five feet nine. He had light brown fur, long synthetic whiskers and a head the size of a Datsun. He wore a long red cape emblazoned with the letter Q for Quality. A very magical cat, Howie walked everywhere on his hind paws. Cruelly, Howie was not entrusted with a dick.

Howie would make the rounds poking his floppy whiskers in and out of each department. A "Howie sighting" was always cause for great fanfare. The workers would scream and holler and jump up and down on their workbenches whenever Howie drifted by. Howie Makem may have begun as just another Company ploy to prod the tired legions, but most of us ran with the joke and soon Howie evolved into a crazy phenomenon.

Of course, this isn't to say that everyone was in Howie's corner. Opinions varied. For instance, Dave Steel hated Howie's guts. He insisted that having a giant cat parade around the factory espousing General Motors dogma insulted his intelligence and demeaned him personally on an adult level. I remember we constantly argued about Howie's existence. One night Dave had really had it with Howie.

"Christ, what's next?" Dave groaned. "They'll probably bring in Fred Rogers to pass out balloons and lollipops."

"Chill out." I laughed. "You're always taking shit way too seriously. Sure, having a giant cat rooting us on is totally ludicrous. But you have to admit the concept is at least humorous in a pathetic kind of way."

Dave bristled. "I don't find anything the least bit humorous about having some suck-ass in a cat's costume roamin' through my place of work. What they are tellin' us is that we are so retarded growth-wise that all we can relate to are characters along the lines of Saturday morning cartoon figures. Bring out Bozo! Hail Huckleberry Hound!"

"Who would you prefer? Einstein and Thomas Edison? Face it, Howie fits the surroundings."

"Fuck Howie. Fuck Einstein and Edison. What do I need this mascot bullshit for? Do they really think I'll perform a better job with a huge cat lurchin' over me? If they really want to charge up all these boneheads, why not bring in some Playboy Bunnies? I'm thirty years old, not thirteen."

"There's only one drawback to your suggestion," I replied. "How long do you think it'd take before some drunked-up redneck mauled one of the Bunnies to shreds?"

"Oh, probably fifteen seconds, tops."

"See what I mean? Dave, it's time for you to get on the winning side. Like it or now, Howie's our man."

"Not this guy's. My fondest wish is that Howie gets his tail snagged in the chain gear and is mercilessly ground into Kibbles & Bits."

On the other hand, my editor at the *Voice* loved hearing about Howie Makem. I can't remember anything that made him laugh harder. He'd double over and clutch his stomach, tears running down his cheeks. Plainly, this was the most hysterical gag Moore had ever heard of. The best part about it was that I didn't have to make up a single word. Everything that I told him regarding Howie was pure fact. I remember the first time I told Mike about Howie.

"You mean to tell me," Moore sputtered between assorted snorts and cackles, "that GM has a guy who walks around the factory... dressed up like a... GIANT CAT! This is their idea of enticing Quality out of their work force?"

"Correct," I replied straight-faced.

"Oh my God, oh shit," Moore squealed. "You know what this means, don't you?"

"The end of Western Civilization as we know it? A communist overthrow?"

"No, no, no. You have to get an interview with Howie Makem for the paper. The Rivethead meets the Quality Cat! Oh Jesus, oh shit..."

"Not a fuckin' chance," I howled. "I'll write you a biography of Howie, I'll put together a Howie Makem diary, I'll interview workers on their feelings about Howie, but I absolutely *refuse* to talk with that... that cat-thing. Not now, not ever. Jesus, who knows what lurks inside that giant furry head?"

Moore kept pestering me to do the interview with Howie Makem. I held firm. The answer was and always would be a definite NO. Just watching Howie trudge by my job waving his big brown paw in my direction was freaky enough. Having to sit down and ask questions of the bastard would have sent me right over the wall. Still, Moore never gave up hope. He pleaded with me every time I went out to the *Voice* for passages from Howie. It became a very large nuisance.

Alas, the matter was resolved in a strange way. Tragedy had apparently struck. Weeks and then months went by without a single Howie sighting. Everyone at work was puzzled. Had Howie been promoted to the front office? Had Howie transferred onto the day shift? Had Howie been kidnapped by Japanese invaders? Worse yet, had Howie Makem, the official ambassador of GM's new Quality push, been unceremoniously LAID OFF? Had it been in the *U.S. News & World Report*?

> The working class the world over is in shock today as it was announced that the General Motors Corporation's beloved Quality cat, Mr. Howard Makem, was officially laid off from his job at the GM Truck & Bus facility in Flint, Michigan. A grieving UAW spokesman told reporters: "The auto industry has lost a dear comrade and a special brother who provided a keen light in an era of darkness." GM Chairman Roger Smith refused comment outside of the admission that he "felt like a lousy hangman." Mr. Makem is reported to be in seclusion at his home outside the small village of Lapeer where a night-long vigil is being held by throngs of admirers and somber linemates.

I remember the day I had to break the news to Mike that Howie Makem had apparently vanished. Christ, it was as if his little brother had disappeared.

"Howie's GONE?" Mike hollered. "Have you asked around? He must be somewhere."

"I don't know where he went," I answered. "All I know is that he's been missing for weeks. The flag outside the plant hasn't been at half mast or anything, so I assume he's still alive."

"You wouldn't be snowin' me about this whole disappearance, would you? I know how loath you are about givin' me a Howie Makem interview. Let's be honest, Ben."

"I can't believe we're having this whole conversation. Howie Makem is missing. I don't know why and I don't know where. Above all, I don't even fuckin' care! If he ever shows up again, I promise to get you an interview. Are you happy?"

My editor leaned back in his chair. "Exceedingly so." He beamed.

It was back to the drawing board for the brainy sorts at

GM Truck & Bus. In light of Howie Makem's disappearance, another inventive Quality concept was needed. They introduced to us the official General Motors "Quality Drinking Glass."

One evening, the supervisors began approaching each of their workers with a little mid-job pep talk. The gist was that if the Quality level reached such and such a figure, we would all receive a lovely drinking glass memento that we could proudly take home to show our kin and prop beside our bowling trophies and eighth-grade diplomas. The glass even provided a wrenching of the heartstrings, for emblazoned on the side was the profile of none other than Howie Makem himself, rest his controversial soul.

Christ, I got all choked up and thought I was gonna bawl. With renewed determination, I began knocking the piss right out of each and every rivet that dared rear its shiny little scalp in my direction. Go, team, go! Forget your house payment. Forget your child support. Forget that trip to Cedar Point. Damn it, do it for Howie!

Sure enough, the boys and I hit our goal. One night after lunch break, Gino came luggin' a case of Quality Drinking Glasses down the line.

"Thanks for the good job, Ben." Gino smiled. "Here's your cup."

At the same time, one of the utility guys was walking right behind Gino asking each worker whether he'd like to sell his Quality Glass for a buck. He mumbled something about wanting to start a collection. I was shocked. I told the guy to get his rotten currency outta my face. No one could have my Howie Makem drinking glass. The gall of some bastards...

I figure that the whole investment in these glasses probably ran GM maybe $35. But, of course, it was the thought that mattered most. After all, when someone works hard all day in a smoky chamber full of sludge, noise, armpits, beer breath, cigar butts, psychos, manic depressives, grease pits, banana stickers, venom and gigantic stalking kitty cats, why not give the guy his own glass.

You can bet your ass he'll soon be needin' a drink.

7

ANOTHER LAYOFF SWALLOWED ME UP, THIS TIME, THE GRAND-
pappy of 'em all. I was out of work for nearly a year, far too
long a span when you stopped to consider Reagan was now
in power. Ron wasn't nearly as charitable as our old pal
Jimmy Carter. He had his own designs on what he wanted
to do with the budget and they surely didn't include funneling any of it into the frayed pocket lining of Joe Lunch-
pail. No more safety nets for the urchins of fickle industry.

On the verge of poverty, Dave Steel and I were really
beginning to sweat it. We began calling up co-workers who
were still clinging to their jobs in the plant. We started hittin'
them up for every two-bit rumor they could hustle down.
Bob-A-Lou informed me that there was some heavy chatter
making the rounds regarding a new product being introduced
at our plant. No one was sure what this mystery vehicle would
be, but the grapevine was practically smoldering. Dave was
receiving the same scuttlebutt from his sources.

We'd both been fortunate up until then. Each time we'd
been shelved, GM reeled us back in just before our benefits were
set to dissolve, so our layoffs seemed more like paid vacations.

But this was before Reaganomics, before the merry-go-round rusted to a standstill. We weren't carefree spuds anymore. We were thirtyfuckin'something and we had budgets that had entwined themselves around those hefty blue-checkered pay stubs.

All we could do was wait. Wait, wait, wait and pray that the simmering rumors were true. Once again, Richard Dawson's eyes began boring tiny little holes in my skull. I'd jump into my Camaro and drive around aimlessly. It wasn't fair. Eleven months of lame luck for a five foot six and a half meat loaf with red eyes and a soul in need of one colossal enema. Seventh Heaven closed for repairs, please proceed to 7-Eleven for as much overpriced beer as you can lug to your car and drive seven miles outta town, plow 'em all down and vomit out the T-top as the crows all scream your name. I was experiencing shoprat withdrawal. From thoroughbred to sawhorse. I became the third-base coach for my brother's Little League baseball team. I volunteered to take retards to the zoo. I conned my way into my own radio show on the city's Public Broadcasting station, playing Black Flag and Annette Funicello records for a small cult of adolescent skinheads.

And then... finally... it was HIM! The date: July 26, 1983. The time: 10:00 A.M. EST. The place: General Motors Executive Headquarters, Top Dog Suite, Detroit, Michigan.

In one fluid motion, GM Chairman Roger Smith reared back in his leather chair, cocked his arm high above his head, and hurled the half-eaten remainder of a lemon-filled jelly doughnut out his fourteenth-story window.

A decision had been reached. A nervous smile crept through and replaced the morning-long grimace. Roger Smith—Chairman of the Bored, honcho of a thousand wretched levers—tapped the intercom button for his secretary.

"Miss Henderson, it is time to place the call."

"Oh, Mr. Smith, surely you don't mean—"

"Precisely, Miss Henderson. Tell him this time we mean it. Tell him to show up promptly and leave his blasphemous notepads behind. Tell him damn the torpedos and damn the Toyotas and damn Iacocca if he gets in our way. Tell him... goddamnit... just tell him we NEED him!"

RINNNNNNNG! RINNNNNNNNG!

...he loves me not. He loves me, he loves me not. He loves me...well, hell yes that squat little gerbil loves me. After all, who else would he rumble outta bed between dreary daymares of life and death and Eve Plumb in turquoise hotpants if not I, the Rivethead, thoroughbred of all throroughbreds, the quickest triggerman this side of the River Rouge.

"Hello."

"Mr. Hamper?" It was that same sultry monotone. I got goosebumps the size of hubcaps.

"Yes?" I responded breathlessly.

"You are to report back to work at the GM Truck & Bus plant tomorrow morning at 6:00 A.M. for rehiring."

"I love you."

CLICK!!!!

Apparently my callback to GM was necessitated when the Corporation landed this enormous contract with Uncle Sam to build a shitload of army trucks. This was the mystery product that Bob-A-Lou and the others had been hinting about. Besides Smith, I now had another man to thank for this swell turn of fate—Caspar (The Friendly) Weinberger. It was this man's dogged lust for a few billion dollars worth of military vehicles that reopened the doors and pumped new life into my sagging shoprat career.

Hey, whatever turned them on. I was just glad to be back. Army trucks? Count me in. Tanks, bazookas, napalm? Hell, it was their hobby shop. I was in no position to argue. Conscientious objection might be a noble path come draft day, but with my meal ticket hangin' in the balance, I was quick to respond "Hell yes, I will go!" Ronnie needed a new fleet of death wagons. It sucked, but so did starving.

As per my instructions, I rendezvoused at 0600 hours in the Personnel office. Just like old times, I fell into a herd of a couple dozen reclaimed shoprats, each of whom were taking long drags from their cigarettes and peering deep into their own separate nowheres. Within moments, a necktie with a pink head attached would enter the room, return our ID badges and guide us back into the Land That Time (and a half) Forgot.

As we waited, I scanned the faces behind me. Slumped in a chair away from the rest of the group was Dave Steel. He was wearing his traditional scowl, looking for all the world like a man boarding a boxcar for Belsen. I had to chuckle. No matter how many times they yanked us in and out of this buggy palace, Dave and I always managed to keep being paired together. I drifted over to say hello.

"Hey, wallflower, what's a semi-educated telecommunications expert like yourself doin' in a place like this?"

"Go to hell." Dave groaned. "As much as this is necessary, I'd almost prefer death."

I felt better already knowing that my reentry into assembly life would be a little less harsh now that Dave was around to glaze the mood with his steady roll call of anguish and inspirational negativism. Misery loves company and a mutual loathing for the same ugly reality might not seem like a very constructive way of dealing with the winds of fate, but sometimes it's the only way.

Along came the bouncing necktie to scoop us up for deployment. Like some proud corporate Johnny Appleseed, he led the way, scattering an occasional rat into one of the boisterous orchards, all the while conferring with a clipboard the size of a storm window. We plunged on through the Motor Line, the Final Line, the Axle Line, the Ten-Items-or-Less Line.

We appeared to be on a one-way, no-frills collision course with the Frame Line—home to several departments, among them the Rivet Line. Dave was in a panic. I feigned dejection, but truthfully I couldn't have been happier.

Ah, the Rivet Line. Just say yes. A nice little spot to settle down and raise up a blister colony. A place where pipedreams spawned and delirium tremens held casting calls. A low spot in the valley where my partner and I periodically returned when the economy began to play boomerang.

Johnny Appleseed brought us to a halt in front of the General Foreman's trailer. He ducked inside to rouse the big boss while we stood outside contemplating our location.

"Mother of whores,'" Dave snarled. "We could wind up right back on the Rivet Line!"

"That would suit me," I said.

Dave couldn't handle it. "What the hell is it with you and those goddamn rivets? The place ain't nothin' but a shithole. I think that you and that Rivethead alter ego of yours are both sick in the fuckin' head!"

"Doesn't it only make sense that I should resume my God-given specialty?"

"Nothing makes sense," Dave stammered as the boss motioned us into his trailer.

The General Foreman forced us to listen to his drab little pep talk about the wonderful new military vehicle we were going to be building. He mentioned how grateful we should be that the government had chosen our plant to assemble all of these army trucks. Without the military contract, we'd all be on the outside a million miles away from any kind of shoprat redemption. To show our appreciation, it was mandatory that we return an immaculate product. Our long-term survival depended on gettin' the boys in the Pentagon all a-twitter.

After the rah-rah was completed, the General Foreman told us to follow along as he escorted us to our new departments.

Panicking, not wanting to leave anything to chance, I suddenly bolted by the rest of the pack and sprang myself at the boss. A lurchin' urchin, front and center.

"Um, Mr. Gibbons, sir?" I said.

"Is there some kind of problem?"

"Not exactly. I just wanted to let you know I'm intimately acquainted with the jobs on the Rivet Line and I volunteer to return to that department."

The General Foreman gave me a puzzled onceover. Shit, he thought I was nuts too. He waved the group to a halt and thumbed through his papers. "What's your name?" he asked.

"Hamper, sir."

He flipped a few more pages. "Well, Hamper, my sheet has you down for assignment in the body drop area."

Oh, shit. Now we were talkin' very dangerous yo-yo slave labor. The body drop area was where the cab portions of the trucks came zinging down on cables from the second floor. The cabs plunked themselves down on their matching frameworks while workers ducked for cover and then humped to fasten the two together. To top it off, this was where Henry Jackson camped his fat Nazi ass the majority of the time. I would kill or be killed within days.

It was time for full-tilt grovel. "Mr. Gibbons, you just spoke to us about the importance of Quality workmanship, a concept I fully embrace. I believe that by returning me to the

Rivet Line, I would have more value to the Company considering the expertise I have in this area."

"Hmm," Gibbons pondered. My knees became butterscotch pudding supported by broken Slinkys. Icebergs danced with suntan lotion billboards. Jets swooped into the sides of skyscrapers. Drunken herds of hippos shinnied up radio towers. And then...

"Go ahead and report to the Rivet Line," the big boss stated. "I'll move someone else over to the body drop area."

I could have kissed the bastard. Instead, I whirled around to find Dave staring at me. He had been hangin' on the fringe pickin' up pierces of my sorry butt-smooching. He shook his head. "That had to be the most pitiful display of brownnosing I have ever witnessed," he said. "To think that someone would actually go out of his way to be sent to the Rivet Line. It's too absurd to comprehend."

"At least I know where I'm headed. For all you know, you'll be stuck heavin' transmissions."

"I'll take my chances," Dave replied bitterly.

The Rivet Line had undergone an extensive facelift as jobs were rearranged to accommodate the production of the army vehicles. The change appeared to be for the better. There were more workers to attend to the extra duties and some of the more aggravating jobs had been busted up into less strenuous routines.

I was placed on a job directly across from the foreman's office and picnic table area. The job turned out to be a cinch. The four-wheel-drive castings and dual exhaust muffler hangers that had been a part of my old pinup job had been slid down the line and were now part of my new job. The big difference was that now I wasn't required to wrestle with the rails or attach any cross members. My groveling had paid off. I could see plain sailing straight ahead.

Meanwhile, management was having all kinds of problems attempting to start up the line. The military vehicles were responsible for introducing numerous new items and it seemed like every time the supervisors thought they had everything covered, some precious new part would turn up missing or defective. The line would budge for just a moment and then some hysterical bossman would come racing down the aisle bellowing "Stop the line! Stop the GODDAMN LINE!"

About the third day into this herky-jerky chaos, I was sittin' on my bench when I happened to glance out into the aisle. Passing through to the foreman's office was Henry Jackson. Shufflin' along right behind him was a very dejected-looking Dave Steel. "Hey, nomad, welcome home!" I yelled. Dave gave me the finger.

After a brief meeting with the foreman, Steel came sulking out of the office headed in the direction of his old rail-pull job. Poor Dave, there was no way to dodge destiny, no escape from the undertow of stubborn fate. His bed was made.

Passing back on his way out of the department, Henry Jackson abruptly halted in front of my bench. He eyeballed me with that evil glint and then came struttin' over. "Well, if it isn't the elusive Mr. Hamper," he hissed.

"Is something wrong, Henry?"

"I've only been searchin' for your ass for three days now. Hamper, you don't belong over here. You were assigned to the body drop area. I suppose you think you're so clever you can just pick your own setup, am I right? Sorry, your ass is mine, Rivethead."

Terrific. Of all the idiots in the plant, Jackson would have to turn out to be one of the slim minority who was acquainted with my Rivethead persona. This didn't bode well at all. Just the way he had pronounced that title told me that I had catapulted right to the top of the Henry Jackson endangered feces list.

There was absolutely no use in tryin' to explain anything to Jackson, so I hollered down the line to my foreman to come and straighten this mess out. As soon as he arrived, Jackson shoved his finger at me and barked "This man does not belong here!"

"I'm afraid he stays put, Henry. The General Foreman sent him over personally."

Jackson helped himself to one of my cigarettes lying on my workbench and glared at me as if I was some kind of repulsive tumor. "Watch your step, Rivethead," Jackson snapped as he took off for the aisle and his next appointment with meddlesome tyranny.

I asked my foreman what Jackson was doing here in the first place. Like me and so many others around me, Jackson was a second-shift fixture. What were we all doing here lumped together on days? My foreman looked at me curiously. He explained that everyone was temporarily workin' the day shift until they got this military vehicle off the ground. I felt very stupid. I was so out of it, I hadn't even paid attention to the fact that the factory seemed to be bulging at its seams and that I hadn't been able to find a parking spot within three blocks of the plant. Something about 6:00 A.M. brought out the dunce in me.

I had another question. "After this is all running smoothly, will I be able to retain this job on the second shift?"

"The job's all yours," the boss replied. "A Mr. Donlan will be your night supervisor."

Damn, things were falling together perfectly. I had a pussy job, an upcoming reunion with Gino Donlan and my beloved second shift, and, until then, a loafer's life sittin' around doin' absolute zilch while the brass sorted through the confusion of the new military vehicles.

Feeling relieved, I decided to stroll down and visit Dave on the rail-pull. I found him sleeping in one of the empty stock bins, a newspaper covering his face. I gave the bin a hard kick and Dave scrambled to his feet. "Let's hit the cafeteria," I said. "You could use a coffee."

"I could use a change of scenery more than anything else," he grumbled.

We went downstairs to the workers' cafeteria. The place was an absolute zoo. Radios blared, voices shouted, fists banged on Formica. Tablesful of old geezers were tossin' spades and suckin' on sausage links. The young guys were lined up by the phones waitin' to rouse their women out of bed with giddy tittle-tattle about how they were all bein' paid to lounge on their butts. There was nothin' like a prolonged line stoppage to goose up the morale of the natives.

Dave and I found a couple seats in the back. Dave was eager to tell me about his brief fling as a desperado. Three days sprung from the jaws of the rivet tips.

"Christ, I was a renegade," Dave mourned. "Just after you fellated that General Foreman into sending you back to the Rivet Line, he sent me upstairs to the paint department. It was great. Just me and these old coots—no noise, no filth, no bustin' ass. I was rivet-free. The foreman even said he might have room for me."

"Let me guess," I injected. "Then Idi Amin showed up to piss on your parade."

"Yeah, that bastard came pokin' around and ruined everything. Right when I thought I'd escaped the Rivet Line once and for all, I spot Jackson waddlin' around the corner like a bloodhound from hell. He must spend a third of his time just seein' to it that I remain miserable."

"Sluggin' rivets appears to be your natural destiny, Dave," I said. "I suggest you stop buckin' your birthright."

Dave crumpled up his coffee up and sent it whizzin' past my head. He folded his arms across his chest and slouched down in his seat. "I was a renegade," he groaned.

We spent the better portion of the next two weeks slurpin' bad coffee, chain-smoking and concocting this ridiculous idea for a short film. We needed something to pass the time. Even though the line was only budging out about one truck per hour, we were required to stay put near our jobs. The boredom made our drowsy morning brains wander to the absurd.

The movie we were discussing was to be a violent blue-collar docudrama called *No Need for the Grievance Procedure.* It would be a collection of short pieces that chronicled the systematic executions of our least favorite shoplords. I can't recall each piece in detail, but I do remember my favorite—the gruesome dispatch of Henry Jackson.

In our scenario Dave snuck up to the glassed-in office where Henry sat and shrewdly welded the door shut from the outside. Dave then commandeered an abandoned fork truck and bore down on the tiny office, scooping it right off the factory floor. Raising the office several feet above the ground, he jostled the cubicle violently. Inside the office, Henry Jackson was slammed to and fro like a mannequin in a cyclone. His head was bleeding badly from repeated bashings with airborne file drawers, stapleguns and the old iron coatrack.

After Jackson was thoroughly marinated, yet still clinging to life, Dave backed up the fork truck and sped off in the direction of the train trench. At this point, the workers all left their jobs and followed behind like so many brainless ghouls in a George Romero flick. Dave had it timed so that a huge cargo train just happened to be barreling down the tracks.

As the train roared its approach, Dave lifted the battered office high above the trench, gave it a few last violent jerks and deposited Henry's welded death cage onto the tracks. Only seconds remained before the crash. Dave hopped down from the fork truck and stood beside the silent assemblage of co-workers. Inside the office, Henry was furiously pounding on the windows, his eyes as wide as Frisbees, his lips mouthing useless final pleas for forgiveness.

Allowing himself a smile, Dave bent over and flicked the butt of his cigarette on top of the office. He waved his hand at Jackson while pointing at his crotch. Just before impact, Dave jumped back and motioned for the other workers to do the same.

SMASHHHH! The train slammed into the office and began pushing it toward the gigantic iron spring at the end of the trench. Seconds later, the office exploded, crushed between the spring and the nose of the locomotive. Glass and paper and hair and bits of skull flew through the rafters. An eyeball casually rolled up near Dave's work boot and he winked at it before kicking it back into the debris.

With nothing left to accomplish, Dave looked at the workers and nodded. Silently, we turned around to head back to our jobs and finish out the shift doing our utmost to produce a fine-quality truck. Henry would have been proud of our commitment to duty.

One morning, tired of movie plotting and fed up waiting for the line to move, I suggested to Dave that we sneak out of the plant and head for my new apartment a couple miles down the road. If we were going to be paid to do nothing, I reasoned that we could do it just as well somewhere else and Dave agreed.

We arrived at my bachelor dump and as I uncapped the beers Dave rummaged through my record crates and found some music to his liking—mainly sixties garage crud like Blue Cheer, the Troggs and the Shadows of Knight. We cranked up the music to a very conspicuous level considering that it was only about 7:30 and most sensible human beings were still tryin' to sleep.

Dave moved over to the window and peeked through my curtains into the parking lot. "Hey, come over here and check this out," he yelled over the stereo.

"Let me guess." I laughed. "It's Henry Jackson with leg irons and handcuffs."

"Stranger than that. It's your neighbors herding off to work. Christ, what a sorry bunch of losers! They should get *real* jobs like ours."

I looked out the window. "They don't look very happy, do they?"

"They look like they're going to their mother's funeral," Dave cracked. He opened the window and started hollerin': "$12.82 an hour! I'm makin' $12.82 an hour to drink Rivethead booze and listen to Rivethead rock 'n' roll!"

"Shit, shut that window. You're gonna have the landlord over here."

We settled back and kept draining the beers. The heavy euphoria of escaping the shop, gettin' loaded, listenin' to jams and knowing we were being paid handsomely to do so was a marvelous thing. Dave was as upbeat and animated as I'd ever seen him. He had found a worn copy of "Open Your Door" by Richard & the Young Lions in a stack of old 45's and played the song over and over and over. Morning spilled into afternoon.

Finally, I had to break the news to him. "We're all out of beer, rail-pull man."

Dave fished out a twenty and flung it at me. He started the record over for the umpteenth time and banged away on my coffee table with rubber spatulas operating as drum sticks.

"Hey, what about work?" I shouted. "For all we know, they might have got the line runnin'."

"Must you always be so negative?" Dave laughed. He was plastered.

Over Dave's drunken objections, we left my apartment and drove back to the plant. We weaved our way in through a side door near the rivet line and looked around. Everyone was gone. The supervisors, the workers, even Henry Jackson. We looked at each other and then our watches.

"Hamper, this is fuckin' spooky," Dave whispered. "Where the hell did everyone go?"

Down in the next department, I could see a skilled-trades worker putzing about on some hunk of machinery. I walked down to talk to him. "Excuse me, you wouldn't happen to know where everyone went, would ya?"

The guy looked at me as if I was some sort of alien. A very

drunk one at that. "Shit, they were all sent home at ten this morning. Not enough parts, I guess."

Dave and I headed for the parking lot. "The one fuckin' day they allow everyone to split early and here we are out there thinkin' we've pulled the great escape," Dave moped. "That means from ten o'clock on, we didn't have the edge on anyone. No matter which route I go, I always end up gettin' rawed."

"Just part of bein' a renegade, I suppose."

Dave ducked into his rusty Vega and rolled down the window. "Very fuckin' funny," he said. "Tomorrow, I'm stayin' put till they release us early."

"You've cursed us already." I laughed. "We'll probably have to work overtime now."

Dave's Vega roared to life and sped off for the north unit exit gate. I stood there for a moment chuckling to myself. A midday hangover was introducing itself to my forehead. I got in my Camaro and drove home. A little while later, my neighbors started arriving home from their jobs. I peered at them through the curtains. They looked neither happy or sad.

A few days later, we were crankin'. The parts to the army vehicles had finally all been located and distributed to their proper spots on the line. Let the war games begin.

The setup called for every seventh truck to be a military job. Management treated these units as if they were gold-studded chariots bound for heaven. If the slightest flaw appeared on one of Uncle Sam's orders, the line would jerk to a halt and a stampede of frazzled bossmen would come racin' with red carpet tourniquets.

All attention was reserved for Ronnie's death wagons. The rest of the trucks slid by like dispensable lumps of Play-Doh. It wasn't the best time to have a truck on order if your name happened to be John Q. Public. I used to sit there and think that if the American auto industry could ever slow down and capture the relentless effort put forth into one of these sacred army trucks, then the day would soon come when we could send all of those Japanese Quality mongers ducking for cover behind the shadow of a *real* marketplace Godzilla.

After a couple of weeks, it became clearly apparent why management was in such a commotion to spit-polish their darling new product. With much ceremony, it was announced that Roger B. Smith and a flock of Pentagon brass were coming to pay us a visit. It was time to unveil the first load of army trucks and Roger himself wanted to be there in person when one General Ball of the United States Army got all goosefleshed at the headlight's first glare.

As the showoff date edged closer, the honchos at the Truck Plant began tumbling around like rivets with their heads whacked off. The panicky pace of the past couple weeks accelerated into one big tremblefest. It was increasingly obvious that if these trucks somehow turned out to be puke-colored lemons, there was going to be one vast necktie party and old Roger B. himself would be the one operating the rope concession.

As for myself and the rest of my co-workers, we were overjoyed about the prospect of Rog's visit. I went out and had a personalized T-shirt made up for the occasion. In big block letters it read: ROGER, LET'S GO BOWLING! I had been on this crusade to commit ten pins with Roger Smith for nearly three years, and I had written several pieces on my quest for the *Flint Voice*. I figured he owed it to me. In turn, I owed it to all of my proud shoprat ancestors. After all, for almost seventy-five years running, the name Hamper and the words General Motors were damn near synonymous.

It was time for some recognition from those blockheads. All I was asking was ten frames of bowling with my boss. How damn American could one get? I reasoned that there were enticements in it for GM as well. We were forever hearing how management and the work force needed to develop more sturdy bonds. Here was their perfect opportunity to put their headpin where their mouth was. We could bring in the networks and press. The entire media would gobble it up. The walls of mistrust would tumble. They'd slap a photo of Smith and me on the cover of *Time*. Jesus, what a vast public relations coup dangled just beyond the yonder three-ten spare!

When the big day arrived, I was pumped. So were all my linemates. Even Dave had dropped his usual scowl and was behavin' giddy. Within a few hours, our big gray barn would throw open its doors for THE MAN. The air was positively electric. History was in the making.

Then, around 9:30, a very strange thing happened. Our foreman came strolling down the line informing us we were

being sent home at 10:00. We all stood at our jobs wonderin' if
our chains were bein' jerked. They couldn't send us home now.
The fuckin' MAN was on his way.

I cornered our foreman as he traced his way back up the line.
"Let me get this straight," I said. "Management is sending us
home in a half hour? Smith won't even BE HERE by then!"

"That's right." He grinned. "By the way, nice T-shirt."

"What's the problem? Did Cab Shop break down again?
Are we out of parts?"

"No problems. They've just decided to give you people the
rest of the day off."

The rest of the day off? TODAY? No problems? Something
reeked big-time. Impromptu generosity wasn't a part of their
nature. And then it dawned on me: the bastards didn't want us
around when Smitty showed. They wanted the factory rat-free!
No unseemly peons pollutin' the promenade.

I was infuriated. We deserved to be on hand. We were the
ones who built all the trucks. It was our labor, our stinkin'
elbow grease, our drudged midwifery that plunked out the
product. Those trucks didn't just show up droopin' out of a
stork's jawbone. How could they ignore the human element of
the project? What was an assembly line without assemblers?

Just before I left for the day, I propped up a sign that
faced out into the aisle next to my job. Chances were some
bosshead would remove it, but what the hell. It read: SORRY
TO HAVE MISSED YOU, KISS MY ASS. SINCERELY, THE RIVET-
HEAD. It was always the thought that mattered most.

When the opportunity came, I wasted no time transferring
back to the night shift. It felt good to be home. The evenings
once again crawled by indistinguishable from each other and
every Thursday Roger Smith would send me a lumpy paycheck as
proof of what a good boy I'd been. The money was fine, but I still
clung to my dream of bowling with Smith. I would never give up.

It was during this period, somewhere in early '83, that the
Flint Voice expanded statewide, resurfacing as the *Michigan
Voice*. I still didn't know how Mike was ever able to pull it off.
Here he was up to his eyeballs in debt and his remedy was to
expand. Love him or hate him (there was no in between in

Flint), you couldn't help but marvel at Moore's tenacious re-solve to keep his publication suckin' air.

Along with the expansion of the *Voice* came sweeping changes. The paper became more political than ever. The boot was given to several longtime staff members, many of whom were close friends of Moore's dating back to high school. New columnists were introduced, intellectual sorts and heavy hitters. Syndicated hotshots were marched in like hired guns. To my total surprise, "Revenge of the Rivethead" survived the face-lift. My editor knew that the core of the readership were blue-collars, so I remained on board as a representative of the average lunk. Besides, by this point in time, I was generating more fan/hate mail than the rest of the staff put together. I bought my first typewriter and droned on.

The timing of the *Voice* expansion jibed perfectly with my new gig on the Rivet Line. My job was such a breeze that I had plenty of free time to write in between my duties. I developed a pattern where I could race through my job in thirty seconds and shoot back to my bench for a luxurious minute and a half of observation and composition. It was like working two jobs at once, neither of which demanded much effort. The best part was that the clock moved by quickly.

What a great scam to be able to sit there, night after night, as much a man of letters as just another weary errand boy. The Rivethead flourished, a peeping Tom buried in pitch-blende. I began peering deeply into the malignant drudgery that entombed those who surrounded me. Their monotonous travail was like ballet for the dead. Something so remarkably unremarkable that I sometimes wondered if I was actually witnessing anything that even qualified as living.

For instance, I could spend an entire shift wondering to myself just what it was that was going through the mind of the poor soul across from me on the steering gear job. He was a young rehire, doomed beyond his own recognition by a job that all the rivet vets referred to as "the end of the line." The setup was a thorough ball-buster, an eight-hour mule train of uphill grind.

The nights rolled on. I'd lean across from the guy and watch the sweat pour off his chin. And, somewhere in this factory town, I could see his wife curled up on a sofa bed awaiting the return of her reclaimed assembly man. It wasn't hard to visualize just how she might shudder when the door flew open each night and in trudged this chewed-up mutation of a football star who, once upon a time, looked awful drooly pastin' petals on the prom float, but now, staring back at her from the other side of the meat grinder, resembled nothing more than a heap of defeat with limbs attached. Dreams died fast around here and, more time than not, there simply wasn't sufficient time to hunt down a decent headstone. One day lured, the next day skewered.

I became obsessed with the steering gear man. He seemed so stoic, so reconciled to the brutish misfortune that defined his routine. I wondered what he thought all night long. I wondered if he ever thought about the fact that only fifteen feet away sat a lazy owlhead perched up on three boxes of unopened rivets—yawning, chain-smoking, doodlin' in his stupid notepad—while he was flirtin' with hernial blowout and draggin' it back and forth like Quasimodo Doe.

The steering gear man never asked about this nor anything else. He just kept bustin' it. I really didn't understand it. The apportionment of duty in the plant was so inconsistent that you would have half of the work force breaking their backs and chugging the work load while the other half were off playing cards, sifting through boxscores and plumpin' down their idle fannies. It gnawed the shit out of some guys and who could blame 'em for bitchin'.

The steering gear man never spoke up. Not for a while, at least. Then, ever so slowly, his resolute facade began to fade. He had found a confidant. It wasn't me. It wasn't anyone. The steering gear man found the bottle.

He chose his spots at first. A few cocktails at lunch, a couple slugs during a line stop. I would lean over to put in my spring casting and the heavy aroma of bad whiskey would hover between us. The booze made the steering gear man sweat more than ever. I'd sneak a peek as he spun in his screws and the poor bastard would be drippin' like a faucet. He'd be hummin' to himself and I wanted for all the world to believe he was happy. If anyone deserved a shot at happiness, drunk-induced or otherwise, it was the steering gear man.

The drinking began to escalate quickly. Oftentimes, he

would arrive at work already packin' a snootful. He began to talk. Not with me, not with any of the other workers, not with the guy who delivered his stock—only to himself. There began a running dialogue that sputtered beneath the din, private confabs and secret asides, a drunken litany of some damn shit that I could never untangle.

The mutterings driveled on as the weeks limped off to the grave. And, layer by pickled layer, the steering gear man began to unravel. He no longer seemed the impervious soldier, the tragic hero of my yellow notebook. It became a regular routine for him to show up for work completely trashed. On these occasions, he somehow managed to stagger out the shift operating on nothing more than ingrained reflex.

Before long, he was gettin' so plastered that we all had to chip in to keep him from falling too far behind. The spring man would tighten down his screws for him while Randy, the left-side muffler hanger man, and I would take turns hittin' his rivets at the front of the frame. These rivets at the front of the frame were right at groin level. The way the steering gear man kept leanin' into the frame for balance scared the shit out of Randy and me. We were afraid he was gonna rivet his dick off leanin' in like that. Vasectomy via rivet gun surely would've been the most painful way of shuttin' down the old baby wand imaginable.

Not long after this pattern of super stupor developed, the matter was resolved in a very ugly way. It happened on a Saturday. I remember the steering gear man showed up absolutely goosed to the gills. Randy and I helped him get rollin'. We were becoming awfully tired of coverin' for his sorry ass. We decided it would be better if we just let him sink or swim, disfigurement or castration be damned.

Twenty minutes into the shift, the steering gear man started yellin' out for our foreman. It was the first time any of us had heard him actually speak aloud. Gino came striding over. Thank God, I thought, the crazy shit was gonna turn himself in. It would've been the wise move.

Gino and the steering gear man huddled secretly for a few moments. Then Gino started motioning for one of the utility men to come over and take the job. The steering gear man untied his work apron, turned it around and fastened it on backwards. He grabbed his lunch pail and headed for the exit, the apron flowing behind him like a burlap skirt. Things weren't adding up.

Gino came walking by on his way back to his office. He was doing a rather poor job of concealing the fact that he was shakin' with laughter. I asked him what the deal was.

"A slight accident," Gino answered, attempting to brush by me.

"A slight accident! He didn't chop anything off, did he?"

Gino shook his head. "Nothing like that."

"What'd he do?" I groaned, "piss his drawers?" I'd seen it happen before.

My foreman completely burst. "Um, something like that." Cackle, cackle.

Something *like* that? Wait a minute. The huddle of secrecy...the bowlegged shuffle...the sudden exit...the *backwards* apron! Jesus, it couldn't be! Not the steering gear man. Not THE ROCK. He was my hero. He was guts galore. Please, don't even tell me that...

"HE SHIT HIS PANTS?"

"Bull's-eye," Gino yukked. "Just remember, you pried it outta me."

I was devastated. For months, I had been praising the stoic gallantry of the steering gear man in the pages of the *Michigan Voice*. The way I saw it, he was one hundred times the hero that any headline-mulchin' fraud on the cover of *Time* or *People* feigned to be. The world was only a bloated bedpan full of shams and leeches wallowing in petty victories that, when sheared down and hung in front of a dyin' twilight, didn't come close to approaching the regal triumph of the steering gear man. Fuck the Donald Trumps and the Ross Perots. The closest thing I ever saw to an authentic American champ for the masses was a sweaty piece of ground chuck in a Black Sabbath T-shirt who strode upon Hades' own loading dock, night after hopeless night, as invincible in his death web as he was invisible to the rest of the feeble globe.

Now he was gone and the myth had been destroyed. The steering gear man proved to be as fallible as the next joker. The boss had to suspend him for intoxication in the workplace. I could live with that. But turdin' in his skivvies? I had to draw the line somewhere. Heroes couldn't go around crappin' themselves. Even the astronauts found a proper way to dump it.

On his return, the steering gear man hopped over to the vacant spring job next to me. I continued to refer to him as the steering gear man in all my columns. He'd rode that bull a long time without ever complaining. That was a conquest that would never be tainted.

The steering gear man's name was Doug. He had very yellow teeth and a tattoo of a rodent on his arm. Above the tattoo, the word "shoprat" was inscribed. It looked like a homemade job, most likely accomplished with a hot coat hanger at the tail end of some ferocious bender. In the summer, when things really broiled, it shined on brightly, but maybe that was just due to infection.

The switch to an easier job seemed to bring Doug out of his shell. He would chat on and on with me as if he were tryin' to make up for all those silent evenings he'd spent luggin' around steering gears. Happy jabber flowed forth. This, I found, wasn't necessarily a good thing.

One afternoon as we were startin' to roll my ex-hero came to me speaking about beards. I mentioned that I never wore a beard because they always made me look like some goofy leprechaun. In response, Doug complained that his beard didn't grow well on his left cheek area. He pointed it out and, sure enough, there was a definite barren patch.

"I know why it's not growing there," he said. I tried to appear puzzled. In fact, I was. "It's cuz when I was a kid in school, I always leaned on my desk like this." He then demonstrated by adopting the thinker's pose, propping his face up with his left fist. "I think sittin' like that all day long, for all those years, pushed all the hair back into my face for good."

I nodded and grabbed another muffler hanger. "Makes perfect sense to me," I lied.

There were those in the immediate vicinity of my job, including Doug, who began to express curiosity as to what I was scribblin' in my notebook every night. I wasn't about to come clean. I had no idea of how they might react if they were to find out I was dissecting their drab little lives for column fodder in a muckraking leftist monthly with a circulation of

60,000 readers. There was the distinct possibility that they wouldn't take kindly to my in-house voyeurism. The few who were aware of my column seemed to really enjoy it. That was fine, but I politely asked them to keep it to themselves. For the time being, anonymity seemed the safest route.

It all ran smoothly until the fateful day that I allowed my editor to talk me into writing a piece about deer hunting, the most sanctified of blue-collar blood rituals. I tried to tell my editor that I knew nothing of this redneck amusement. He persisted and I gave in as usual.

The resultant article was nothing more than one long cynical defamation of deer hunters. I celebrated the fact that these yahoos often ended up shootin' each other's brains out in their orgasmic frenzy to go boingin' some Bambi. I chuckled about all the oldsters who huffed their way right into cardiac arrest in the frigid autumn air. To hell with 'em. I liked deer just fine. The whole idea of slingin' a deer carcass over the hood of your Buick seemed rather unhinged.

My big mistake was including one of the good old boys from the Rivet Line as a central character in the article. His name was Polson, one of the banana sticker Cro-Mags. He was forever singing the praises of the National Rifle Association, a tired old tune that he often enlisted when tryin' to buffalo a fellow linemate into buying some stupid $15 membership into his gritty boys' club. We managed to get along pretty well considering we hated each other.

The day after the issue with my deer hunting article came out, I was horrified to learn that someone had brought several copies of the *Michigan Voice* into the plant and was spreading them about. I knew that eventually someone would show my piece to Polson and he'd go apeshit. I gambled with my own ploy. Rather than wait around for the inevitable, I decided to present the article to Polson myself and act as though I'd intended to give him a harmless ribbing. Perhaps by doing so, I could defuse any confrontation. I should have had my brain X-rayed instead.

Twenty minutes after presenting Polson with his personalized copy of the article, I heard the unmistakable sound of jackboots thumping up the line. It was Polson, all right. Six feet two, eyes of blue, 245 pounds of snout and gristle. The veins in his neck looked like phone cables. It was stupid, but I thought I'd try to humor him. "Hey, Rambo, so what'd ya think of..."

I made it that far and would have gone further, however windpipes are such nagging mechanisms. They require a flow of air in order to have much success with speech. At the moment, mine was being used for a concertina.

"I should kick your worthless faggot ass!" Polson shouted. There was really no need to yell. Our mouths were almost touching. "I bet all your candy-ass writin' pals think you're clever. Let me tell you what I think. You're nothin' more than a dumb cunt with diarrhea mouth. The only way you can get your garbage printed is by suckin' up to commie assholes who've got nothin' better to do but sit around, all doped up, tearin' this country down."

When Polson was finished with his critique of my vast writing talents, he wadded up the article and flung it at my feet. As he stormed away, I thought to myself how wonderful it would be to somehow wedge his fat head in between the iron pincers of my rivet gun. To pull the trigger, over and over, watching as that thick cranium of his splintered like a moldy coconut.

When lunchtime arrived, I drove up to the liquor store with Dave to grab a cold forty-ouncer. I slammed it down quickly, hardly pausing for air. Dave, who worked right beside Polson, couldn't resist the urge to comment on my situation.

"Christ, have you ever got Polson seein' red. I'd keep my eyes open the rest of the shift. A few of his redneck pals are down there eggin' him on and gettin' him stoked. Oh, by the way, did you know that you're a faggot-commie-pinko-candy-ass-punk-rock-dope-fiend?"

"You don't say." I managed to laugh. "I hope none of that gets back to my pastor."

We headed back into the factory. I glanced over at Polson as I passed his job. Dave had been right on the dime—our little spat was far from finished. Polson's eyes bore through me as if I were a twelve-point buck. As I walked on toward my job, I began thinking of new hobbies outside of the writing field. Projects that wouldn't require the use of one's arms and legs.

The horn blew and everyone resumed their duties. I kept

one eye on my job and one eye glued down the line. From my vantage point, I could see several rednecks fuelin' Polson's rage. They'd pick up a *Voice*, read a section, and point in my direction. I would have stood a good chance paired with any one of those miserable shits. But Polson was out of my league. That maniac could've whomped on a grizzly.

Suddenly, it was time for round 2. Out of the corner of my eye, I could see Polson jumping the line and heading in my direction. He had another copy of the *Voice* balled up in his fist. Damn, what I wouldn't have given for a stun gun and a can of mace right about then.

Polson stormed up to my job and pinned me against my workbench. Despite appearances, he wasn't here to dry-hump. He spread the deer article open and slammed his fist on it. Meanwhile, my job was going down the line unattended. It wasn't my greatest concern at the moment.

Polson started in. "Where in the hell do you get off writin' that I rented my wedding tux from *Outdoor Life*? Listen, shitbag, I'll have you know I was married in my MARINE DRESS OUTFIT! And what about this part where you state that the NRA stands for Nuts Run Amuck? Where do you come up with this crap?"

"Just a joke," I answered. "Can't you take a simple joke?"

"This whole goddamn article is a joke. Do you realize if it wasn't for dues-payin' members of the NRA, the deer would overpopulate and starve to death?"

Christ, not that stale serenade. In other words, I was supposed to believe that out of the boundless mercy of their hearts, these wildlife assassins were willing to trek 200 miles to the northern timbers to blast large holes in deer bellies, all in the name of preservation of the species. I guess part of it made sense: if you were dead, it was unlikely you'd be crowdin' anyone's rump out of the chowline.

"If you ask me," I injected foolishly, "I think you just enjoy killing things."

"And faggots are at the top of my list!" Polson exploded.

It took Al, our no-bullshit Quality man, and a couple other beefy sorts to pry the bastard off me. The ruckus brought Gino out of his office. He hustled over and instructed us to settle our differences elsewhere. He wasn't at all pleased that we had been letting our jobs sail by incomplete. GM didn't give a shit about dead deer or humorless rednecks or commies. They needed all available muscle attending to the production of recreational vehicles and military gas hogs.

After work let out, I prepared for an ambush that never came. Polson sped off in his pickup and I went out and got miserably drunk. From that night on, we avoided each other completely. He went back to his gun manuals, I returned to my little yellow notepad.

When Mike Moore got wind of my close call he suggested that I make Polson a running character in my column. My editor surely loved to stir up trouble. "Fat fuckin' chance," I responded. "All these bikers and tough men and gun freaks belong in someone else's diary. I'm supposed to be on shoprat detail, remember?"

Mike nodded and put his chin on his fist. I was tempted to tell him that such posture was a proven element in the stunting of one's facial hair. Instead, I said so long and headed for the factory where several thousand rivets were waiting to be pummeled. It was nice to be needed.

Go to any General Motors plant in Flint. Turn your back to the building and gaze directly across the roadway. I guarantee you'll be peering at a tavern, perhaps several of them. This bit of truism is as unfailing as spotting a bail bondsman's office across from a jail or a motel next to an airport. Find a factory, you'll find a bar.

Our local version of this concept was a long, dark room located right on the ribs of the train tracks called Mark's Lounge. It was here that the coverall brigade would retire each night to suck 'em down and spoon-feed one another a thousand years' worth of their dead fathers' lies. The conversation always consisted of shop talk: denunciations of tyrant supervisors, unwanted mandatory overtime, sore joints and dreary labor. Second verse, same as the first.

Dave and I quickly adopted Mark's Lounge as our post-shift sanctuary. In a way, we were outsiders. We enjoyed the atmosphere, the red Naugahyde booths cloaked in darkness, the ice-cold beer—however, we weren't much into jabbering about what we'd just left behind in the factory. Nine tedious hours of nothingness spoke for itself. Mostly, we'd end up staring at the natives and listening to the trains roar by like herds of thunder. Where all those trains were headed at that time of morning was anyone's guess. Their destination was the private mystery of important men.

Night after night we'd descend on Mark's Lounge searching for a booth in the most remote corner. Night after night the very same waitress would inquire as to what we were drinking. This always pissed me off. Couldn't she get it through her stacked beehive that we were confirmed Budweiser addicts? It seemed as though everyone else in the bar had their brand of libation tattooed on their foreheads. Hoss would roll in and a bottle of Pabst would hit the bar before he was seated. The same went for Clem and his Southern Comfort. Ditto old Marty and his tall beaker of vodka and orange. Why was it that we always had to go through the customary ordering procedure as if we were out-of-towners fresh off a tour bus?

"What is it with us?" I'd gripe to Dave. "We must be the most insignificant dullards on the face of the planet."

"We're just not part of the hierarchy yet," Dave reasoned. "We haven't beaten anyone up, we haven't offended anyone's girlfriend, we haven't thrown up on the carpet. There's nothing for them to remember us by."

I sat and stewed. "Well, how many of these guys in here are published writers and host their own radio shows?"

"Look around you." Dave laughed. "Do any of these gearheads look like readers of leftist literature or fans of the Butthole Surfers? My advice to you is that you find someone you can handle and pick a fight."

I surveyed the bar. Nothing but big boys with big thirsts. "All right, once I'm done whuppin' *your* ass, I'll puke in the middle of the bar and ask the first broad I see whether she'd be willing to give birth to my mutant offspring, Rivethead Jr."

Dave got a chuckle out of that one. That's all we were really here for: cold beer and stale jokes. Last call would always come too early on these nights. They'd boot us out, drunk and invigorated. Dave would go home to hurl kitchen utensils back and forth with his old lady and I'd go home and attack my typewriter like I knew what the fuck I was doing.

Due to his wife's grousing, Dave couldn't always attend the

nightly retreats over to Mark's Lounge. I would locate surrogate drinkin' pals, usually guys I knew from back in my Cab Shop days. It wasn't the same. Even drunk, these guys were way too serious. All they liked to talk about was the factory and financial planning. Most of them had a couple of kids and still had thousands in the bank. I was single and had $235 in my savings account. I had enough money to buy a complete set of tires for my car. I always used that as a barometer for fiscal security.

One night I'm up at Mark's, it's in the vicinity of last call, and I'm all by my sweet lonesome propped up next to the Beer Nuts display at the end of the bar. Some damn fool keeps playin' "The Heat Is On" by Glenn Frey. I hate Glenn Frey. I hate him and all the rest of the Eagles.

All around me are the sounds of my co-workers yapping it up and tossing 'em down. Just another night with the shoprats—clutching our paroles, maddened with thirst, looking for any good reason to laugh at ourselves. One thing we don't need is goddamn Glenn Frey advising us on the heat. It's hot, we realize. It's hotter than a cobra's dick. It's all brains afire and radioactive crotches and smoldering flesh piled high at the watering hole. That old factory labor in the midst of July is all you'll ever need to greet the heat. The only thing that gets most of us through is the knowledge that when it's all over there will be several tall cold ones aimed right for the gullet.

I'm about to pack it in when up strolls this tanked palooka whom I recognize as a friend of Dave's. The guy's a complete alkie, the waitresses know his brand by heart. Despite the heat, he is wearing a Mark's Lounge softball jacket. I hate softball.

"You've gotta tell 'em about the barbed wire," he slurs. This guy routinely mistakes me as some kind of champ of the underdogs. He's seen my Rivethead columns and assumes I'm deeply committed to THE CAUSE, whatever that might be. "You've gotta get that in your paper," he insists. "Tell 'em about the GODDAMN BARBED WIRE!"

I give a slow nod. "They should know," I reply. This always seems to make him feel better.

As long as I've known this character, the only topic we've

ever discussed is the barbed wire fence that surrounds the GM Truck & Bus plant. It must annoy the hell out of him. Others complain about the overtime or the boredom or the humidity but, with this guy, the conversation never varies. Always and forever, the barbed wire.

"It doesn't make any sense," he insists. "The barbed wire all faces *in*. The shit's pointed right down our throats. They don't wanna keep others out, they wanna KEEP US IN!"

He's right, of course. And here I always figured that the barbed wire was just so much precautionary neckware strung around the grounds to ward off would-be Empire looters. Just the Company's paranoid way of pissing on its boundaries. Hey, you never know who might drop by and try to pilfer the cookbook.

Silly me. Just one look will tell you that GM designed their security fencing with one guarded eyeball on their own work force. The barbed wire *does* face inward. Maybe they believed that we were all double agents plotting to swap the recipe for our cherished military vehicle to a carload of Russian Intelligence parked on the dark side of the trainyard. The ingredients to Ronnie's new death wagons, even up, for a dozen cases of Stolichnaya 100 proof.

Maybe they all lived in fear that one hot July evening we'd be smitten with road fever and roam our bunions elsewhere. We'd all toss off our gloves, rub axle grease all over our faces, load up our coolers full of car stereos and carburetors, and flee over the West Wall.

As we marched on toward freedom, the bullhorns would blare: "WARNING! WE COMMAND YOU RIVETERS TO HALT!" (The shriek of gunfire over a backdrop of Glenn Frey music.) "REPEAT! THIS IS YOUR FINAL WARNING! HALT IMMEDIATELY OR NO MORE MICROWAVE POPCORN FOR SIX MONTHS!"

Maybe there's nothing to it at all. Maybe some construction boss just hung the blueprint for the security fencing upside down. An honest mistake. Then again, maybe GM just strung up all that confounding barbed wire to give us Midnight Plowboys something to chaw on in between the beer nuts and the swizzle sticks: the long wait for death and the heat to go off.

THE BIG CONTRACT WITH THE PENTAGON, COMBINED WITH THE
sudden rebound in truck sales, enabled more shoprats to be
recalled from indefinite layoff. Consequently, the Rivet Line
began an overdue blood transfusion. We embraced new workers
from closed factories in Saginaw, Bay City and Lansing. Off
went the disgruntled rednecks in quest of lighter workloads. In
came the greenies to swallow up the vacancies. You could feel
the atmosphere of the department recharging.

The new guys fit in well. Jerry, Herman, Dickie, Tony,
Hogjaw, Willie—an easygoin' bunch who worked hard, partied
hard and weren't opposed to mixing the two together. We were
all around the same age—mid-twenties, single, unshackled.
The only surprise to this new group was the inclusion of a
female, a very unfamiliar species in our area.

Of course, we'd seen this happen before. The results were
always the same: an honest attempt, a few hours of overmatched
jousting with the rivet guns, a huddle with the foreman and a
quick reassignment. Why they even bothered movin' women to
the Rivet Line is beyond me. The success rate was abysmal. I
think they just liked to keep the ladies guessin', taunting them

with hectic visions of brute labor. GM was big on useless gut checks.

It turned out that the new female was to be replacing the guy next to me. The idea suited me fine. God knows I was sick to death of this idiot. His name was Kirk, a nice enough sort, but I had grown terribly weary of his nightly blabber. All he ever talked about was how much he hated his ex-wife and how much he loved bow hunting. Several times I was tempted to ask him why he didn't just combine his two obsessions and be done with it.

Henry Jackson ushered my new neighbor over to her job. He went through the obligatory demonstration of splintering a board between the pinch cycle of the rivet gun. "Darlin', that could have just as easily been your hand," he smiled. My neighbor wasn't smiling. She looked downright terrified. This made Jackson grin all the wider.

"That could also have been a bully's neck," I heard myself mutter.

"You say something, Rivethead?" Henry Jackson demanded. In the background, I could see my new neighbor stifling a laugh. It felt good to have momentarily broken the tension.

"Just mumblin' to myself, Henry."

Jackson whirled around to resume his confab. After a few more minutes of bosshead oratory, he took off down the aisle. Somewhere in a distant alcove of the plant, there were more greenies to intimidate. More nerves to unsettle. More useless machismo to dump down the gills of the unsteady and vulnerable.

Kirk began the slow process of breaking in his replacement. His job wasn't all that tough, but it did involve a dangerous procedure—the buildup of the military cross members. Affixing the skid plate to the cross member called for plenty of caution. As with everything else that went onto these military trucks, the skid plate was double the normal thickness. It had extremely sharp edges that jutted out from the cross member at an awkward angle. One slip, one momentary loss of grip, and the skid plate could carve your arm to the bone or, if dropped, swipe off a couple toes.

The new female wasted little time pullin' up her sleeves. By lunchtime, she had already mastered assembling the cross members. She was also doing an impressive job of hefting the finished product onto the frames and bolting them down. However, she wasn't having nearly the success with the riveting portion of the job. She'd grab the gun, wrestle with it, sway with it, curse at it and invariably slice the rivet. Exasperated, she'd throw up her hands and grumble.

I could sense that a visit from Dr. Rivethead was in order. I let her mangle a few more rivets before wandering over and introducing myself.

"My name's Ben. For better or worse, I am the local guru regarding the defiant nature of the rivet gun."

This brought a smile. "My name's Janice and, for better or worse, I'm a total klutz."

"Believe me, so is everyone when they first get ahold of one of these guns."

As Janice looked on, I began to demonstrate the proper riveting technique. I passed on all relevant advice. To wit: Resist the urge to arm wrestle the gun. The gun will pin you every time. Do not yank the gun. The gun will cooperate better with a nudge. Wait until the rivet is aligned. If you strike too early, the rivet will wind up creased or double-headed. Become a passenger. Let the gun do all the work. Be patient. Glide instead of lurch. Close cover before striking. Induce vomiting. You can lead a rivet gun to water, but you can't make it surf. Blah, blah, blah...

By the end of the shift, Janice was gettin' the feel for it. Her ratio of bull's-eyes to beheadings was running ten to one in her favor. Not a bad average for a greenie. It would come. It always did if you just relaxed. All one really had to do was get over the fact that he or she was navigatin' a stubborn hunk of cast iron that packed up to 17,000 pounds of pressure per square inch and wasn't awfully picky about its menu. It would just as soon devour Mozart's fingertips as a boxful of rivets.

Janice thanked me for my bit of tutelage. Then she paused. "So you're the Rivethead guy," she said. "I've heard about your columns. My girlfriends think you're a riot."

"Basically, I'm just a peeping Tom. It helps keep the clock moving."

"I can see how that might be handy around here." Janice laughed. "I'll see you tomorrow."

"I'll be here."

The arrival of Janice turned out to be a real blessing. She was intelligent, warm and witty. She was also just as twisted and desperate as the rest of us when it came to engaging in the assorted hijinks we used to bludgeon'the ruthless minute hand. We quickly became comrades in the battle to destroy the monotony. Mainly, I would babble, she would laugh. We were fond of discussing our fates.

"Monkeys could be doing this," Jan observed and gazed around at the crew. It was a little sad. "I guess they already are," she surmised.

It wasn't easy for a woman on the Rivet Line. They were under constant siege by legions of moronic suitors. Almost every guy down there perceived himself as some kind of rodent Romeo. A woman working in the midst of so many men was looked upon as willing prey. Personality, looks, marital status hardly mattered. If it had tits and ass and jiggled along, it was fair game. Being that she was young and attractive, Jan was swarmed nightly. She deflected them nicely, defusing their advances with talk about her husband and snapshots of her little boy. Sooner or later, the vultures would hang it up and drag their libidos toward the next shapely bottom.

There was also another dreary side to this situation with women on the line. Due to the fact that Janice and I spent so much time together goofin' off, it was commonly accepted that we must be involved in some gooey love affair. Whenever Janice and I would slide out at lunch to race up to McDonald's, we'd arrive back to a chorus of oooohs and ahhhhs. The consensus was that we were fleeing at every given opportunity to find someplace to hump ourselves silly.

It pissed me off. Not that I really cared what others were dreamin' up. It just bothered me that it was impossible to be close friends with a female in the factory without a bunch of dick-for-brains assuming that sex was the only bond. Maybe they were all jealous. Maybe they were confused as to why the new gal on the block would choose such a bland gigolo. Regardless, I could have done without their lousy assumptions.

We'd get over to the bar after work and it would start up. How large are her tits? Is she a screamer? Does she prefer it on top? Is her old man suspicious? When can we expect an in-depth article on the proper method of jumpin' factory snatch? Yuk, yuk, yuk. I'd sit there and drain my Budweisers, smiling wearily. At least it beat talking about foremen and financial planning. When I'd tire of the conversation, I would simply agree with everything that was being said.

"Yep, you boys are right. If I don't slow this thing down, my dick's gonna fall off. But, at least I'm gettin' a female. It must be rough on you other guys having to make it with each other every night out in the parking lot. Come to think of it, *that* would make for an interesting article: 'NOT HAVING ENOUGH WANTON WOMEN TO GO AROUND, MY SEX-STARVED LINEMATES WERE FORCED INTO A SHAME-LESS HOMO JAMBOREE—GOBBLIN' EACH OTHER UP, STROKIN' EACH OTHER'S MULES, TWEETIN' LIKE TURTLEDOVES—SO OUTRAGEOUSLY CORRUPTED BY THEIR OWN LUST FOR SUMMER SAUSAGE THAT THEY PLOWED OVER ONE ANOTHER IN A VILE FEEDING FRENZY FOR ANY OLD CHUNK OF GENITALIA THAT SPRUNG FROM THE SHADOWS OF THEIR FOGGED-OVER FAG WAGONS.'"

Before long, we'd be back to talkin' about the usual stuff. Why doesn't Jack Morris just keep his yap shut and pitch the fuckin' ball? How come Michelob makes you fart so much? Why don't they kill the bastard who keeps playin' that Glenn Frey song? Why won't Roger Smith go bowling with us?

Why? Why? Why?

Exit Dave Steel. During the mad scramble of those who wanted to escape the Rivet Line, he had filed for transfer to Work Inspection. My nagging attempts to persuade him to stick around fell on deaf ears. Once the paperwork came together, he was gone in a wink. Dave couldn't believe that I wanted to remain. "I believe you are in dire need of psychiatric help," he suggested.

Dave was way off. After years of being bumped in and out and around the plant, I was never more convinced that this is where I belonged. Tot lot for the toothless. A footstool lackey for the Rivet Lords. A snot-nosed megaphone for the rodents. Comfortable in my stinkin' placement—glad only to scrawl it down, to sleepwalk to the next greasy errand, the next smudged-up paycheck headed for the whiskey man's till. Departure was nonsense. Departure was treason.

After Dave had transferred, I occasionally visited him on his new job. I couldn't find a solitary reason to envy his relocation. All Dave did all night was shuffle back and forth poking an occasional dipstick into some half-hidden hole and yawning like a hippo in the mud. His neighbors resembled Stepford Wives at a linen sale. It was fuckin' eerie. No revelry, no pranks, no communication, no turmoil, no nothin'. No, thank you.

Thus began a constant routine between the two of us of sniping at each other's jobs. I would condemn Dave for wanting to become a part of this silent mausoleum. I assured him that the clock would eventually tear him apart in such a lifeless outpost. Dave would counter by insisting that the Rivet Line was a lake of fire, a dungeon full of lamebrains and misfits who looked like they were all fresh off triple homicides. On and on it would go. Denouncements, slander, scorn. The trouble was clear. Neither one of us could understand each other's motives for the paths we had chosen.

The simple truth was that Dave had zero use for humanity. Had he been able to swing it, he'd probably have taken a job sittin' in a shanty on top of the factory roof fiddlin' with a busted Etch-a-Sketch all night. Camaraderie was a useless priority for Dave Steel. I was his only friend and, half the time, I think that was one over his limit.

For myself, comradeship had developed into a must. I needed drinkin' buddies and fellow clock maimers. The Rivethead was no working class hero. Not by a long shot. He was only a conglomeration of the hucksters and slickers around him.

Folks like Janice. Within weeks of her arrival on the Rivet Line, we had grown to depend on each other for assistance in knockin' down the humdrum. She became my personal sounding board. On each shift I would write for a couple of hours before lunch. When I was finished with whatever I was working on, I'd hand my stuff over to her. Being that she walked that same murky strip, she was an excellent barometer for what needed to be said and what should be scrapped. She could tell when I was on to something. She also knew when I was just ramblin' on. Several times I used her suggestions for themes in my *Michigan Voice* column.

Then there was Jerry, the lady-killer from Bay City. I'd never seen a smoother operator. I quickly dubbed him the Polish Sex God—a handle he was enthralled with, always pestering me to fork over any articles I might write containing references to his title.

In the absence of Dave Steel, Jerry became my new beer chum. We often worked out this scam where we would volunteer to work a couple hours overtime cleaning up the department. As soon as the line stopped, we'd race for the brooms. Jerry would start at one end of the department and I would head for the other. We'd begin a furious system of kicking, sweeping, sliding and hiding the night's debris under benches and stock pallets. We worked like absolute maniacs for about fifteen minutes. Our boss had us written down for two hours. However, our boss was long gone and, soon enough, so were we.

We'd scram over to Mark's Lounge with an hour-plus still ringing on the overtime meter. This was a much more agreeable way of earning extra cash. Dark lights, cold beer, shootin' pool and, without fail, an encounter with a bunch of tipsy bimbos. Jerry sure knew how to spin that web.

I can remember one night whisking off for the can and by the time I returned, the Polish Sex God was holdin' court. He had one chick in his lap and another one draped on his shoulder. These women were buying *him* drinks. I tuned in on some of the conversation and wanted to puke.

"Doreen, has anyone ever told you that you're a ringer for Natalie Wood?"

"Are you serious? She's gorgeous!"

"Precisely my point." Jerry grinned.

Only the fact that we were bein' paid twenty-some dollars an hour made this charade tolerable. Doreen was Natalie Wood like my grandma was Angie Dickinson. Jerry tried interesting me in taking the two bar babes out to his van with him. I was as horny as the next guy, but I did have some requirements as to who, when and where. This scenario included none of them. I told Jerry that I'd just meet him back at the time clocks at 3:00 A.M. to punch out our badges. I sat by myself and savored the beer. I suppose there were much worse ways of makin' a living than gettin' sloshed while your buddy was bouncin' around the back of his van with the new Natalie Wood.

I got together with Doug, Eddie, Dick and Jerry and we created this grand diversion that we called Rivet Hockey. Rivet Hockey could best be described as a combination of foosball, soccer, the Civil War and every Charles Bronson movie made after 1972. It was total mayhem, a Neanderthal free-for-all that was both violent and one hell of a lot of fun.

The game was simple. Position a rivet on the floor, scope out an opposing linemate, and kick the rivet as hard as possible toward the linemate's foot, ankle or shin. In Rivet Hockey, pain was the payoff. To connect on a direct hit to a tender tibia, to exact blood through an opponent's pant leg, was equivalent to kicking a fifty-yard field goal in the Rose Bowl. Remorse was forbidden. Revenge was encouraged. Ruptures were illegal. Every rat for himself.

As for selecting a Rivet Hockey victim, you had to be very cautious not to put the scope to a linemate who saw no redeeming humor in having his legs and ankles blasted by screamin' chunks of metal. There were some of our neighbors who just weren't buyin' Rivet Hockey. They were only here to make a buck. These grumps gulped coffee, gnawed on salami sandwiches, pawed through girlie rags and sat out the death march of the minute hand.

We had problems with one guy we all called Mighty Joe Young. No one knew his real name and no one was about to ask. He looked like some kind of science project from Muscle Beach—250 pounds, invisible neck, hands like hams and a scowl as big as Utah. Unfortunately, they plopped Mighty Joe right in the middle of our battlefield. His presence began to alter everyone's game plan. Our savage line drives were exchanged for wimpy high-percentage pokes. The whole deal began to reek of cowardice and retreat. No one wanted to risk peggin' this monster in the flannel shirt.

As self-appointed commissioner of the North Unit Rivet Hockey Association, I felt obliged to act. I gathered up all the players and we retreated at lunchtime to Jerry's van for strategy and Budweiser. Janice tagged along to take down the minutes.

I began. "Listen, guys. My father was a shoprat. His father was a shoprat. My father's father was a shoprat. I'm bettin' that your fathers and their fathers were shoprats." The guys all nodded. So did Janice. "The point is this. We come from very noble stock. Realizing this, do you believe for one moment that our forefathers would have put up with this crap? Here we've hit upon a great diversion, one that'll distract us from that goddamn clock, and we're backin' down like a bunch of panty-waist bank clerks. Wouldn't our fathers have embraced Rivet Hockey and fought to the bitter end for its survival? Huh? *HUH?*"

My co-workers pulled on their beers and pondered. I forged on.

"Well, I think the answer is obvious—HELL NO, THEY WOULDN'T! They would have thought Rivet Hockey was a bad fuckin' joke. And that, my friends, is precisely my point. WHEN THE HELL DID WE EVER DO ANYTHING OUR FATHERS WANTED US TO DO? NEVER! After all, we're workin' here, ain't we? My suggestion is that we go back in there and kick the shit out of some rivets!"

My hokey speech worked. Mighty Joe was soon conquered. He still wasn't real fond of bein' pegged with a misdirected rivet, but I think he began to realize that our malice wasn't directed at anything that walked on this earth or chewed on lunch meat or wore a flannel shirt. Shit, we liked just about everybody. Our only adversary was Father Time. And by slammin' rivets up against each other's shins, we were only out to jump that bastard and maim him something silly.

Eddie was responsible for another one of our favorite amusements. He called it Dumpster Ball. To play, all you did was round up some empty boxes, fold in the cardboard flaps, set the box on its side, and attempt to kick it on a high enough arc that it would clear the center of the dumpster next to the wall across from Eddie's job.

Dumpster Ball wasn't as easy as it might seem. It took practice to get those boxes airborne. There was a certain art to the required motion and, before long, Eddie was givin' out lessons. He would demonstrate the proper approach and follow-through. He was damn near automatic, smooth as Jan Stenerud, powerful enough to occasionally deposit one of the boxes into the rafter stratosphere. We called these moon shots and they were truly breathtaking. Everyone in the pack had some goofy talent and, for whatever it was worth, Eddie's was Dumpster Ball.

In time, we all started to get the feel for it. We'd hustle through our jobs and race down to polish up our kicking game. All of us kept improving until we were able to give Eddie some decent competition. Thus began Dumpster Ball wagering and, with it, Eddie's mysterious backslide from the very sport he had invented.

The problem was Eddie simply got the yips whenever money was on the line. We'd bet a dollar a field goal, ten chances per taker. I don't know whether it was a fear of losin' a few bucks or all the pot he was smokin' (I used to get contact highs just lookin' at his eyes), but Eddie just couldn't hit for shit when it mattered most. Eddie would become so enraged that sometimes he'd kick a box so hard the damn thing would explode into scrap the moment it met his toe. This was a very impressive feat, but hardly any way to win your money back.

To lessen the stakes a bit, we started kicking to see who would have to bring in the alcohol on Friday nights. Kickin' for booze revitalized Eddie's game. He had an edge on us. Where we all drank vodka or Jim Beam, Eddie's drink was Hennessy. A fifth of that stuff ran about twenty bucks a pop. With such a cost discrepancy running in his favor, Eddie relaxed and soon his towering blasts were once again penetrating the dumpster's gut, bangin' a good forty feet up the wall.

Eddie was the only guy in the department who could match me drink for drink. The Polish Sex God was good with the beer, but couldn't handle the hard stuff. Hogjaw could knock back anything, but had problems with the long haul. Doug had already shot out his belly and Tony lacked stamina.

Fridays became special. Eddie and I would start knockin' down the bottles early in the shift. Whenever we'd get caught short, I would arrange for Jerry and Janice to cover my job while I snuck up to the liquor store. I always enjoyed this trek. It excited me to know that I was up to something that was rigidly forbidden. I was leaving the department without permission. NOT ALLOWED! I was wandering off plant grounds without punching out. NOT ALLOWED! I was intoxicated during working hours. NOT ALLOWED! I was smuggling alcohol onto GM property. NOT ALLOWED! I never once got nabbed and it made me feel like laughing at the bossmen but... NOT ALOUD.

The only problem with Eddie was the more he consumed, the more maudlin he became. We would sit in my Camaro after the shift was over, uncapping a new bottle or finishing an old one, and Eddie would start running all this worthless shit at me concerning race-mingling. It was stupid. So what if we were different colors? I listened as Eddie let it out.

"Ben, we're all brothers. We all bleed red. Why the hell we gotta fight?"

"Goddamnit, Eddie, who's fightin'? We certainly aren't. We're drinkin'. This is supposed to be fun, remember? Why bring up that bullshit? It doesn't concern us."

"The thing is, I never spoke with any white folk until I was fifteen. Where I come from, the two just don't get together."

"Well, shit, I wasn't exactly Don Cornelius's houseboy. Listen, Eddie. If some of these bastards got their heads stuck up their asses, that can't be our problem. As long as we hit it off, who *cares* what those idiots are up to."

"Yeah, I suppose," Eddie replied, content to drop it for the moment, but hardly convinced of anything that would smooth his doubts on the matter.

The summer rolled on and we broiled in the heat, smuggling our fair share of amusement wherever we could find it. Jerry had decided to try out the lock-nut job a few spots down. Taking his place was one of the college kid "interns" GM hired each summer to cover for guys who were off on their vacations. His name was Mark, a chubby kid bound for med school. For the time being, he belonged to us. We taught him how to play Rivet Hockey and Dumpster Ball. We even got him to sample an occasional beer. Before long, he fit right in like a true-blue rivetling.

I remember one day I was just mindin' my own business, molestin' yet another series of rivets, when our little greenie started yellin' "Holy shit... HOLY SHIT!" I looked over at Mark and he was motioning frantically over my shoulder. Could it be? Roger Smith? Had he relented and come to answer the dogged plea of the Hamper ancestry? Tonight, we bowl?

I turned around slowly. What I was gazing at was not Roger Smith. Standing only ten feet behind me was none other than Howie Makem, his big swollen cat head teetering in the haze. The men began to howl deliriously. It had been a few years since the last known Howie sighting. We continued to roar our lungs out as Howie Makem strutted down the aisle and out of view.

"THE DEAD HAVE RISEN! THE DEAD HAVE RISEN!" I shrieked. I looked over at Mark. His mouth was hangin' open like an oven door. He appeared to be in a state of shock.

"What the hell was THAT?" Mark cried.

Introductions seemed in order, yet how did one go about telling a traumatized bystander that the large CAT he'd just seen strolling near his job was the living messiah of the masses and the secret to a Quality work plan all wrapped into one blur of fur? My guess was you didn't even try.

"That was a big cat, Mark. He must be lookin' for that mouse we've been seein' around here lately."

Mark asked for a cigarette. I had never seen him smoke before. "Oh," he said.

After that sighting, I saw Howie on a few more occasions. The news appeared to be bad. For one thing, Howie looked absolutely terrible. He seemed to have fallen prey to some dreadful disease. One night, I actually saw Howie propped up in a fork truck, waving his feeble paw back and forth, apparently too weak to complete his rounds on foot. I screamed "Howie!" and that gigantic noggin of his tilted toward me, a hideous mask of pain. It hit me right there at my workbench: My God, I think Howie's dying!

How true it all appeared. Just another giant struggling valiantly against the gravedigger's spade. Death didn't give a shit. Death never paused for John Wayne. It chewed on him like a warm Swanson dinner. Howie, nine lives and all, was not immune. All our heroes died.

Just about the time we were preparing weepy eulogies for the ultimate passing of Howie Makem, he came firin' out of the chute again. What the fuck was GM up to? Howie was more alive and antimated than ever. It was all too much. Even I, possibly Howie's greatest fan, began to cool in my affection for our schizophrenic mascot. We didn't want drama, we needed something to laugh at.

A severe Howie Makem backlash developed. Instead of the customary cheering that greeted Howie, he was now bein' heckled unmercifully. Whenever he appeared in the vicinity of the Rivet Line, he did so at grave personal risk. We would load up on rivets and toss them at his generous skull.

A horrible realization began to bother me. After a Howie sighting, I'd lean back on my bench and think to myself: SOMEONE is in that head. SOMEONE whose wife and kids lie sound asleep in another part of town while the stars shine down and the trucks pile up and Daddy haunts the halls in his kitty costume. SOMEONE who was forced to go through twelve worthless years of the American Education System only to wind up jerry-riggin' the same old acid flashback night after night. There should be exemptions made for men who aspire to do nothing more than dress up like huge house pets in the middle of factories.

Another thought began to occur to me. If Howie Makem was allowed to roam the plant as the spiritual ambassador of the Quality Concept, why wasn't equal time being provided a likewise embodied representative of GM's FOREMOST preoccupation—the Quantity Concept? An elusive second self that would lurk among the shadows and pounce upon any worker who dared cause any kind of stoppage in production.

I decided I might like the role. What the hell, the job would allow for plenty of maneuverability and I could work at my own pace. It turned out that Janice had a friend who worked over in the audit area. Through information passed on by this friend, I learned that this was the privy location of Howie Makem's costume. I was doubly excited to hear from Jan's source that Howie actually had a SPARE head stashed away somewhere in the audit room. It was my resolute intention to swipe the spare cat head, paint the eyes a violent red, attach large fangs to its overbite, and carve the word QUOTA on its forehead.

With this accomplished, I, the Quantity Cat, would set out to terrorize all those who were responsible for assembly line downtime. How many times had I heard the woesome lament:

"For each minute the line is down, the Company loses another $10,000." I would fix all that. I would call myself Howie Rakem, Quantity Cat. Howie Rakem would ambush workers at stoplights. Park next to them at drive-ins. Claw their bedroom windows during the sex act. Hiss at them in booths at Mark's Lounge. No man would dare shortchange the coffers knowing that Howie Rakem was on the prowl. To reward my gallant service, I would finally be allowed to go bowling with Chairman Roger.

Sadly, I must report that it never worked out. It wasn't due to a lack of effort. Countless times I made it as far as the very closet where Howie stored his heads, but the goddamn thing was always padlocked. According to Jan's source, this was due to the fact that a few months back some vandals had made off with Howie's legs and torso. All the Quality people were left with was a couple of disembodied cat heads. This helped explain Howie's frequent bouts of absenteeism.

Or did it? Now I was really confused. Just because Howie no longer had a body, what was preventing him from putting on the head and performing his rounds in jeans or coveralls? The way I had it figured, as long as you had a head, you had a Howie. Right? RIGHT?

Nope. Janice explained: "The Quality people feel that the workers won't be able to relate to Howie without the full presentation. In other words, without the paws and tail and the fur—"

"STOP!" I injected hysterically. "Let me guess. You're about to tell me that without the paws and tail and the fur... THE WORKERS WON'T BELIEVE THAT HOWIE IS AN ACTUAL... um... CAT! Don't lie. That's what you were about to say, wasn't it?"

Janice began to shake with laughter. She had a rough time gettin' it out. "Exactly!" she howled at last.

It was all so silly. I brought home over $400 a week for accomplishing nothing. When everything went just right, I had absolutely no recollection of what had transpired moments before. If all went according to plan, I would be eligible for a tidy retirement plan in the year 2007.

The Quality people had no need to worry. For the life of me, I would believe *anything*.

*   *   *

"MANDRELL SISTER ORDERS A SUBURBAN!" the headline announced. I had in my hand a fresh copy of our in-plant propaganda sheet, the *Truckin' Tribune*. It was September 19, 1985, and I was relaxing at the picnic table near my job, waiting for the line to start rolling.

I continued with the article. I wasn't sure why, but I found the topic mesmerizing. "Today, Flint Truck Assembly will produce a Suburban for well-known singer and performer Louise Mandrell. The unit is loaded, has four-wheel drive and is black and silver with gray inserts. The order originated in Scottsville, Ky."

I put the paper down and sat there for a moment. Louise Mandrell. Today. Suburban. A warm sensation streamed through me. I picked up the *Tribune* and read the article several more times. I was becoming infatuated with the entire concept. A clear vision of lovely Louise plowing right through the Kentucky dusk, her hair unfurled, her bronzed legs stretched full, goosin' that big black chariot through a bend in the brush where the critters all leapt in the glow of her ramblin' fog lights. It was pretty damn romantic.

Carefully, I sliced the article from the *Tribune* with my box-cutter knife. As I was doing so, Doug was taking a seat at the end of the table to mark his production schedule for the day. I scooted over. Information this urgent had to be shared.

"Dougie, have you seen today's issue of *Pravda*?" I asked. He shook his head and continued marking his manifest. It was never a polite idea to interrupt a linemate as he was totaling up his schedule. This kind of outside interference could cause omissions and oversights that would show up in errors later in the job operation. Schedule-marking was a solemn, all-absorbing event.

Big shit. I flung the article down in the middle of Doug's manifest. "You *must* read this, right *now!*" I insisted.

Dougie picked up my clipping and read it through. He didn't appear to be much amused. After all, this was a Friday afternoon and no one really thawed out until about lunch break when the horn would blow and we'd gallop off to the liquor store.

"Didn't she get mashed in a car wreck?" Dougie replied while returning to his schedule.

I moaned. "Naw, you're thinkin' of her sister, Barbara, the gloomy blonde. Louise is the frisky one. The brunette. The sister who does all those White Rain hair spray commercials."

"Doesn't she play the fiddle?" Dougie mused. Now we were gettin' somewhere.

"You better believe it," I yelled.

"So what about her?"

"WHAT ABOUT HER? Is that all you've got to say? Jesus, Doug, you just read the article. You must realize the significance here. Today we will be building a truck for a goddamn celebrity. Someone we can attach a face to."

"Sorry, I still don't get it. Fill me in later, I've got to finish marking my schedule."

"The hell with your schedule," I exclaimed while shoving off.

Soon, the line began to roll and we moved to our stations. In between jobs, I raced up and down the line apprising my co-workers of the impending approach of the Mandrell Sister Suburban. I dangled my clipping in front of their faces in hopes that it would generate for them the same type of enthusiasm I was delighting in.

Their reactions varied. While some appeared marginally enthused, the majority merely shrugged and peered back at me as if I'd finally teetered over the brink. Alas, my reputation as one who was given to occasional flights of madness, gibberish, delirium and amphetamine prattle had preceded me.

However, not this time. I was clean. I was in complete control. I understood completely the whence and the wherefores. I understood that Louise Mandrell was having a General Motors four-wheel Suburban built today. It was to be loaded. It was to be black and silver. These were inescapable truths. I couldn't help it if it was a Mandrell Sister as opposed to someone who would have been more shoprat vogue—someone like Merle Haggard, Richard Petty or Traci Lords. At least it was SOMEBODY!

The basis for all this mania was simple. For nearly a decade I had toiled away for the GM Truck & Bus plant. In all this time never, but never, had I encountered one human soul who had either purchased, ordered, leased or even hot-wired a General Motors Suburban. Every night the frames would roll by—thirty-eight jobs to the hour—and it would mystify the hell outta me as to where all these beasts were headed.

My Rivet Line pals were just as confused. We would often look up from our jobs in the middle of another shift and ask "Who buys all these things?" Obviously, someone had to be doin' it and we were tremendously grateful to them. We had mouths to feed and bar tabs to resolve. Still, it often seemed like the trucks we were assembling just vanished out the door—thousands of them, millions of them—lurching into some enormous black hole out by the train tracks and barbed wire fences. What a peculiar way to turn a profit.

Enter Louise Mandrell. She was *real*. On any given day, you could see her cavorting across American television with a canister of goop aimed squarely at her stylish mass of tresses. She lived, she breathed, she sawed an angry fiddle. No longer could there be any denial. What we had here was an actual entity who was able to confirm for us that what we were doing every night resulted in some kind of tangible cause and aftereffect.

There still remained one bitter disappointment. Our plant newspaper hadn't revealed any information as to which job was to be the Mandrell Suburban. I made a couple of futile attempts to wangle the job number out of the management boys but, to no great surprise, was met with an assortment of lame utterances like "I have no idea" and the old standby "Hamper, just do your job."

Another factor working against me in my pursuit to identify the Mandrell Suburban was my work area itself. The Rivet Line was just an ongoing series of clone-like black frames. Each one was a duplicate of the one that went before with the exception of the occasional army vehicle. I doubted rather strongly Louise was gonna get her claws on one of those. The information that the Mandrell Suburban would be black and silver, that it would have gray inserts, that it would come loaded, was totally useless to all of us on the Rivet Line. Everything that went our way was identical.

It still turned out to be a better than average shift. At random intervals through the night, I would holler down the line to my co-workers: *"This* one could be it. Let's give it the rivet!" Dougie would whip into a frantic air-fiddle solo, the Polish Sex God would start making humping motions, Janice and I would genuflect and we'd give it our best. Above us, the clock would swirl by. Another day, another diversion.

Not all diversions were of an amusing nature. I recall one that really gave us fits. GM and the union got together and installed these mammoth electronic message boards in various locations around the plant. They only sprung for about a dozen of these boards and, wouldn't you just know it, with all the available acreage around the factory, they just had to point one of these bastards right at me. It hung about five feet above the picnic table directly across the aisle from my job.

The messages they would flash ranged from corny propaganda (green neon bulb depictions of Howie Makem's face uttering shit like QUALITY IS THE BACKBONE OF GOOD WORKMANSHIP!) to motivational pep squawk (A WINNER NEVER QUITS & A QUITTER NEVER WINS!) to brain-jarring ruminations (SAFETY IS SAFE). The board also flooded us with birthday salutes, religious passages, antidrug adages, audit scores, limericks and the occasional abstract gibberish. (One night the board kept flashing the phrase HAPPINESS IS HORSES alongside a rather grotesque-lookin' rendering of a horse head. If I had any idea what it meant, I'd gladly pass it on.)

I remember the first day the message board went into operation. For the entire shift, it beamed out one single message. They never erased it. We kept waiting for another phrase to come along and replace it. No such luck. The message blazed on brightly like some eternal credo meant to hog-tie our bewildered psyches. The message? Hold on to your hardhats, sages. The message being thrust upon us in enormous block lettering read: SQUEEZING RIVETS IS FUN! Trust me. Even the fuckin' exclamation point was their own.

Talk about a confused bunch of riveters—we had no idea whether this was some kind of big bro Orwellian brain-dunk or just some lowly office puke's idea of a nimble-witted gibe. Whatever it was, we were not especially amused.

Just for a moment, let's imagine that you worked for the sewage department. One day you walk into work to discover that the boss has erected a giant neon sign right next to your job that insists SHOVELING TURDS IS FUN! Or, let's pretend you're a shoe clerk. You arrive at your workplace to find a huge billboard that pours forth the adage SMELLING FEET IS RAPTURE! How would you react to such derisive lunacy? You couldn't accept this as normal. Not in a billion years. C'mon, c'mon. WHAT WOULD YOU DO?

Well, I know what I did. I cut myself up a chunk of cardboard, took a big red felt marker and etched down the letters CKED. I then crammed a wad of tape on the back of it, stood atop the workers' picnic table and slapped those four letters over the N in the word FUN. I hustled back to my job and turned around to gaze at my handiwork. Oh yes, this was much better: SQUEEZING RIVETS IS FUCKED! I was such a stickler for accuracy. My proud correction remained up there for about three hours until Gino, fearing the wrath of overlords, ripped it down amidst a chorus of heavy booing. It was all right. Gino was cool. Any other foreman would have torn it down immediately and reprimanded me for some muddled violation of Company policy.

This whole incident with the new message board disturbed us. We wondered exactly who was in charge of this vile effrontery. Were these the same deplorable loons, the same demented pimps of propaganda that had shamelessly spermatized the Howie Makem saga? Did these fuckers really believe that squeezin' rivets was "fun"? If so, why weren't they all down here having the time of their lives? They'd have gotten no protest out of us: "Here you be, Jenkins, another dozen rivets to squeeze! Head 'em out! More fun than a whore with three tongues!"

I had several definitions of fun. Riveting was nowhere on the list. Taking in a Tiger game from the right field overhang was fun. Listening to Angry Samoans records while gettin' sloshed was fun. The episode of *Bewitched* where Endora hexed Dick York with elephant ears was fun. Dozing past noon with the phone off the hook was fun. Having sex in a Subaru was difficult—however, that was fun too. Squeezing rivets was *not* fun. It paid the rent and put Fritos in our kids' bellies, but there was no way you could classify it as fun. Not yesterday, not today, not tomorrow.

It made us wonder just what our precious union's involvement was with this brain-rapin' contraption. They were coinvestors in the purchase of all these message boards. Weren't they obliged to be on our side? How could they sit idly by and allow GM to glut the screens with hysterical lies? Since we paid their goddamn salaries, you would think they'd have some balky mulehead assigned to monitor the mucus. A representative of the workin' Joe who would step in and tell GM: "Hey, you chuckleheads. If you dare beam 'Squeezing Rivets Is Fun!' ever again, we reserve the right to broadcast 'Squeezing the Plant Manager's Balls Is a Hoot!'

I believe the thing that grated us most about the giant message board is that it never once supplied us with anything we didn't already know or couldn't have cared less about. The possibilities for useful data were certainly there. For instance, why couldn't they flash the nightly lottery number? Several of us had money ridin' with Frankie, our in-plant numbers runner. Why couldn't they post updates on scores from the Tiger and Piston games? What could be more harmless and righteously American than lettin' us check in on our local sports heros? Why couldn't they run silent footage of the Three Stooges or Tom & Jerry cartoons? No lyin', we'd have settled for home movies of Roger Smith's valet sortin' through his sock drawer.

All we got was the same daily bullshit. I had a creepy suspicion that the message board was slowly driving us daft, especially Eddie. His job was situated just such that the messages were staring him right in the face. Several times I caught him glowering at the board as if he were on the verge of goin' bughouse.

Eddie and I began firing rivets at the screen. We'd rear back like Seaver and Gooden, throwing our arms out in a desperate attempt to shut down the madness. It was useless. The damn message board must have been made out of Kryptonite. Once in a great while, Eddie would peg it hard enough to make one or two of the words temporarily disappear. Everyone would begin to applaud when, suddenly, the letters would heal up and reappear.

It ate at Eddie. At times, he seemed to be hypnotized to the board during which he would engage in absurd conversation. I still recall the night he motioned me over to answer a question. His eyes were pinned to the center of the green neon.

"Ben, what's the difference between No Lead Gas and Unlead-ed Gas?"

"Are you serious, Eddie?" I chuckled.

"Could you just tell me the FUCKIN' DIFFERENCE!" Eddie shouted. He was serious.

"Well, I always assumed that the two were just the same."

"Then how come my car runs better on the goddamn No Lead?"

I had no idea. I slid back to my job and hit a few rivets. It wasn't any fun.

One of the guys from the plant called me up one morning. It was just after 11:00 A.M. and I was still tryin' to snooze off a hangover.

"Get outta bed and switch on Channel 5," the voice demanded. "Your damn bowling buddy is holding a press con-ference. They broke right in on *Hour Magazine!*"

"Why?" I mumbled.

My informer wasn't sure. Something to do with plant closings and little pink slips fluttering down on the heads of the working class. There had been rumors of such. I went in and turned on the television.

It was him all right. Roger B. Smith, my elusive bowling foe, GM's resident reducing plan guru. Perhaps the only fella in the entire Western Hemisphere to possess eight million freckles and yet absolutely no sense of humor whatsoever. He looked like Howdy Doody presiding over a hangin' party—a fiendish combination of power, dread, panic and too much rouge.

Evidently, I had tuned in just after Rog had revealed his roll call of plants headed for extermination. The walking papers having been served, it was now time for the heavy Q & A. The media swarmed in on The Boss, a great sea of gnats luggin' minicams and mic cables. The ultimate American game show squirming to life with 30,000 potential urchins lined up behind Door Number One.

I sat there in my underwear wondering if I would be among them. I wondered what else I could possibly do for a living. I had no training, no skills, no degrees, no connections. I drank too much to fit into most occupations and I wasn't ambitious enough to have a shot at the rest. Above all, I didn't like poking my head into society. People bothered me. That was the best part of my factory job: never really having to relate to anyone or anything other than the awkward-lookin' rivet apparatus that hung from the rafters next to my job. We understood each other. We got along just fine.

While I was reflecting on all of this, Roger was doing his best to explain everything to the media. It was very apparent that as far as public speakers went, Smith rated far down the dais, say, right behind a garden hoe or a doorknob. I could sympathize a bit. I'd be a nervous wreck too if I had his lousy job. Shredding people's livelihoods to bits before it was time for lunch had to jangle one's nerves.

What I found most alarming was that Smitty appeared totally confused with the subject matter itself. Specifics like when, where, who, WHY? Jesus, spit it out, boss. Your ass is covered. You ain't one of the gang bein' upchucked curbside.

Befuddled, Smith began to deflect most of the questions over to his sidekick, GM President Jim McDonald. Now here was a guy who ate decimals and divisors for breakfast, lunch and dinner. A real chatterbox in banker's blue. Jimbo babbled on in the kinda cool-daddy corporate jumble-thump that plain old numbskulls like you and me and the owl in the tree could never hope to untangle. If he was clarifying anything, it still managed to sail about ten feet over my head. (I remember a year or so later, during GM's angry brawl with EDS, it suddenly dawned on me why these stiffs ached so bad in their urge to rid themselves of Ross Perot. It had nothing to do with his loud criticisms or his uppity swagger or even his beguiling hickoid funkiness. Pure and simple, THAT SON-OF-A-BITCHIN' BILLIONAIRE DARED SPEAK PLAIN OLD ENGLISH! Show that goofball the gate!)

I went into the kitchen and opened a can of beer. On the way back, I overheard what had to be the unquestioned highlight of the entire press conference.

A reporter in the back of the room leaned forward and, quoting Smith, hollered: "How can the elimination of 30,000 jobs IMPROVE job security?" Hey, this hack was on the beam. Even the Rivethead hadn't caught how hopelessly inane this statement had been. Remaining completely stone-faced, Roger

Smith glanced at the reporter and reasoned: "For those who are left, their jobs will become that much more secure." Ouch.

That cinched it. The guy in charge of the largest corporation in America had a brain the size of a fuckin' lima bean. Not that he was lyin'. It only figured that *anytime* you were able to dispose of 30,000 workers you were going to be able to provide a more secure base for "those who are left." What had me rockin' in my recliner was Smith's casual infusion of flat-out genocide as a harmless means of streamlining the roster. He launched this verbal septic log so nonchalantly, one was left with the distinct impression that Smith actually believed that what he was saying would send a soothin' gush of relief through the rattled wits of the blue-collars. Man, some guys had balls large enough to use on a demolition crane.

For those who are left. That sounded awful damn grim for a solution that was intended to come off as some form of reassurance. It was entirely possible that Roger Smith had missed his calling in life. He could have been our ambassador to Ethiopia: "A food shortage, you say? Nooo problem. Simply exterminate a vast portion of your population, stack 'em out of view where they won't upset anyone's appetite and, PRESTO!, vittles aplenty for THOSE WHO ARE LEFT."

I swear, somedays it just doesn't pay to get outta bed.

As it turned out, one of the ten targeted plants for elimination was Flint Truck & Bus. The plan was to close down Line One, the Pickup Line, and move it down south to a new facility in Pontiac, Michigan. Tastes great, less workers! New robots, less filling! The end result would mean the eventual slashing of 3,500 jobs at our plant.

This disclosure tended to fall in step with GM's stubborn desire to keep its work force forever herding southward. Consider this scenario: at least half of the guys around me on the Rivet Line were refugees from closed plants in Saginaw or Bay City. They had to drive south forty or fifty miles a day to barely hang on in Flint. Now, from the information I was receiving, in order to retain my job I would have to sign some transfer sheet and steer my nose fifty miles to the south to the plant they were constructing in Pontiac. The people in Pontiac were probably headed for the plant in Fort Wayne, Indiana. The folks in Fort Wayne were no doubt being packed off for new jobs at the factory in Shreveport, Louisiana. Meanwhile, these Cajuns were being prepared to duck under the border and tinker for a while in Mexico. Notice a trend here? Precisely! Sooner or later, we were all gonna scrape our heads playin' limbo with the Equator.

And I bet it wouldn't end there. Nope, GM would have us all down there by the mid-nineties and the robots would be working out just fine. They'd have some massive burial pit ready and, before any of us could whip off a letter back home, we'd all be fifty feet under some godforsaken desert, laid out elbow to elbow with absolutely no recall rights to anywhere but the bottom of a dusty plaque hangin' over the middle urinal inside Mark's Lounge.

One thing was for certain. I had absolutely zero interest in signing up to work at this newfangled gulag in Pontiac. I felt by doing so I'd be bailing out on my ancestral destiny as the last in a long line of kin who had spent their entire earning years in the factories of Flint. If they were bringing down the curtain, so be it. I simply felt I had to be there when it ended.

Naturally, Dave Steel thought I was nuts. "Forget this town," he told me. "GM is movin' us south and anyone who chooses to remain behind will be freezin' their ass off waitin' in line for food stamps and government cheese."

Tony, our repairman on the Rivet Line, was of the same opinion. He talked constantly about the supposed benefits of transferring to Pontiac. Tony: "With our seniority, we should be able to land gravy jobs. I hear the place is supposed to be climate-controlled. On top of everything else, they won't even have a Rivet Line down there!"

Hold on a second. No Rivet Line? Jesus Christ, what kind of alien broomshack were they building down in Ponti-yuk? NO RIVET LINE? No Rivetheads? No Rivetettes? Don't tell me those damn robotics had finally eaten away at the one and only profession I'd ever been able to nurture, conquer and dominate? It was like tellin' a pollywog there was no such thing as frogs.

To hell with resettling. I'd been at GM long enough to grow accustomed to their habit of hollerin' "Earthquake!" at every little speed bump on the road. It only made perfect sense that if General Motors was offering me a rubber raft in one hand, chances were way more than likely that they had to be packin' a harpoon in their other paw. I would call their bluff and stay put. Go ahead and bring on that World Van you've been whisperin' about. I know you frauds are hidin' something up your sleeves. I won't be takin in. Furthermore, I won't be taken away.

The day arrived when we were scheduled to accept or refuse our transfers to the upcoming plant in Pontiac. Group by group, they called us down to the small conference room adjacent to the workers' cafeteria. I walked down with Tony and Kirk, who were heatedly debating which was the better option. I found myself beginning to flit from one line of thinking to the next. The plain truth was that I was a complete wuss at decision making. Maybe that was one of the reasons I chose to become a shoprat in the first place. GM always made your decisions for you.

Inside the conference room, union reps and recruiters from Pontiac were seated behind long rows of tables. They all wore large name tags as if we really gave a shit who they were. Kirk, Tony and I stood in line waiting to be popped the offer. I spoke with Kirk. He was starting to vacillate as crazily as I was. Stay put or venture south? It was an enormous decision, one that would affect the rest of our careers. We both were able to agree on one thing. The only prospect more dreadful than having a job at GM was *not* having one.

My name was called and I slid into a chair across from some stern-lookin' union shill. I told him I had severe reservations about leaving my hometown and forfeiting all rights to ever return to Flint in the future. He asked for my seniority date. "Seven nine seventy-seven," I replied.

The union man shook his head. "If you stay here, you'll be out of a job within two years."

"That's a long time off," I said. "Things could turn around in that span."

He seemed angry that I would quibble with his assessment of the situation. "Anything's possible, but your safest bet would be to transfer down to Pontiac."

I looked down the tables at Kirk. Further down, I could see Tony. Both of them were scrawling their signatures to the transfer contracts. Reluctantly, I followed suit. Though the plant wasn't even entirely built yet, though it would be another two years before I ever set foot inside that cretin farm—I was now signed, sealed and delivered as sole property of the Pontiac Truck & Bus division, Union Local 594. I walked back to the Rivet Line feeling like a rotten Judas.

That very same night, I found that I couldn't sleep. I felt as though I had made a terrible blunder. I turned out all the lights in my apartment and stood at the window drinking bourbon from a plastic mug emblazoned with the motto: WE MAKE OUR OWN HISTORY—50 YEARS, UAW. I stared at the apartment building across from me. Nothing was going on. Just a bunch of self-assured Americans tucked beneath the sheets with three hours to go before the alarms started to ring and it would all unwind again. The meetings. The deadlines. The parking spot. The boss. They were truly amazing specimens. They adapted to everything.

The next afternoon, I got to the plant early. I was a man on a mission. I had changed my mind. I would not go south. I stormed through the lobby and into the workers' cafeteria. I fixed my gaze on the little conference room that held my treasonous contract with the poachers from Pontiac. I would resolve this matter quickly. I would rant and rave until they fetched that fraudulent contract and let me rip it apart. I would declare myself a loyal domestic, a devoted Flintoid, a rock-solid pillar on the listing hull. I would throw the doors open and...

HUH? The room was totally dark. I flipped on a light switch and peered around. The room was entirely empty. No tables, no chairs, no files, no ashtrays—NO CONTRACT! I went back into the cafeteria and pulled one of the servers aside. "Could you tell me where all of the transfer people have gone? It seems they've stepped out somewhere."

"What transfer people?" replied the moron in the hair net.

"The transfer people who've inhabited that back room all week! Where'd they go?"

"How should I know. I just work the grill. I don't know any transfer people."

This had a bad aroma to it. One day ado, the next day adieu. It was spooky. Where in the hell did those cradle-lootin' nomads disappear to? I wandered out of the cafeteria perplexed as to my next move. As I did, I half expected to turn around and catch a glimpse of Rod Serling ducking out of one of the phone booths, his hands knotted at groin level, his mocking sneer poking out of the plume of his eternal Winston. I could almost hear him:

"Witness if you will an enigma, a frustrated punster besieged by his lack of an appropriate punchline. We may call him the Rivethead, a self-designation currently on very tenuous footing, obscured amongst the nervous shuttle of those who would waver between embarkation and a fostered urge to remain. For here amidst the impossible din, amongst the sooty backdrop of this macabre garden, nothing is a sure bet. Nostalgia is as worthless as a slug nickel. A reconsideration only an old key prying hopelessly against an exchanged lock. However, a contract remains a contract, a coward still a coward. Now witness if you will a man's desperate attempt to undo that which is done, a man in need of what is known, a man's march through darkness into the Transfer Zone."

I raced upstairs to the Rivet Line looking for Gino. I found him in his office going over a stack of paperwork. I didn't bother to knock.

"Tell me something, Gino," I blurted. "Where in the fuck did those transfer people from Pontiac go? Their office has simply vanished."

"Yesterday was their last day," Gino answered. "They won't be back until next spring or summer. What happened, did you miss the boat or something?"

"No, the damn boat ran my ass right over! I signed their rotten transfer contract and—"

"You've changed your mind," Gino finished for me.

I told Gino about how I had panicked. About how the union guy had claimed I'd be out of a job in two years if I didn't sign on. I told Gino that I'd been struck with this vision of myself cramming sugar paste into the butt end of cream sticks for three bucks an hour while the repo men tap-danced down the boulevard with my end tables and record collection in tow. I told him I was possibly the biggest fuckup either of us had ever met.

"Did they mention to you that, once you signed on, the contract was irreversible?"

"Yeah," I moped, "they stuck that right in at the top."

"I'm afraid you're locked in. Let me ask around and see what I can come up with."

"I'd appreciate it."

Gino wasn't able to find a single loophole. Nor was I. For weeks, I went around shaking down every union rep and boss-type I could find. Their only response was to ask me if I had inked the transfer sheet. Once I admitted that I had, they simply shook their heads and wished me luck. GM wasn't in the habit of lettin' a sucker off the leash.

Pontiac was in the offing. I had a couple of years before I shipped out. Two years of Rivet Line mania. Two years of the spectacular and the absurd. I didn't intend to waste a minute of what was left on the meter. All aboard for clown time. The mayhem was only beginning.

9

It wasn't every afternoon that I received long-distance phone calls from folks at the *Wall Street Journal*. I didn't remember having any friends who worked there and I was certain that I didn't owe these people any money.

All the same, there was this guy on the line from Chicago who needed to talk with the Rivethead. He said his name was Alex and that he had enjoyed the piece I had written for the December issue of *Harper's*. He mentioned that he was working on a story for the *Wall Street Journal* about blue-collar writers—whatever the hell they were. He seemed convinced that the Rivethead qualified as such. (In time, I was able to surmise that a "blue-collar writer" was just about anyone tricky enough to get his junk into print without having to stay sober, suck ass, show up at house fires, hold a degree or learn his way around a word processor. Nothin' to it. Hi Mom!)

This Alex guy was full of questions and I did my best to supply him with answers. "What do your co-workers think about your articles?" he asked.

"The ones who can read seem to like it."

"What has been management's reaction?"

"They only react when I fuck up a rivet. Very seldom, I might add."

"Where do you take your lunch break?"

"In my car."

"Is that where you take down notes?"

"That is where I take down beer and wade through chronic lines of bullshit."

"Do you consider yourself a factory worker or a writer?"

Yechhh.

Why anyone at the *Wall Street Journal* would be intrigued by all of this snooze was beyond me. What was happening? Had all the E. L. Hunts and Teddy Turners knocked off early and disengaged their cellular phones? Had the movers and shakers suddenly petrified? Was I the last available mortal for the angleworms of the press mob to collide against? January always brought out the bleak.

I had to cut Alex short. It was time to go hit rivets. Before I hung up, Alex mentioned that he would like to come to Flint to continue our conversation. Like to come to FLINT? Obviously, I was dealing with a journalist accustomed to lowbrow thrills.

Whatever his goals were, Alex said that he would be arriving in town the next week. He asked that in the meantime could I see what I could do about obtaining a pass for him to accompany me to my job at GM Truck & Bus. He was very excited about the idea of catching the Rivethead in the midst of his mooring. Confused, I agreed to give it a try.

Having never been in this position before, I had no idea of my first move in gaining clearance for an outside visitor. Through eight-plus years on the assembly line, no one I knew had ever expressed an interest in watching me swing my dead ass around while pinchin' a rivet gun. For this, I was extremely grateful.

Not that the situation didn't occasionally come about with my linemates. Every now and then, one of the workers would feel compelled to bring in his wife or his children or some dolled-up galfriend as if by showing them the horrible nothingness of the layout proved indubitably, once and for all, that he'd endure any kind of daily martyrdom in return for their fondness and favors.

I can remember right after Hogjaw got married. Two days into his goddamn honeymoon, he came paradin' his bride through the department, showing her the different jobs, demonstrating various machinery and introducing her to all his shoprat chums. It struck me as one of the saddest things I had ever witnessed— inside or outside a General Motors facility.

I decided to approach my foreman to see if he knew the proper formula for obtaining an official visitor's pass. I described for him the mysterious "blue-collar writer" angle and banged him over the head a half dozen times with the phrase "for inclusion in the *Wall Street Journal.*" Gino looked unimpressed. It was apparent that the *Wall Street Journal* wasn't a part of his regular reading rotation. "The *Walleye Journal?*" Gino mulled. "Why do they wanna know anything about you?"

He had me there.

I could already see that securing this pass was going to be a real task. Shit, why couldn't someone representing *Motor Trend* or *Hustler* come to visit me? They'd be sure to give those folks the run of the roost and my co-workers would be buyin' my lunch straight through to the next model change. *The Wall Street Journal? The Walleye Journal?* It all amounted to one fat zero.

My foreman decided he would have to take it up with his boss. That meant dickering with the Penguin. No sweat, I figured. Surely that bloated autocrat would be duly impressed that the businessmen's Bible wanted to pass the poop with one of his devoted underlings. I returned to my job feeling semiconfident.

A couple hours later, Al came over to spell me. He told me that I was wanted on the phone in the foreman's office. It was Gino calling from over at the Penguin's place.

"What the hell did you say the name of that paper was— something about walleyes?" I made the necessary repairs with the paper's name and hung up. I began dwelling on the little liquor store near my apartment. How good it was gonna feel to do some trade with those people tonight.

The Penguin wound up telling Gino that his "hands were tied." Accordingly, we would have to go through Labor Relations to get permission for Alex to visit. Gino found someone to cover my job and, reluctantly, we hiked off for the Labor Relations office.

At this point our story really begins to fester into a cesspool of terrible dreams. I'm telling you I was on mighty strange turf for a riveter. An alien frontier full of neckties, wingtips, belt beepers, bright lights, serious cologne and high command. Well-groomed fly-boys sucking on silver pens with pictures of children propped like tombstones on their desks. From nowhere and everywhere came the strains of Muzak—"Eleanor Rigby" and "Mandy" moanin' in the boneyard. If there had been a window, I'm certain I would have jumped.

One of the high rollers from Labor Relations motioned my foreman into a glassed-in office. I was told to stay put. Inside the room I could see two men wearing very solemn expressions as they chewed it over with my boss. Now and then, their heads would bob and they would peer out at me as if they half expected I might try to filch an ashtray or pee on the carpet. It occurred to me that these men were aware of the Rivethead. It promised to be an uphill battle from here on out.

When my foreman returned, he said that we would have to go through Salaried Personnel. "They told me that their hands were tied," Gino added. This euphemism was growing stale. Why couldn't they just substitute the truth and admit their spines were putty.

The following Monday, Gino got in touch with Salaried Personnel. He was told to call back on Tuesday. Tuesday spilled into Wednesday before we were told that we would have to take up our request with General Motors Public Relations. In a stunning development, they had explained to Gino that their hands were *not* tied, however their feet were webbed and their heads were hollow.

By Thursday, the day the *Wall Street Journal* was to arrive, the situation was still unsettled. It was ridiculous. I probably would have stood a better chance tryin' to smuggle Ted Bundy through a sorority house. Had I known beforehand just how difficult this visitor's pass would be to secure, I would have skipped all the red tape and simply instructed Alex to bring along some filthy duds and a three-day beard. With 3,500 workers on our shift, he could have easily waltzed through the door and taken up residency anywhere he damn well chose to.

Alex Kotlowitz arrived at my place around noon. He was disappointed to hear about the problem with the visitor's pass. I assured him it wasn't due to any lack of effort. I recounted the path so far, adding that the ball now seemed to rest in the hands of GM's Public Relations office. Alex decided that it might be best if he gave them a call and explained his harmless intentions.

"Good luck," I said. "If you hear the term 'hands are tied,' you know you've dialed correctly."

Public Relations listened to the request and told Alex to call back in an hour. I decided that this was a good time to start drinking. We drove to a bar. In one hour, Alex called them back. They insisted they needed more time and to try back in another hour.

"Those idiot paranoids must be tearin' the place apart looking for my file." I laughed. "Next time I talk with Owen Beiber, I'll be sure to mention this appalling demonstration of botchery. Goddamnit, heads will roll!"

By the time I had to leave for work, they were still stringing Alex along. He said he'd continue with his attempts on the phone and hopefully see me later inside the plant. "These people must really have it in for you," he added. "I've had easier times entering federal prisons."

I arrived at work just as Dougie bellowed out his resounding "ALL ABOARD!" As was custom, Eddie shouted back "SHUT THE FUCK UP, FOOL!" Rituals were rituals. The line began to roll and, just as it did, Gino came over to tell me that he had just received a call from the Personnel office. They had wanted to know what kind of worker I was—company man or misfit, friend or fraud. The boss said he assured them that I was fine GM timber. You couldn't force a fib out of Gino.

Moments later, the phone rang again. This time they wanted to see me down in Personnel on the double. This was not the best of times to be huffin' beer breath so I crammed a handful of Certs in my mouth. I trekked off hoping this would be the end of it, regardless of the outcome.

No doubt about it, this time I was deep inside the GM digestive tract. I weaved around corners and wandered down hallways that seemed to extend underground for two miles east of the plant. I had to stop and ask directions countless times. The further along I went, the brighter the lighting became, the larger the glass tombs expanded.

I paused for a cigarette and some self-examination. Why, I wondered, had I ever set myself up for this? What had pos-

sessed me to get lippy in print when, sooner or later, I had to
know that I'd become entangled in my own sarcastic web and
be beckoned down a long hallway toward the very core of everything I most wanted to avoid in life? Why couldn't I be like all my
other buddies and have normal hobbies like snowmobiles, softball
and reefer? Why was it that I wanted to carve out Phil Collins's
eyeballs with a linoleum knife? How come I never watched
Michigan Replay with Bo Schembechler? Why hadn't I become a
disc jockey or an ambulance driver like I was supposed to?

They were waiting for me in Personnel. I shook hands with
a man in a three-piece suit and he ushered me into his office. I
assumed that this man had to be someone extremely important. His desk was easily the size of my dining room.

The questions came. "Precisely, why does this reporter want
to enter our facility?" I explained that Alex only wanted to ob-
serve my routine and ask my boss and co-workers a few questions.

"Why is it that this man has a particular interest in *you*?" I
laid the blue-collar writer junk on him and mentioned that I
wrote a column. Thankfully, he was obviously unaware of the
Rivethead.

"In this column, do you ever broach the subject of General
Motors?"

Uh-oh. I began scratching an imaginary itch. A certain
evasiveness was my only hope. "Well, I suppose I've occasionally made small references to the fact that, yes, I'm a factory
worker."

All was silent for a few moments. I could sense a stalemate
between the big cheese and little rat. I lit a cigarette, took a
long drag, and was alarmed to notice a NO SMOKING sign on
the desk. I quickly rubbed out the butt on my work boot as the
Personnel chief stared into space.

Finally, he spoke: "You know, we just can't be too careful.
We've been burned on stuff like this before." I nodded like I
knew what he meant.

Just when I was beginning to feel all was lost, he stood up
and announced a compromise. One of his young assistants was
introduced and it was explained that this guy would accompany
Alex throughout every portion of his visit. First, the game
rules: "My aide will monitor all conversation between your man
and any member of management. If at any time an inappropri-

ate question is raised, my man will intercede and terminate the interview. At that point, your man will be escorted promptly from the plant."

Your man, my man. My man, your man. I felt like I was playin' Milton Bradley's Stratego.

Alas, Alex made it inside. With his ever-present guide lurking nearby, he looked like a captured fugitive. It was quite hilarious. We exchanged smiles and he went about his interviews.

The grapevine must have been buzzing, for within moments of Alex's arrival none other than Henry Jackson came strolling down the aisle to toss in his worthless two cents. I could see Alex and Jackson holed up in Gino's office. Not surprisingly, Jackson was doing all the talking.

After Alex managed to escape the brilliant ejaculations of Henry Jackson, he made his way over to my job for observations in riveting. With no member of management in the immediate vicinity, his guide gave us some breathing room, standing out in the aisle like some rigid Aryan lawn jockey. I used this opportunity to ask Alex what Jackson had been dumping on him.

"He was very insistent that you were all his boys," Alex stated. "He expressed a certain fondness for you, claiming he was a big admirer of your writing talent."

"That bastard's a lyin' ass. He hates my fuckin' guts! I hope you don't print a word he told you. Henry's about as corrupt and insane as they come around here."

Just then a guy named Joe, the department's resident dopehead moron, came buttin' in. Alex took him aside and began interviewing him regarding my blue-collar writing expertise. I shook my head and returned to my job. If Joe had read anything in his life, it was probably only the price tag on a coke spoon or a joke on a cocktail napkin. Jesus, this was beginning to suck.

"Well, what did Dopey have to say?" I asked Alex on his return. "Keep in mind that he has never read a single word I've written."

"He told me you were right on, that your columns were right on, and that the thing he liked best about them was that they were—"

"Right on?" I moaned.

"Actually, he used the word heavy."

I suggested to Alex that he interview some riveters who actually read my stuff. I pointed out Janice, Terry and Dick. He went to them and began jotting down insights. I hoped he was getting what he was after. Chicago was an awfully long way to come for "right on" and "heavy."

A few weeks later, Alex Kotlowitz's article about blue-collar writers appeared on the front page of the *Wall Street Journal*. The piece used the Rivethead as its main subject; however there was also mention of a few other scribes of labor—a longshoreman from San Francisco, an assembly worker from Ohio, some poor bastard who worked in a pickle factory—men who I assumed were just as bored as I was. In cases such as these, literature was just an accident waiting to happen.

In the center of the page was a truly demonic-lookin' sketch of the Rivethead. I looked like a drugged land turtle or a droopy mongoloid. My head came to a sharp point. Even my girlfriend Amy was shocked. "Truly hideous," she remarked. "You look like a Korean version of Dick Nixon."

"What's done is done," I replied. "It is time to begin looting the paper boxes. I will need a copy for every man, woman and child on the Rivetline. Also, several copies for my ancestors and a few more for future propaganda purposes."

Amy and I spent the early morning ransacking every *Wall Street Journal* box within the city limits. She'd swerve up to a machine, I'd bail out, slap in the coins, and snatch up a handful of copies. "Drive on," I ordered. "After today, all this international coverboy shit will rapidly dissipate into wasted nostalgia. Only one man per day gets his face on the cover of the *Wall Street Journal* and today that wretched face belongs to me."

When we were done, I thanked Amy for her part in our petty larceny spree and lugged the newspapers into my apartment. Once inside, I grabbed a couple Buds from the fridge and sat down to make a thorough scan of the article. I found myself fascinated by the remarks of the longshoreman. He described in detail how he would have to protect all these loads of hides from armies of maggots by scooping steer manure onto the center of the skin before it was folded and tied. There was a brief passage from his writings, very good stuff, where he described the stench connected with his occupation. "People actually flee from you," the longshoreman wrote. Jesus Christ, and I thought bangin' rivets was a bleak gig. At least the only manure I had to deal with was what flowed forth from Henry Jackson's mouth or the messages on the neon propaganda board.

Reading on, I came across a disturbing part of the article. "The vast public has not seemed very interested in reading about work," noted a New York University expert on the blue-collar trend. "Work is not considered a hot literary topic."

Though I felt angered, I was hardly surprised. After all, who had time to wade through the murky pathos of an average Joe like the longshoreman when the best-seller list was clogged with *real* revelations of the here and now. Momentous dispatches like "Oaf Surfin' with Belushi's Lukewarm Corpse" or "I Slept with Shemp Howard." The "vast public" *wanted* to know about turds and maggots, but only the name-brand variety who hid behind ghost writers in the display windows of the local book mart.

If the "vast public" weren't entirely satiated by the trendy grief of others, they merely got a hold on their own. How many gold-diggin' knotheads had spun the web of the ever-popular self-help book? Everyone but the Hillside Strangler and my mailman, that's who! Face it, the plain truth is that most Americans feel left off the bus if they can't hitch up their rattled psyches to some fashionable new malady bein' bandied about on Phil and Oprah. The longshoreman or the guy from the pickle factory were survivors and survival didn't play very well within a nation drenched to its Valium-gobblin' core with luckless visions of self-hate and unendurable dejection.

Kotlowitz finished up his story by referring to me as "the Mike Royko of the rivetheads." Given a choice, I'd have preferred "the Mark Twain of Mark's Lounge" or "the Johnny Holmes of the second-floor cushion room." Mike Royko? Shit, they buried his grunt in the middle of the editorial page. Not many shoprats bothered with that portion of the paper.

It was time to retreat back to bed. The Rivet Line would be beckoning soon enough and I had to be properly rested. I was almost asleep when the phone started ringing. It rang and rang. Whoever was on the other end wasn't giving up. I stumbled to the kitchen and grabbed the receiver.

"Yes," I said.

"Is that you, Hamper?" a voice shouted.

"Yes," I repeated.

It turned out to be some guy I had gone to high school with. Matt somebody. I hadn't spoken a word with this individual in over a dozen years. In fact, we never talked way back then. We had never even liked each other. Hell, I hated the bastard's guts and he'd hated mine.

"Is there something I can do for you?" I asked.

Matthew somebody explained that he was a stockbroker nowadays living in San Francisco. He was calling me to express his dumbfounded shock at seeing my swollen face staring back at him from his morning's *Wall Street Journal*.

"Christ, I thought my eyes were playin' tricks on me," he said. "What the hell would Benny Hamper's face be doin' on the cover of *Wall Street*. I thought maybe you rolled a bank or something.

I always hated people who called me Benny. "I understand," I replied. "I have to go to back to bed now. Nice chatting."

I never did get back to sleep. Every time I got close to noddin' off, the phone would ring. A Flint television station suggested an interview. A lady representing a film production company in Los Angeles called. A book agent buzzed in. A few more jerks from high school called. I couldn't understand it. Since we seemed to be having an impromptu class reunion on my phone, where were all the cheerleaders? Coverboy or not, those sluts still hated my ass.

In a startling gesture, my old man called me from Florida. Some bar patron had shown him the article. The old man was already in the bag. He mentioned that he was proud of me and asked if I really looked that ugly. He also had words of advice: "You better watch your ass, son. Those big boys have no sense of humor. Just look what they did with Hoffa."

I assured my father that what I was up to would hardly incite either the union or GM to want to do me bodily harm. I was only writing a column for an underground newspaper.

"Don't be too sure," my old man countered. "They've got the muscle to shut you down. Do you own a piece, son?"

"*A piece?* As in *gun?*"

"Well, I ain't' referrin' to no piece of ass!" My old man hadn't changed a lick. The more he drank, the more he indulged himself in flights of old-school machismo.

"I've gotta get ready for work now, Dad."

"Just remember to watch out for those bastards."

"Will do," I replied.

I was almost out the door when the phone rang again. It was my editor calling from the *Michigan Voice*. "Listen," Mike said, "some producer from *60 Minutes* just called out here for you. He said he wanted to talk with you and that you should get in touch with him immediately."

I scribbled down the number, grabbed a can of beer and began dialing.

"*Sixty Minutes*," a voice answered.

"Um, my name is Hamper. I was told you were trying to reach me."

"Oh yes, Ben. My name's Joel Bernstein. I enjoyed the article about you in this morning's *Wall Street Journal*. It sounded like something we might be interested in pursuing for the show. If it's all right with you, I'd like to fly into Flint next Tuesday so we can get together. How does Tuesday work out on your end, Ben?"

I paused and took a large swallow of beer. I looked over at the calendar. Tuesday was blank. Friday was blank. March was blank. September was blank. Every day of the year was blank. "I think Tuesday would work out fine," I answered.

"Great. I'll give you a call when I get to town."

I finally made it into work. One of the guys from first shift had already tacked up the *Wall Street Journal* on the bulletin board. Several of my linemates were gathered around readin' the piece and joking about my face. I wormed in between them.

"One outrageously handsome rivetling, huh?" I snickered.

"Goddamn, Hamper, your face looks like a mudheap," Joe replied.

"Who's your hair stylist, Beldar Conehead?" Al needled.

The Polish Sex God stepped in. "Shit, whatever you do, don't gaze into those swollen eyes! Prolonged contact with that satanic gaze could cause unspeakable damage to one's soul."

Dougie wanted to know who Mike Royko was. I told him he was some guy who loved softball and wrote about minor social injustices and made twenty times the money we did.

Janice was reading the article at her desk. Dave Steel stood there reading over her shoulder. As I approached, Dave started shaking his head. "I can't believe how much mileage you're gettin' out of this factory drivel. This guy acts like you're fuckin' Steinbeck or something."

"Mama didn't raise no blockhead." I laughed. "Find a gimmick and milk those udders!"

Right then, the horn blew. The line began to lurch and Dave sprinted off for his inspection job. The rest of us reached above our heads for our rivet guns.

"ALL ABOARD!" Doug shouted.

"SHUT THE FUCK UP, FOOL!" Eddie responded on cue. Ah, home sweet home.

I bought two cases of beer for the guys that night. We got stupid and rowdy and started acting like a bunch of Cub Scouts in a titty bar. It was forty souls vs. that old stubborn time clock and we beat its ass rather soundly. Nothing like a strange new distraction and a bellyful of beer to nudge on the night.

The Mike Royko of the rivetheads. Hell, whatever. It kept us laughin'. All I knew for certain was that for one crazy shift in the midst of a frigid Michigan winter the crew had plenty to gnaw on. Something that brought us closer, something silly and offbeat, something that reached out for the rivetheads and spoke their names, something that attached our oily grins to a small piece of the puzzle, a visibility or something, and something was better than nothing.

On Tuesday, Joel Bernstein called to tell me he was staying at the Hyatt Regency in Flint. He asked that I come down and join him for lunch. I had a bad feeling about this encounter. I had problems with strangers, especially when sober, and from what I'd seen of *60 Minutes*, these guys didn't appear to be the most amicable bunch of bubs on television. I should have insisted on Mark's Lounge. There was something in that dark Naugahyde shack that made me feel almost human.

I drove downtown and waited for Bernstein in the lobby of the Hyatt. He came down the elevator carrying a large duffel bag. He looked more like a paratrooper than an influential television producer. "Ben Hamper?" he asked.

"Um, yes," I answered, fumbling to light another cigarette.

"Let's find a restaurant. We can talk over lunch."

We took a table over in the corner of this glitzy eatery on

the main floor of the Hyatt. There were plenty of plants and too much sunlight. I felt exposed and nervous. Bernstein sat across from me in total silence. I stared out the window at the derelicts who were trooping by on the Saginaw Street bridge. I wondered how I was doing so far.

Finally, Bernstein spoke. He asked if I would describe some of the recent subject matter contained in my Rivethead column.

I mentioned such things as GM's deceptive Quality hum-bug, their annoying habit of promoting only suck-asses and snitches, their reliance on childish propaganda gimmicks and their southbound extermination scheme. I mentioned the Howie Makem farce and the brainwashing message boards.

Bernstein's face became visibly red. "I'm telling you right now," he huffed, "I didn't come all the way out here to do an anti-GM piece. I have no axe to grind with those people."

"Well, if you read the *Wall Street Journal* story, you had to know I took the view of an assembly worker. What did you think I was writing about? The glorious advent of robotics?"

"I'm just explaining that I have no interest in doing a rip job on General Motors."

"Fine," I said, "let's talk about something else."

We sat there for several minutes without speaking. Jesus, what was wrong with this guy? Here he represented the most popular muck-slingin' television mouthpiece in all America and he seemed to be taking the stance that GM was some sort of hands-off sacred cow. The thought occurred to me that GM was probably their leading sponsor, their most consistent meal ticket.

Our conversation resumed, a confrontational tone firmly implanted:

"If you're such a popular writer in this town, how come no one has come over to greet you?"

"I can only assume they're intimidated by the presence of such an esteemed visitor."

"Do your columns elicit *any* reaction from your co-workers?"

"In most cases, mainly laughter."

"Then you are an ENTERTAINER!"

"Aren't all writers?"

"From what you were saying a minute ago, I was under the impression that there was some type of social significance to your writing."

Outside the window, a vagrant was pushing an old shopping cart across the bridge. I looked at him closely. He seemed utterly content. There was no hint of anger or discord. There was no sign of crossfire. There wasn't much of anything. I swelled with a sudden sense of envy.

The interview was headed nowhere. It seemed increasingly evident that, besides his producer's title, Joel Bernstein was sworn to another duty—to run interference for the impending spine-removal tactics of a Mike Wallace or an Ed Bradley. If you managed to weather his test run, perhaps they would fly in the heavy artillery and your mama would get to see you squirm in prime time.

I knew I'd failed the test run when Bernstein pointed out my obvious discomfort with simple conversation. It was true. Talking with people that I really didn't know tended to make my insides twist and shout. Maybe that's why I had taken up typing.

"How would you handle it if Harry Reasoner was sitting in my place and the camera was rolling in on you?" the producer demanded.

By this point, I'd ceased to give a shit. "I'd make sure that I was drunk," I replied.

Bernstein almost flew out of his chair. "NOT ON *60 MINUTES* YOU WON'T!"

So be it. To be honest, it all sounded pretty farfetched from the outset: beer-stoked Rivet Line smartass cavorting across the Quasars of the Free World... Diane Sawyer dodgin' filthy palms next to the pool table in Mark's Lounge... the steering gear man sermonizing atop a crateful of lugnuts... Howie Makem bounding through the murk like a ridiculous drum major... Rivet Hockey and Dumpster Ball bein' thrust upon a confused republic weaned on tee ball and putter golf. Do not attempt to adjust your set. Do not attempt to call your cable company. That rumble you hear is only Edward R. Murrow swiveling in his grave.

We gave it up and Bernstein walked with me out to my Camaro. He mentioned that there was always the possibility that a segment could be worked out at a later date. He handed me one of his business cards and told me to stay in touch. I said I would. Both of us were liars. As I drove off around the corner, I flung the card in the direction of a couple bag ladies standing on Saginaw Street. May it serve them well, I chuckled to myself.

Alongside the debacle with *60 Minutes*, I managed to cross wires with folks from National Public Radio, Random House, Esquire, Embassy Productions, Playboy, Penthouse, Voice of America and *U.S. News & World Report*. Each of them rang up needin' a piece of this week's rage—the Autoworker/ Journalist. I understood. Having your face displayed on the front page of the *Wall Street Journal* lent a sudden legitimacy to whatever the hell you were doing. All at once you were pronounced fit for active duty in the phone directories of the Mighty Big. It just happened to be my time. Next week it would be the Fry Cook/Opera Tenor or the Bank Clerk/Porn Stud.

After a few weeks, the phone calls went away. I returned to sleeping past noon, safe in the knowledge that the hounds had picked up a new scent out on the power lines. It was fine with me. After all, I already had my hands full. There were muffler hangers to attach, spring castings to insert, rivets to be mashed. There were clocks to duel and antics to explore.

Idiot labor may not have been much to fall in love with, but it beat the hell out of flailing around on someone's conference line. High wages, low thought requirement, beholden to only those you chose. What the rest of the world wanted was their own problem. Ambition maimed so many of them. I'm sure they had their own reasons for grasping for the next rung, but it all seemed so bothersome and tedious.

In contrast, working the Rivet Line was like being paid to flunk high school the rest of your life. An adolescent time warp in which the duties of the day were just an underlying annoyance. No one really grew up here. No pretensions to being anything other than stunted brats clinging to rusty monkeybars. The popular diversions—Rivet Hockey, Dumpster Ball, intoxication, writing, rock 'n' roll—were just reinventions of youth. We were fumbling along in the middle of a long-running cartoon.

Having asserted this, it always came as a personal shock and frustration whenever a core member of our cast slipped away. I felt betrayed and abandoned. The Rivet Line may have been a shithole but, for chrissakes, it was *our* shithole! I couldn't grasp the flimsy rhetoric of those who became bent on relocation. All I could understand was my obstinate devotion to the setting. Relocation was the equivalent of graduating. It seemed so futile and adult-like.

Jerry and Janice decided to move on. Neither were especially excited to go, but they had fallen victim to that weird undertow that sometimes swirls by in a shoprat's career—one that murmurs deceitful lies, one that maintains that a change of scenery will induce a grand rebirth. Assembly lines being the monotonous hangouts they are, confusion often takes advantage. You can outwit yourself. You can envision things that aren't really there. Persecution preys on pondering minds. Right becomes wrong. Suddenly, one man's sandbox becomes another man's quicksand.

Jerry left first, opting to take his pastel muscle shirts and heat-seeking libido onto the first shift. This left a tremendous gap in our Rivet Hockey league, not to mention a string of forlorn barmaids and a half pint of Root Beer Schnapps under the passenger seat of my Camaro.

I tried to talk some sense into him, warning him at great length about the dealings that awaited the Day Men—the alarm clocks, the brutal hangovers, the rednecks decked out in camouflage goon suits, the endless lunkspeak about trout bait, Willie Hernandez, faggots, spooks, kikes, dykes, nips, spics, hemorrhoids, Jesus and power tools.

The Polish Sex God would have none of it. He argued that now he would have his workday over by 2:30 P.M. and be able to prowl for kicks and chicks the rest of the night.

"It doesn't work like that," I told him. "First shift only works for the married guys. They have a very rigid system—rush home, drink three beers, eat supper, watch *Wheel of Fortune*, hop the old lady and be sound asleep by 9:00. Clean, decent American living. A bar hound like you will never beat the clock. You'll miss so much work, your ass will be out on Van Slyke within a month."

Jerry left anyway and maybe it was best for all concerned. Lately, he had developed this terrible knack for hijacking his co-workers at lunchtime and not returning them for the completion of the shift. What would happen is that we'd all pile into his van at lunch break, begin hammering the beer and stare off silently into the city lights. Five minutes before we were due back on our jobs, Jerry would rev up the van and turn to whoever was crammed in back. "Who wants to go back in there?" he'd demand. For those who wanted to avoid certain penalizing, this was a cue to haul ass. Halftime desertion was something Jerry never joked about. You either bailed out or were taken hostage. Terry, Herman and I often went along. Eddie, Doug and Al always scrambled for the door. We had much more fun than they did. We had the penalties on our records to prove it.

The night Janice left, I had a lump in my throat the size of a croquet ball. For three years, she had been my neighbor, my soundboard, my confidante and best friend. When she had first arrived on the Rivet Line, Janice was vulnerable and naive. There were times I thought she'd never make it. I was dead wrong. She transcended the token female role and became one of the boys—a description she was utterly comfortable with.

On Friday nights, we had this routine where I'd pull my car up close to the exit doors and the two of us would sit there drinkin' beer while scrutinizing the workers as they fled from the plant. We laughed like idiots, pretending to be able to forecast their destinies. Janice handled the women and I covered the guys. It went something like this:

"Take a look at this goof," I observed. "Not a lot going on here. He will drive home cautiously, take a long shower, eat two chicken pot pies and tune in an old episode of *Kojak*. This man should be put on life support. No wonder his wife joined a motorcycle club and never said goodbye."

Janice would spot one. "A definite party bimbo. I predict she is en route to a large house where she will become intoxicated on sloe gin and make a complete ass out of herself dancing to the *Big Chill* soundtrack. Eventually, she will wind up having intercourse with the first guy who offers her a long line of cocaine."

After the parking lot had emptied and all the beer was gone, we would go have breakfast at some greasy diner. Amidst the clamor of our drunken co-workers, we would drink black coffee and talk for hours—about anything, about everything, about nothing at all.

On that last night as Janice prepared to crunch her last rivet, the croquet ball in my throat had grown to the size of a grapefruit. I tried to appear busy and unconcerned. It would be over soon and Janice would stop by and say something sweet. I was sure I'd begin blubberin'. Not that Janice wouldn't understand. She's probably start bawlin' too. I just didn't want the rest of the crew to catch the Rivethead in the throes of some Jimmy Swaggart meltdown.

However, Janice surprised me. Instead of deliverin' some hopeless gush, she snuck around my workbench and began singing. The tune was "Forward to Death" by the Dead Kennedys, one of several warped ditties I had polluted her with. I got a big grin on my face and joined in on the raucous chorus: "I don't need this fuckin' world, I don't need this fuckin' world—this world brings me down, I gag with every breath, this world brings me DOWN, I'm looking forward to DEATH!"

We hugged each other and laughed. It was like being paid to flunk high school.

When it came time to fill the vacancies left behind by Jerry and Janice, we got lucky. Henry Jackson, always in a mad quest to break up the chemistry of the Rivet Line by importing snitches and milksops, bungled the opportunity and sent us down a pair of jokers who fit right in.

Jerry's replacement was a small black guy named Jehan. He came to us with excellent credentials. For the past several weeks, Jehan had been on this dogged mission to keep the line down. He worked one of the rail-pull jobs at the start of the line situated right beneath one of the stop buttons. Whenever the mood struck, Jehan would reach above his head and smack the button. He'd keep the line down until the supervisors started closing in. You had to admire that kind of suicidal derring-do. When Jehan was finally busted, Henry sent him down to our area away from any stop buttons.

The guy who took Janice's job was a big German hulk named Paul Schobel. He'd arrived with the latest batch of refugees from the closed plants in Saginaw. He was absolutely ecstatic about his placement on the Rivet Line. Paul's last job for GM had been working in a foundry, which was a lot like being sentenced to work in Satan's private bakery. He was glad to be here and we were glad to have him, especially me. I had plans for Mr. Schobel. I was baking something too.

I watched in wonder as Paul quickly pulverized his new job

into a brief nuisance. He steamrolled through the entire event. The cross members looked like twigs in his arms. The rivet gun became his bitch. He choked its neck like a dead flamingo. It was all so beautiful. The guy was a plowhorse. After all those years in the foundry, the cross members and rivet guns must have seemed like birdies and badminton.

As I watched Paul tromp through the motions, lights flashed in my head. The strategy I had been cookin' up moved straight for the front burner. My mind began chanting restlessly: "It is time to double-up... time to double-up." It was all spread out in front of me. That golden loophole, that glorious lifeboat, the ultimate clock-killer, autonomy for two. It would be a cinch. Paul with the brawn, I with the blueprint.

One night I invited Paul out to my Camaro. It was time to run this thing by him. We drank a couple of forty-ouncers and began to discuss details. "Paul, after lunch I want you to cover my job."

"Do *your* job? Who the hell is gonna do *mine*?"

"I will. It's important that you learn my routine, especially the sidewinder gun. It's a bit stubborn at first, but I have no doubt you'll be able to tame it."

Paul looked at me perplexed. "What in the fuck is this all about, Hamper?"

"It's all about freedom, you fat kraut. We combine our two jobs into one setup. When I'm handling the setup, you can get lost. The same goes for me when you're up. Think about it, Paul. It sure beats sittin' round all night crucified to the time clock."

It took about three hours for Paul to conquer my job. He had little trouble with the sidewinder gun or, for that matter, anything else. If some portion of the job played nasty, Paul just sucked in his gut, let out a growl and bullied the issue into quick submission. The horizon was wide open.

However, there were a few details we had to tend to before unveiling our system. First, we had to take into account all the cross members Paul was required to build each shift. There was no way either of us could keep up with the line if we had stock to build. We agreed that we would have to build up the required amount of cross members before we could begin doubling jobs. This meant getting to the plant extra early and bangin' them out ahead of time.

Another matter to be considered was supervisional reaction to our setup. This wasn't the Cab Shop where any two hustlers who could put together a scam were free to flee. This was the Rivet Line where hittin' the lam still meant sluggin' a young sheep. In this region, doubling-up was as much a novelty as shag carpet. I wasn't too much concerned with Gino. He'd already taken a shine to Schobel and he knew, when it came to hittin' a good rivet, I was the cream of the crap. Henry Jackson was the one who posed the definite threat. We would have to watch out for him.

On the eve of our new arrangement, Paul and I retreated to my Camaro for beer and briefing. There were a few loose ends and precautions I wanted to make my partner aware of.

"Before we crank this gimmick up, we need to get a couple of things straight. First off, no more drinking on the job. If I'm gone, there'll be no one around who can give you a piss call."

Paul rolled his eyes. "Hey, lecture your own ass. You and Eddie are the ones gettin' tanked every night."

"Not startin' tomorrow. Complete sobriety while working. If we work this right, we'll have plenty of time off to go drinkin'."

"Understood," Paul replied.

"Another thing," I continued. "Absolutely no more weed smokin' with Jehan and Dougie. Every time you get stoned, your eyes get bloody and you get this stupid, guilty look on your face."

"Hey, smokin' dope relaxes me. What if I wore a pair of sunglasses like Eddie does?"

"Just say NO, pothead. One more idea. I think it wise that we leave each other the phone numbers of where we'll be at. I will normally be at my place, Mark's Lounge or my girlfriend's. If Henry Jackson comes snoopin' around, have someone call me and I can be back here within ten minutes."

"You're forgettin' something. Where am I gonna go when *you* are working?" It was a valid point. Paul carpooled from Saginaw with two other guys. He only had his own vehicle two times per week.

"I'll take care of it. On the nights you have your car, you

can leave at lunch. On the nights you don't, you can use my car and apartment. I've got extra keys I'll give you. I'll also give you a map of some of the better bars around Flint and directions to where the whores hang out."

"That's sure gonna beat workin' in the foundry."

"That's sure gonna beat workin', *period*," I added.

The system worked just as smoothly as I had hoped. Schobel and I clicked perfectly. Even Gino was duly impressed. He looked the other way and kept his distance. The only thing Gino said to me regarding the setup was: "I don't even want to know where you two disappear. Don't even tell me!" I faithfully obliged my supervisor.

Henry Jackson was easy to dupe. He always came callin' early in the shift while we were still racin' around buildin' up cross members. The occasional times he'd pull a surprise raid later in the shift after one of us had vanished, we'd be ready. Tony would holler down the line from his repair post: "Asshole! Asshole!" That was our cue to spring into a new formation. Cam, who worked on the other side of Paul, would slide down closer to Paul's area and Doug would work up the line toward mine. Henry would strut by, take a quick glance and be satisfied that everything appeared positioned normally.

It was like 1978 all over again. Four hours' work, eight hours' pay. Once again there was that certain exhilaration knowing that your job was being nursed along in able hands while you howled at the screen in Mark's Lounge after Lou Whitaker had blasted a hangin' curve into the right field upper deck. Such things seemed to make more sense than manual labor. To lie there in your sweetheart's bed, shakin' off the post-ejaculatory sweat, gigglin' like a schoolboy, a paroled hedonist smiling from a third-story window far removed from the numbness and drudgery of Greaseball Mecca.

Above all, I liked the idea of outsmarting all those management pricks with their clean fingernails and filthy bonuses. They weren't much competition but, all the same, they couldn't earn their paychecks outside the walls drinking and fucking and evading and watching home runs sail on through the twilight. However, I could. I was a career opportunist. My time card was germinating in the corporate greenhouse, ladling out the loot to an emancipated hooligan who regularly dipped beneath their radar screens and hid himself in the red Naugahyde like a clever fox full of someone's mutton. They were in THERE! Only an earthquake could bring them out. I was out HERE! Only an emergency phone call could bring me in.

And goddamnit all, it did. RINNNNNNG! RINNNNNNNG! It was a Monday night. I was sitting around my apartment watching a game and eatin' a pizza. Schobel and I had been working the scheme for a few months without the slightest hitch. The world was our Slinky. Then, the phone call. Hell's own jingle bells. RINNNNNNG! RINNNNNNNG! I got up and answered it.

It was Schobel. He was talking low and fast, "Ben, I'm sorry about this, but you have to get back to the department RIGHT NOW! I'm afraid we're in deep shit."

All at once it hit me. Something terribly wrong had happened. This wasn't any lousy Henry Jackson headcount. This was real disaster. PAUL SCHOBEL WAS TALKING TO ME! How could Paul be talking to me and still be covering our jobs?

"Paul, where the hell are you?" I screamed.

"I'm down in the plant hospital. I told 'em I had to call my wife. They're running me over to McLaren Hospital for surgery on my arm."

Instead of asking Paul how he was doing or how badly he was hurt, the humanitarian in me opted to blurt: "SHIT, WHO THE FUCK IS DOING OUR JOBS?"

"Gotta go now, honey." The meat wagon must've arrived. "Do what I asked. Love you."

I drove with my knee and dressed like a contortionist. I blew through three red lights and screeched into the No Parking zone at the plant gate. I sprinted past the guards and time clocks and raced up the stairs to the Rivet Line. I attempted to walk leisurely to my job. I doubt I was fooling anyone.

Al and one of the spare utility men were covering our jobs. Al looked at me with what appeared to be a mixture of woesome pity and brooding contempt. The message was clear: I was a cooked rat, I was thoroughly doomed, I was popular as a leper, and I had better concoct one helluva spiel mighty quickly.

I grabbed my gun and waved them off. "Where's Gino?" I mumbled to Al.

"He's still down in the hospital," he said.

"Has Jackson been around?"

"Haven't seen him since before lunch."

Eddie wandered down. "Shit, Ben, I ain't ever seen so much blood in my life. It was shootin' straight outta Paul's wrist like a gusher. They mopped most of it up but there's still some down there if you wanna check it out. Damn, blood was flyin' everywhere. It looked like a damn shark attack. The funny part is that Paul never said as much as ouch. He just—"

Per usual, Jehan's dope had woven its way deep into Ed's skull. "Fuck all that, you weed-suckin' ghoul. I don't want to hear about the mess. Just tell me what HAPPENED!"

"It went down fast. Paul was puttin' a military cross member up on the frame and the bitch slipped off. Paul caught the skid right across the wrist. Took it right to the bone. When they picked up the cross member, the skid plate still had a chunk of Paul's skin hangin' off it."

This certainly wasn't the time to go pointin' blame, yet I found myself steamed over the cause of the accident. From what Eddie had described, I knew exactly what had happened. Paul had been guilty of making a very stupid and dangerous blunder. I had seen him pull this stunt before and pleaded with him to knock it off. The rule was this: when a cross member begins to slip or tilt off the frame, let it fall! DO NOT TRY TO CATCH IT! Tryin' to grab hold of a military cross member as it tumbled off the frame was as bright as reachin' for a runnin' chainsaw. Unfortunately, Paul couldn't help himself. It was a reflex thing. The cross member would slip and he'd play fetch. For this error in judgment, my partner was now at McLaren General Hospital having his arm reassembled.

The part I was really dreading was now on its way. Down the aisle I could see Gino Donlan makin' his way back to the department. He didn't look like the happiest man in the world.

Instead of jumping into my shit, Gino simply walked on by as if ignoring me. This lack of cognition made me even more uncomfortable. A major ass-chewing was in order. A flock of penalties were in the balance. I wanted it over with. My foreman chose to let me walk that long, lonely plank as if I really needed more time to ruminate about the damage done.

Finally, he came strollin' over. "I would assume you know what this means," Gino said. "You can forget about the doubling-up right now."

And, that was it. No screeching, no interrogation, no penalties, no suspension. Gino seemed to realize that I felt bad enough. What had really saved my butt was the fact that Henry Jackson didn't ever find out about the particulars behind Paul's accident. He was still in the dark about our comings and goings. It got me to thinkin'. Maybe someday in the faraway future we could restore this crashed bird back to its natural glory. It was a long shot, but, maybe.

Paul stopped in to visit the Rivet Line the next day. He'd just been released from the hospital and his arm was in a gigantic sling. He had torn right through the arteries and tendons in his right wrist. He showed us the maze of stitches. It looked horrible.

Paul pulled me aside. "The damn doctor says I'm finished hittin' rivets. However, I'll be back. Give me a few weeks and we'll be smokin'. They'll never shut us down, partner."

That big German was nuts. "Don't worry about it, Paul. Just heal that arm up and they'll find you a real pussy job. Forget about this place. You don't wanna return here."

Wrong. Six week later, a month ahead of schedule and against doctor's orders, Paul Schobel was back on the Rivet Line. I swear to Jesus the guy was a plowhorse. That very same night we sprung into our old routine. I pleaded with Paul that we should work it in gradually. He wouldn't hear of it. Gino stood in the doorway of his office staring at us.

"I assume you know what this means," I yelled over. Gino just shrugged. His face did everything it could to keep from smiling. It failed miserably.

A hazy morning in the middle of May. It's around 3:00 A.M. and the mood inside my Camaro is rather strained. For the second consecutive evening, Dave Steel has snapped the E string off his guitar while plunging into the crescendo section of "Mussolini Chews Red Man," a pivotal song from our upcoming rock opera about General Motors factory life.

As Dave begins tearing apart my floorboard for a replacement string, I hit the pause button on the tape machine and fish two more beers out of the Igloo cooler. The smokestacks stare down, tombstones older than God. We're parked beneath one of the huge vapor lamps at the far north end of the GM Truck & Bus employee lot. Nothing out here but the barbed wire, the possums, an occasional freight train and two off-key and off-duty shoprats. It's a long, long way from Abbey Road.

We are sitting out here working on our shop opera or, as we've come to call it, "shopera," a thirty-tune rock opus concerning the real dealings of assembly line labor. So far, we've completed five songs to our liking: "Rat Like Me," "He's a Suck-Ass," "Banana Sticker Republic," "Are You Goin' in Tonight?" and "You're on Notice." Three rockers, a ballad and a miserable dirge.

Despite the obvious drawbacks of trying to write and record inside a car, I've insisted on these surroundings for two main reasons. First off, we'd grown awful tired of the old bitch who lived below Dave callin' the cops every time we plugged into his amplifiers. The cops would come and Dave would try to explain that we were dedicated composers emoting our wretched angst against a world that saw us as nothing more than blockheads and lackwits. The police were not impressed. Dave was finally faced with turning it off or bein' evicted.

The second reason for our whereabouts was a decision I had made. Despite the hardships, I was convinced we should retire to the scene of the theme itself. My hunch was that if our proposed rock opera about shoprats were ever to stand a chance, it would have to be fertilized directly on the threshold of Greaseball Mecca. It was the musicians who belonged in studios. It was the poets who belong in bungalows. We laid claim to neither. Just a couple of nine-year prostitutes of the Industrial Cycle sniffin' around the back forty for an exorcism you could dance to.

Dave and I had already been messin' around for the past year in our own little grunge quartet called Dr. Schwarz Kult. (The name came courtesy of Dave's shrink.) We had done quite a bit of recording down at the studios of WFBE where I did my weekly radio show. Admittedly, our entire playlist was just a bunch of aimless ranting: "Hotbed of Sin," "Bowling for Teenagers, "Drinking Makes Sense"—anything to annoy. We put out one cassette appropriately entitled *Entire Mire*, refused to play live, never practiced, got bored and disbanded. It was silly. Here we were in our thirties, dolin' out a bunch of sonic mulch that only appealed to a handful of miscreants who could've been our kids. What we needed was a purpose.

That purpose turned out to be General Motors. Not solely General Motors, but all forms of blue-collar moil and toil. The more we thought about it, the more sense it made. What it came down to was simple truth and authenticity. During the past few years, Dave and I had become terribly weary of hearing a number of these flimflam rock 'n' roll mongers pluggin' up the airwaves with their detached meanderings of "da average man, man." Goddamn millionaires mewin' all over the dial about how bad the grind was. When? Where? How? They should have all been forced to write songs about cocaine orgies and tax shelters and beluga caviar. Leave us alone.

Average man? Shit, Billy Joel wasn't "livin' here in Allentown." He was twirlin' tongues with Christie Brinkley in some high-rise china cabinet. If that's average, how come the steering gear man wasn't bangin' Cheryl Tiegs? Why weren't Dave and I playin' leapfrog with the Landers sisters?

And what about Bob Seger? He might've been from our neck of the woods, he might have put out some hot-ass groove before sellin' out to housewife drivel but he *sure* as hell wasn't "makin' Thunderbirds." He was buying them! Probably by the lot load. Get outta here, ya four-flusher.

Hey, when was the last time you saw a photo or video of John Cougar Mellonfarm when he wasn't strategically positioned within a five-foot radius of: a) corn on the cob b) a manure rake or c) some dilapidated porch brimming with Jed Clampett clones and pregnant Negresses? C'mon, Johnny, you don't mean to tell us you lug all those things into the Jacuzzi with ya, huh? Go inseminate a tractor, bub.

Then, of course, there's Springsteen. Who says you can't be 297 places at once? The guy has made untold zillions hoppin' to and fro in his house of hallucinations, always emerging on release date as either a construction worker (*The River*), a garage mechanic (*I'm on Fire*), a minor league batting instructor (*Glory Days*), the kindred spirit of Charlie Starkweather (*Nebraska*) or some other pockmarked casualty of Crud Corners. No wonder this guy's concerts run on to half-past never. It takes a heap of time to sing from A (aviator) to Z (zincographer). Yo, Boss, you didn't happen to have an older sister named Sybil by any chance?

Before everyone gets cranky and wants to assail me as the bastard spud of Albert Goldman, chill a moment. All right, maybe it's true these rock stars have dandy intentions but it just doesn't wash. For instance, you wouldn't call a heart surgeon to your house to steam-vac your carpet. Why entrust the blues to a bunch of off-whites? These fickle chameleons oughtta clear out and take their lousy method acting with 'em. We don't need them to serenade us on how tedious and deprived our lives are. If need be, we can do it ourselves.

At least, this was the belief Dave and I were operating under. Workers should perform the songs of workers. Let assembly workers sing about assembly lines. Let waitresses sing about waiting tables. Let garbagemen sing about garbage. No more hired tongues. No more rummaging tycoons. No more surrogate songsters. No more Bruciemania. No more false prophets. Get real.

The night after our clumsy recording session, Dave and I are sitting in a corner of Mark's Lounge attempting to gather inspirational fodder for our shopera. We've found this watering hole to be a great source of relevant information. At times, I've been able to snatch lines from conversations and use them verbatim in a song. Unfortunately, it's Friday, and that means disco night at Mark's. Neither Dave nor I have been able to completely figure out this hideous phenomenon. As a rule, all shoprats hate disco music. Still it's right back here every Friday. It's an amazing hoot to watch the rent-a-jock tryin' to coax one hundred baffled shoprats onto the dance floor with loud bait like "Hey, you weekend warriors, let's get it down to some Culture Club!" Talk about your uphill battles. There's maybe five females in the entire place.

As the reflections of the disco ball paint ghoulish images across the faces of my linemates, I can't help but think to myself that this reeks of the moronic effrontery I would expect from GM. Goddamn, doesn't that goofy little rent-a-jock realize that our feet fuckin' ache? All we needed now was Howie

Makem to hit the floor wearing a sequined glove and three dozen gold chains. Needless to say, there isn't much dancing. There is severe drinking, however.

I turn my chair around to escape the vision. "Average man is a myth," I remark to Dave. I am getting stoned and obnoxious. "They've hired mercenaries to sing his song. The shit on MTV is as safe as strained carrots. Any bastard in this bar could do better. The radio is hopeless, just a holding tank for miserable shits who don't wanna offend or defy or speak the truth. They're too bland to even suck. And in the face of all this deception and betrayal, Michelob Light has the balls to ask us commoners 'Who SAYS you can't have pinstripes and rock 'n' roll?' I'll tell 'em who! The peons they've got stuck down in their brewery with six more hours to go before the sweat subsides and the gears quit grindin'. The brewers, the fry cooks, the shoprats—that's who! Pinstripes and rock 'n' roll. What's next? Tuxedos and cock fighting?"

Dave just nods wearily. He picks up the bar napkin he's been writing on during my tantrum and reads: "Don Johnson, asshole deluxe, is making a rock 'n' roll record. It will no doubt be an enormous hit with his millions of dedicated fans."

"No doubt." I laugh.

We grab a six-pack to go and head back to the truck plant's employee lot to see if we can come up with anything. Dave picks up my pawnshop Alvarez acoustic and begins strumming our anthem, "Rat Like Me." I fiddle with the knobs on the tape machine and fall in on the second verse: "Wilbur lost his teeth one night in the pit/When the track took a jump and the oil pan bit,/Tommy lost a finger to a sheet metal goof/And they fed it to the pigeons on the North Unit roof./Rat . . . rat . . . rat . . . they're all rats like me." Shit, we missed the amps on this one.

As far as ratings go, I'm not much of a singer. My guitar playing could be described as primitive. Dave is much better, he's at least adequate. Neither of us worry about it too much. We know we can work any damn guitar better than Springsteen could work a month around here.

••••10•••••

By the summer of '86, things were really beginning to unravel on several fronts. Mike Moore called me out to the *Michigan Voice* office whereupon he informed me that he was very close to accepting the top spot at *Mother Jones*. He seemed unusually subdued, almost morose. I felt the same way. I hadn't a clue as to what a *Mother Jones* even was. Were we talking about a chain of rib joints or a blaxploitation flick?

The damn thing turned out to be a magazine. Apparently, the publication was in dire need of revitalization, having been neutered along the trail and allowed to flounder in gutless yuppie dross. Moore was their choice to restore the rag to its old muckraking intensity. Well, if anyone knew how to rake the muck it was our man Mikey.

"Shit, your own national magazine," I remarked. "Sounds like a solid career move."

"Yeah, I suppose," he said.

"Then why the long face?"

"It would mean leaving Flint. San Francisco is a long, long way."

Flint for Frisco? Most locals would've somersaulted naked through a barn fire for that type of option. Not Moore. He had this goofy love affair with Flint. I, for one, could empathize with him completely. For as sure as he was being beckoned to the West Coast, I was beginning to hear the first faint boot stomps of those rat-snatchers from Pontiac. They were startin' to reel in those rotten transfer signatures. It was looking more and more like Mike and I were on our way out of the city limits—one half torn, the other fully shredded.

A couple days later, Moore called to tell me he had decided to accept the editor's position at *Mother Jones*. I was hardly amazed. It was the right decision. Now it was my turn to feel subdued and morose. Without Mike Moore, the pliers were applied to the damn uvula and the next sound heard would be the *Michigan Voice* becoming the *Michigan Mute*. I wondered what would become of my festering literary hobby. By no master plan of my own, I had become extremely reliant on the Rivethead journals as an outlet for a good deal of my frustrations and malcontent.

Just before he was to leave town, Mike phoned me. He had a proposal he wanted to discuss. "If it meets with your approval, I would like for you to get started on your first article for *Mother Jones*. I'm hoping to use it for the cover story of my first issue."

"I'm gonna be writin' for *Mother Jones*?" I sputtered. "Wait, you mean I'M GONNA BE WRITIN' FOR MONEY?"

"Eight hundred fifty dollars a column," Mike replied. "The cover story will probably net you sixteen hundred."

Jesus, lug that headstone back beyond the boxcars, Quasimodo. The Rivethead once again walks among us! Go home and have that typer greased. Put the Budweisers within arm's reach. Fall to your knees! We have witnessed the resurrection of the gimmick that wouldn't die. Fetch those tattered teats, those chapped udders, those benign and bottomless milk sacs. Farmer Rivethead is taking his cow to market. Do not question the outlandish logic behind such a command. Far dumber shits have hit gold, I swear it.

Further oddness was to follow. On his last night in town, Moore came to see me on the Rivet Line. His flight to San Francisco was to leave the next morning and this is how he had chosen to spend his final hours in Flint. I was puzzled. Certainly, there had to be more attractive options—dinner with old friends, one more TV interview, a family farewell, gettin' drunk, gettin' laid, gettin' some sleep, ANYTHING.

After my initial sense of confusion, I think I understood. For a guy who was born and raised in this Greaseball Mecca, there could be no more fitting place to go to round up an apropos swan song for one's formative years than the oily altars of General Motors. Although Moore had never worked in the factory it didn't necessarily exclude him from being a semishoprat. The same went for everybody else in this town. There were chunks of these people orbiting from one end of the building to the other. The laughs and tears of their ancestors' struggle were entombed here. The good times and the bad times and all the messy in betweens.

For Mike's visit to the truck plant, I made sure to advise him on the appropriate wardrobe. "Wear those faded jeans you always have on, put on your Tiger cap and, please, leave those ugly bifocals at home."

For extra precaution I insisted on the following: "If anyone happens to stop you, tell 'em your name is Henderson and that you work in Cab Shop. If they pester you for identification, tell 'em that your ID badge is upstairs in your lunch bucket. Refrain from using large words. Itch your testicles freely. At all times, act surly and miffed."

I waited for Mike in a predesignated area of the North Unit parking lot. I was working on a quart of beer and had an extra one waiting for him. He didn't drink, but I thought it only proper to extend the quart of beer as a ritualistic courtesy to one who would soon be entering the mind stomp of an American assembly line. Beer helped keep things in perspective.

Tardy as always, Moore came screechin' up in his faithful Honda. Uh-oh. Rare was the time you gazed upon a Japanese import in this sprawling car kennel. When you did, they were usually very easy to identify—busted-off antennas, boot heel indentations on the quarter panel, key scrapes along the paintjob, broken mirrors, broken windows. Freedom of choice in one's particular mode of transportation ended rather abruptly at the entrance gate to most GM assembly plants. There were plenty of flag-totin' vandals still takin' night classes at the John Wayne Institute for Insecure Bigots.

"Couldn't you have borrowed your girlfriend's car?" I asked Mike as he hopped into my Camaro.

"She drives a Toyota," he replied. Sheesh.

"How about a cold quart of beer?"

"You know I can't possibly down that much beer. Hey, you sure my car's safe out here?"

"Does your insurance cover mindless vandalism and freak disasters?"

"I guess."

"Then she's as safe as a cock in a jock," I lied. "Have a drink, you'll loosen up."

"I told you, I can't drink that much beer."

"Looks like you've given me no choice." I uncapped the other quart and began poundin'.

I went inside the plant first and told Mike to follow behind me a minute later. We met down at the time clocks. He seemed momentarily mesmerized. "Man, I wish I had a time card to punch in one of these."

"Well, you can't use mine. That would stop my pay. Try using your Visa card. You never know, it might wipe out your balance."

When we made it up to my job, Mike took a seat on a crateful of spring castings. I flipped over my garbage can and sat down next to him. My editor couldn't stop smiling. He looked up and down the line as if this was some kind of breathtaking moment in history. Perhaps it was.

"This is where you *write?*" Moore asked. "What about all this noise?"

"You don't even notice it after a while. It's like real discordant elevator Muzak."

I introduced my editor to several of the regulars. Paul seized the opportunity and began showing Mike photographs of his prized motorcycles. Hell, the way Mike was grinnin', you would have thought he was gazin' at nude snapshots of Ginger and Mary Ann.

My editor wanted to meet the steering gear man. I had to break the news to him gently. "He's not available, Mike. He checked himself into a detox ward last week."

His next request was to catch a glimpse of Howie Makem. I explained that Howie had no set schedule. "Howie makes up his own hours. Besides, he rarely patrols this beat anymore since Herman beaned him on the head with an empty pint of McMasters."

Mike Moore's final request was to hit a few rivets. I tried to talk him out of the idea, but he was practically foamin' at the mouth. "Shit," I moaned. "If Henry Jackson were to come stridin' through here, my ass would be crammed through a keyhole."

My editor began to beg. "C'mon, just a few. Please... PLEASE!"

I showed Mike how to grasp the gun and navigate the tip to the target. I warned him not to pull the trigger until everything was aligned. He was really smiling now. I lit a cigarette and stepped back. Moore positioned the gun squarely atop the target and drove home a perfect rivet. The guys applauded and he hit a few more. Hell, he looked like a natural.

"Thanks," he said.

Anytime.

Things began moving quickly. Craziness pervaded. Not only did I have this sudden invitation from my editor to take the Rivethead to a national forum, but I was being tapped on the shoulder by other unlikely sources. A man from *Penthouse* magazine kept calling wanting me to write "an autoworker's view of sex on an assembly line." I told him that such an article would have to be pure fabrication. He said that would be fine, that I could use a pseudonym if I preferred. I had to decline. It was absurd: "Mel brandished his walloper as Kate's ample melons glistened in the piss-colored haze. He mounted her as the rats looked on, sweltering loins pulsing in the..."

A woman from the *Detroit Free Press* called. She was aware of the demise of the *Voice* and wanted to know if I'd be interested in ladling out my factory grunt for their Sunday magazine. I told her about my upcoming move to *Mother Jones*. She then asked if she could run a variety of my old *Michigan Voice* pieces and reprint any further *Mother Jones* articles. I inquired about payment for such and the numbers she responded with seemed remarkably generous. Be my guest,

I told her. Welcome to the Rivethead's sensational bar tab rummage sale.

Soon after, another woman phoned. It was the lady I'd talked to a few months earlier from *Esquire* magazine. She was calling to inform me that I had been selected to appear in *Esquire*'s 1986 Register, "a compendium of the nation's brightest young minds and high achievers under age forty." She offered her congratulations and said that a photographer would be arriving in Flint within the next few weeks to get some pictures. Either I was improving or it was a sluggish year for phenoms.

I called Dave Steel. "Prepare yourself," I cautioned. "The Rivethead has just been selected as one of this country's brightest young minds by *Esquire* magazine. I think it only fair to warn you that this bizarre turn of events conclusively indicates that the ruination of Western Civilization is now in full swing."

"I would have to agree," Dave replied. "The moral fiber of this land is in deep jeopardy."

Things on the Rivet Line were also runnin' wacky. In the span of ten days, two workers had been bitten badly by their rivet guns. One guy lost his ring finger and the other one had broken all the bones in his right hand. Neither worker was ever to return.

As for the guy who smashed his hand, the aftermath was both sad and ridiculous. Within ten minutes of the mishap, Henry Jackson was over at the scene of the accident rantin' his fat ass off to all within ear shot about how he was gonna put this individual on notice for "careless workmanship in the job place." Even those of us who were used to Jackson's ill nature were dumbfounded. Here a man had just been permanently maimed and Henry's only concern was to see that the guy would be promptly penalized. There were some things you saw and heard inside a factory that made you bristle. There were some things you saw and heard inside a factory that made you want to throttle a prick by his neck until your wrists snapped.

Crazy, crazy, crazy. There was the night I was up in Cab Shop visiting Bob-A-Lou. We were just shootin' the shit when a fight broke out down the line. Like everyone else, we dropped what we were doing and headed for the action. It

ended as we got there. The two combatants were already bein'
separated. That's when we noticed the blood. It was streaming
out of the one guy's neck like he'd opened a faucet. He'd been
slashed badly and the fella who'd sliced him stood there,
bug-eyed and sweatin', breathin' very hard with the blade
danglin' at his side: mad at the world, mad at the machines,
mad at the walls, mad in the head. He looked around at us, then
went bolting away through the snaking lines of the Trim Shop
area. As long as I live, I'll never forget the vision of him
sprinting in the distance like a panicked gazelle, insane and
desperate, disappearing like a phantom into the industrial
underbrush.

Bob-A-Lou told me later that the two of them were back to
work, side by side, gettin' along just fine. The victim had
gotten his neck stitched up and the other guy had received two
weeks off plus probation. It seemed more than odd. Was there
any other workplace in the world where you could have a go at
killing someone and be back at your job within fourteen days as
if you had simply made a minor error in judgment? I doubted
it. Imagine if this scenario had taken place at IBM or Sears.
The cops would have been everywhere, the TV stations would
have descended and the knife wielder would've been lookin' at a
minimum of five to ten in the state pokey for attempted
murder. But this was GM. The Sign of Excellence. Quality,
Commitment and Cutlery. Boys will be boys.

Just as discouraging as smashed bones and slit throats was
the sudden decision by management to remove Gino from his
supervisor's role on the Rivet Line. It made no sense whatsoever. No other foreman in the entire corporate dog pen could
possess Gino's knack for overseeing the daily traumas on the
Rivet Line. The sacred Quality meter bore this out. For all of
the horseplay and hijinks that went along with the area, the
Rivet Line always remained near the top of the Quality ratings. Why would they want to tamper with a working marriage?

The explanation we were given was that Gino had become
"too close to his work force." GM often employs this screwy
logic whenever a supervisor and his crew develop a bond that
won't allow for proper amounts of hostility and mistrust. They're
quick to fill you up with all their newfangled bluster about
"team concept" and "consensus decision making" while, at the

same time, they insist on elevating the most inept suck-butts they can dredge up to ensure that everything proceeds at a level of useless antagonism.

The Rivet Line was far from perfect. We all had our share of shortcuts and bits of petty disobedience. Gino was aware of it all and drew us a bottom line. Build good trucks. Hit good rivets. Cover your damn job and we'll cover each other's backs. Just give me a good job. If you hang, you'll hang yourself. The way it should be. We were gonna miss old Gino.

Enter the new boss, a self-proclaimed "troubleshooter." He had been enlisted to groom the Rivet Line into a more docile outpost. As he told Schobel and me on his first night on the job: "I float from plant to plant. Whenever GM has a specific problem spot, they call me in to clean up."

With a tight grip on the whip, the new bossman started riding the crew. No music. No Rivet Hockey. No horseplay. No drinking. No card playing. No working up the line. No leaving the department. No doubling-up. No this, no that. No questions asked.

No way. After three nights of this imported bullyism, the boys had had their fill. Frames began sliding down the line minus parts. Rivets became cross-eyed. Guns mysteriously broke down. The repairmen began shipping the majority of the defects, unable to keep up with the repair load.

Sabotage was rather drastic; however it was an effective way of getting the point across. We simply had no other recourse. Sometimes these power-gods had to be reminded that it was we, the workers, who kept the place runnin'. If you started reamin' your men at every turn, sooner or later it was all gonna come back to you. There would be a bigger honcho than you, with a larnyx twice as loud, just waiting to chew your ass to ribbons as the forty greasy serfs you thought you had conquered would be lined up for last call with grins on their kissers and shrugs on their shoulders.

This new guy was nobody's dummy. He could see it all slippin' away, his goon tactics workin' against him. He pulled us all aside and suggested that we return to our old methods. The guy was no troubleshooter. He was a scared little lapdog whose hand had been called. Very quickly, the big boys moved him out to try his hired-gun charade in some other corner of the works.

We had won this particular go-round, but we all knew the big boys would be returning to the drawing board.

Our next supervisor was selected from our very midst, a popular ploy. GM would promote a boot-licker whose allegiance could be twisted by power and money, clear his rap sheet and send him back to his home base as a kind of in-house spy. The rationale was that this creepin' Judas would have an inside track on all the systems and schemes of his former linemates.

The scab they promoted was a veteran co-worker of ours named Calvin Moza. Within hours of his appointment, Moza had put Schobel and me on notice for doubling-up, Doug and Terry on notice for kickin' rivets and three other workers on notice for bench banging. (The banging of the benches was a ritual performed right before break or the end of the shift, a tribal celebration that had gone on for years.) These were all "violations" that Calvin Moza had indulged in just the previous week. But, now, he was one of *them*. There was nothin' worse than a fuckin' sellout.

When Moza nailed Eddie for bangin' on his bench, it was too much to take. I motioned for Moza to come over to my job. I took out my hammer, smiled, and proceeded to go apeshit on my bench top.

"You're on notice again, Hamper," Moza shouted above the clamor.

"Fuck you! YOU'RE THE ONE ON NOTICE!"

Almost instantly, the sounds of hammers, drifts, chains and pipes came crashing down in gorgeous unison. Moza braced himself against my bench, his head whipping back and forth. You could pretty much tell what he was thinking. How can I put forty workers on notice at once? To do so would require more paperwork than any one man could peddle. We banged on and on. Finally, Moza fled for the sanctuary of his little glass office.

It was only the beginning. For the next eight days, we made Calvin Moza's short-lived career switch sheer hell. Every time he'd walk the aisle, someone would pepper his steps with raining rivets. He couldn't make a move without the hammers banging and loud chants of "suckass" and "brown snout" ringin' in his ears. Calvin Moza got everything he deserved. There simply was no room for pity when dealing with a hypocrite who was about as pure as freshly driven snot.

When they led him away on the final day, he looked like he'd aged a decade. They buried his sorry ass in some remote corner of the South Unit. Once again we had turned back the Big Boys' attempt to saddle us with an intimidator. All it took was a unified effort and a healthy dose of anarchy. Together we stand, divided we might as well transfer to the Fender Line.

We didn't have nearly the success with the next guy they threw at us. His name was Sanders—a diehard prick, a full-fledged sadist, a corporate pit bull. We gave it our all, but this brickhead took it in stride and spit it back out. I had the distinct suspicion that we were locking horns with something that didn't even qualify as human.

In the weeks to come, we fired everything we had at Sanders. We ran bad shit. We heckled him unmercifully. We stole the hubcaps off his car. We put everything from Alpo to acid in his sandwiches. We banged on our benches until our arms and ears throbbed.

We walked out at lunch (penalty). We threw rivets and globeballs everywhere (penalty). We insisted on doubling-up (penalty). We blasted the radios (penalty). We refused to clean our areas (penalty). We refused to wear our safety glasses (penalty). We blew whiskey in his face (penalty). Recognize a pattern? If not, you most certainly deserve a...

PENALTY! The damn word must've been Sanders's middle name. It proved to be the key to his success in breaking us. Plain and simple, the bastard lived for paperwork. He'd have made somebody a fine little stenographer. Sanders never ranted or raved. When trouble brewed, he merely went reaching for his arsenal of Bic ballpoints. That was all it took. Before long, the aisles were plugged with pink paper carbons from his penalty file. We'd been corralled. The revolution fell apart.

Paul and I had been penalized several times for attempting to double-up. We simply couldn't help ourselves. We knew what waited on the other side of that wall and it was a helluva lot more attractive than what was stacked in front of us. In the end, we had to surrender. We couldn't keep buttin' heads with Sanders's penalty machine. At the rate we were being written up, the two of us would be fired within a month.

"Jesus, we should off the bastard," I remember Paul fuming. "This is ridiculous."

"No, killing him would be ridiculous," I replied. "The penalty for murdering your foreman is three months off without pay. Let's just pray he develops arthritis in his writin' hand."

Schobel and I finally reached a pansy agreement with Sanders that would allow us to double-up just as long as we didn't leave the department. It sucked. This arrangement was like being told you could vacation in the Bahamas but couldn't leave the plane.

I went back to my flipped-over garbage can and the world of blue-crud journalism. Paul made a crude hut out of some cardboard boxes and slept half the day. Our alcohol consumption hit levels that caused even us concern. We were beaten and desperate and bored like never before. It felt as though something was about to break.

Sadly, it did.

Wednesday, July 16, 1986. There was nothing particularly askew on this date, noting to remotely suggest that this shift was to be any different than the few odd thousand that had gone before. I weaved my way through the rivet guns and cross members, the waltz of the unblessed, awaiting the next frame and the one after that. Thirty-seven frames an hour. Thirty-seven clumsy muffler hangers. Thirty-seven rear spring castings. Thirty-seven invitations to dance.

First break arrived and I plopped myself down at the workers' picnic bench for a smoke and a glance at the box scores. It was precisely 7:08 P.M. As I stared at the paper, the words and numbers started swirling together. I stood up. I could feel a numbness in my arms and legs. I began having major difficulty trying to catch my breath. I stepped away from the table feeling totally disoriented.

A stroke, I figured. I'm having a FUCKING STROKE! Thirty-one years old, a mere minnow in the scheme of the dream, and here comes the big daddy death rattle himself, smug as can be, marchin' right down the center of Screwball Lane. What kind of filthy, poetic injustice was this? Choking over dead like a sack of yams only ten yards away from some moron's half-tinkered embryo of a Suburban. To top it off,

Sanders would probably write me up for expiring without permission. I can joke about this now. However, I can assure you, I wasn't then. I was too busy searchin' for air.

I remember racin' into the phone booth, though I wasn't sure why. I wasn't sure of anything. All I knew was that I didn't want to die. Then it occurred to me. I had to dial for help. That's why I was in the booth. I was in such a state that I couldn't remember the phone numbers of my best friends or family. I hit zero and told the operator I was having an impossible time dialing. I had her ring my girlfriend's apartment. No answer. I should have guessed. As their men stood crackin' and crumbling in barbed wire vomitoriums, the women were all out at the mall tryin' on shoes.

I suddenly remembered that Mike Moore was back in town to sell off all the junk left behind at the *Michigan Voice*. I had the operator dial out there, praying that they hadn't disconnected the phones yet. After a long wait, Moore answered.

"Goddamn, listen to me, Mike. I'm in a phone booth on the Rivet Line and I believe I'm having a stroke or a nervous fuckin' breakdown. I'm losing my vision, my arms and legs are tinglin' and I can hardly breathe. Help me!"

"Try your best to calm down," Mike advised. "It sounds like anxiety. The best thing you can do is to get the hell out of there. Go home immediately, then call me back."

I stepped out of the phone booth into a nightmare. Everyone's head seemed enlarged. Their eyes seemed to converge on me. I made it to my workbench and grabbed my keys. Paul was buildin' up some cross members and I approached him. I had to notify Paul I was going. By now, I could barely speak. It felt like an elephant was sitting on my chest. I wasn't aware of it at the time, but tears were rollin' down my face.

"I have to leave," I warbled. "Tell Sanders I puked or something."

Paul didn't press the matter. He could see things were seriously amiss. "Don't worry about Sanders," he said. "Just take off." His voice seemed to be coming out of a transistor radio.

I bolted out of the factory and into the sweet outdoors. It was a great relief to be free from that freak show. My memory was shot. I spent about fifteen minutes trying to locate my car.

When I did, I sped straight for home. The two-mile drive seemed to take hours.

My mind was completely unhinged. I paused at street-lights and snuck glances at people in neighboring cars. It was hideous. I saw insects driving sports cars and frogs driving station wagons. They all seemed to be staring at me. WHAT THE HELL WAS GOING ON? I was the Rivethead. I had only wanted to check out some box scores. I didn't belong here driving around as bugs and amphibians peered at me like I was an alien.

I turned on the radio thinking some music might soothe me down. The Beach Boys were singin' "Wouldn't It Be Nice," a great song if you could escape the irony of the title. I began to sing along: "Maybe if we think and wish and hope and pray it might come true..." Jesus, I started bawlin' like a newborn. Even Brian Wilson was takin' a poke at me. I slapped off the radio.

I arrived at my place and called Moore. "At least we know it's not a stroke or heart attack," he said. "My guess is some kind of nervous breakdown. Do you have a doctor?"

"No," I answered.

"Then I will give you the number of someone you can call. Do you remember Darlene Shea? She's always been a fan of your writing."

"I don't need groupies, I need a damn exorcist!" I shouted.

"Darlene is a physician, a very good one. Call this number first thing tomorrow and tell her that you must see her at once."

"What if I'm going insane?" I asked Mike.

"Then I would say you're comin' around to your old self."

It was a long night. I paced back and forth through my apartment, unable to think straight, unable to talk on the phone, unable to relax. I tried to watch television but all they were showing were sitcoms featuring large flies, frogs and lizard-things. I went through a fifth of Jim Beam and several beers. The alcohol at least helped me to pass out. As I slid off to sleep, I kept thinking maybe I'd wake up to find that this had all been part of some terrifying dream.

I got up the next morning feeling much better. Except for an unusually brutal hangover, I felt like my normal self. My arms no longer tingled, my vision was clear and, best of all, my heart was beating at its usual pace. I looked out the window to catch a peek at my neighbors. They looked ugly and beaten and full of malice. However, they didn't look at all like insects. Whatever it was that had overtaken me the previous day at work had surely passed through my system. I didn't bother calling the doctor. I was cured. I went back to the Rivet Line, a very grateful rat.

The shift went by without incident. Of course, Sanders wrote me up for walking off my job. He asked what had happened to me. I told him that I had come down with stomach flu. Sanders said that he hoped I was feeling better. He crammed the penalty into my shirt pocket and marched off.

On Friday, two days after my bizarre crack-up, I got to work and was loading my stock bins full of muffler hangers and rivets. Another day, another dullard. We had about fifteen minutes before the line was to roll. Dougie was done building up his springs and walked over. He began chattering about some trivial matter when, clear out of the unholy blue, everything suddenly flipped. Here we went again! My arms and legs started tinglin' and shakin'. My heart joined in, an atomic bongo thumpin' some blue streak lick. Doug was still yappin' when I grabbed for my keys and hit the aisleway. I didn't wanna be around when he switched into a grasshopper or something.

I sped home fully realizing that Wednesday had not been the strange fluke I had hoped it had been. I was fucked up in a big way. This wasn't like havin' a broken leg. A broken leg would heal. You could retain all your senses. Who knew about this shit? Who knew what it even was?

Hopefully, Dr. Shea. I got her on the phone and tried my best to describe what I was experiencing. I doubt that I was even making sense. She had me come straight to her office.

We talked a while and she came to a preliminary diagnosis. "Ben, you appear to be suffering from severe panic disorder. This condition often manifests itself in the symptoms you are currently experiencing—the rapid heartbeat, numbness in the extremities, distorted vision, feelings of paranoia, disassociation, hopelessness—they all fit the pattern. What I will have you do is two things. I will prescribe a medication called Inderal.

Whenever you feel an attack coming on, take one of these pills. They should help steady your heartbeat. Also, I am going to recommend that you immediately make an appointment with a Dr. Lee at the Holly Road Mental Health Clinic. He is very knowledgeable in dealing with this kind of disorder."

It was one hellish weekend. The panic attacks descended on me one after another like sharks to a rib roast. I took the Inderal but its effects were minimal. If it slowed my heart down any, it sure as hell did nothing for the war going on inside my head. Mostly, I drank. I drank and paced from one room to the next. I was looking for something. I was searching for my shit.

On Monday morning, I called the Holly Road Mental Health Clinic. I asked for an appointment to see Dr. Lee but was told he was booked up to the twenty-third century. The receptionist said that a Dr. Kilaru had an opening the next day. I told her to write me down. In my shape, I'd have settled for Dr. Seuss.

Dr. Kilaru was a very short man, very pleasant and extremely dapper. Obviously, this loony business lent itself to the big buck. He was also very Indian. I had trouble making out his accent. Fortunately, I was called on to do most of the talking. The doctor listened intently, occasionally jotting notes, as I told him about my ugly metamorphosis from Rivethead to Rancidhead.

When I was finished, Dr. Kilaru put down his notepad and spoke. "Ben, you are suffering from rather intense episodes of panic attack syndrome. This stems from a condition called acute anxiety. There is not always a set pattern to when or where these attacks may occur. For treatment, I am going to recommend weekly psychiatric counseling and medication. I will prescribe for you a sedative called Xanax. This should help a great deal. You may still experience small amounts of anxiety. However it's the episodes of full-blown panic we are out to avoid."

I couldn't have agreed more. For the past four days, I had been wondering if I'd ever be able to leave my apartment again. I asked the doctor if it was safe to assume I was not going insane.

"That is a frequent fear expressed by those who suffer

these attacks. Often, a person will become convinced that he or she is having a complete breakdown, a heart attack or actually dying. You have a serious disorder. However I believe your sanity is fully intact."

I had Dr. Kilaru write me out a medical excuse for the next couple days. What I needed was a few days off to check out this Xanax stuff and to make absolutely sure it would keep the demons at bay. After the previous week, I simply couldn't afford to hit the Rivet Line with anything less than a happy, healthy cerebellum.

The Xanax seemed to work well. Bolstered by my new pharmaceutical pal, I rejoined the fray. At the slightest hint of unsteadiness, I would scramble over to the drinking fountain and gulp down more medication. I would have swallowed cat puke, it didn't matter. I knew just one thing. I'd seen walls sweating and ceilings sag. I'd seen close friends of mine transform into various insects. I'd seen that great lake of fire roll down the aisle. If it were to spill over again, I was damn sure going to be clutchin' on to something buoyant.

Mike Moore called me in August to tell me my article for his first issue of *Mother Jones* was being well received by the folks at the magazine. He wanted to know if I could take a couple weeks off in order to do some promoting for my cover story. For the first time in years, I headed off on vacation.

At one point, Mike and I did two newspaper interviews, three radio talk shows, three television guest spots in five different cities in the span of twelve hours. We crisscrossed the state from head to heinie. My futile requests to hit a bar somewhere in the middle of this marathon were quickly shot down. I sucked down the Xanax like Tic Tacs. The interviews all followed the same basic format. Moore would harangue everything under the sun while I sat at his elbow like a real numbskull. Anytime I was called on to speak, I'd mutter something decisive and profound like "There aren't enough windows in the factory" or "I once saw a guy incinerate his pet mouse with a brazing torch."

A few days later, the promo guy from *Mother Jones* called to tell me they had scheduled a series of television and radio interviews in Chicago. I was told that I would have to make this trip solo because Mike was busy back in San Francisco. I immediately balked. There was no way I could pull this off alone. After much grumbling, they consented to pay Dave Steel's way to Chicago.

We arrived there in the afternoon. The schedule called for me to do a live television interview at 6:30 the next morning. Dave and I both agreed that I'd never be able to function at that early hour. He suggested that we stay up all night and indulge in a nocturnal bar crawl of Chicago nightlife. Finally, someone who spoke sense.

We hit several blues joints and got back to our hotel around 3:00. Only a few more hours to go. I kept drinkin' and tossin' down the occasional Xanax. Dave was as drunk as I'd ever seen him. He insisted on ordering a pizza. When it finally arrived, he took about three bites out of it before hurling it, along with an empty fifth of rum, over the balcony and into the hotel swimming pool eight floors below. "Swish!" Dave yelled.

"Cool it, Laimbeer. Our mission still lies ahead of us."

"Gimme a bourbon," Dave snarled.

We sat around drinkin' Jim Beam and water. Dave kept playin' with the TV set until he ran across a channel that was showing *Lost in Space*. It was the episode where Dr. Smith found a machine which allowed him to pump out these armies of cyborgs which looked exactly like him. Old Zach was havin' a great time. Alas, Dr. Zachary Smith's plans fell through. The end of the show found him squattin' on this Styrofoam boulder weeping: "All I wanted to do was rule the universe." Dave and I cracked up. Dr. Smith should have been the Chairman of General Motors.

Around 5:00, Dave started primpin' for the TV show. He showered and shaved and began styling his sacred pompadour. It was hilarious. He had a hair blower contraption the size of a bazooka.

"Hey, I was under the impression they wanted me on the show." I laughed.

"They may need a stand-in seein' as how you're drunk and doped silly."

"They'd never buy it. You look more like George Hamilton than a shoprat."

Dave shook his head. "At least brush your teeth and comb your hair."

By the time we arrived at the television station, I was pretty wasted. The door guard looked at me and refused to let us in. I stepped aside and let Dave do the explaining. Finally, a sweet-lookin' gal appeared and ushered us upstairs to the set. Apparently, she hadn't seen the cover of *Mother Jones* yet. She kept complimenting Dave on his writing flair. I injected that not only was Dave a decent writer, he had hair stiff enough to dent beer kegs. Dave flipped me the bird and the two of them walked on ahead of me.

Remarkably, the show turned out fine. I didn't slur too badly or toss in any four-letter words. I remember the stage guys were laughing so hard that their cameras were shakin'. They were especially fond of my wrought-up tangent about going bowling with Roger Smith. As the segment ended, I stood up and almost fell straight on my face. The host gave me a big handshake and invited me to come back on the show whenever I came to Chicago.

My nerves were growing steadily worse. The Rivet Line, once my fortress and private lair, was now nothing more than a huge galleryful of paranoia and mayhem. All I did was stare at the clock, a suicidal gesture in itself. I threw away my notebook. There was no inspiration, there was nothing.

As if things weren't bad enough, they announced that the first group of transfer signees would be heading off for Pontiac within a month. Tony and Dave's names were on the list. I had drawn a temporary bye. Tony was elated. Dave was his usual uncertain self.

Meanwhile, in the wake of my *Mother Jones* piece, the phone began to ring again. A producer for *The Today Show* called expressing an interest in doing a feature on the Rivethead. This was getting downright silly. I had a notion to tell him the Rivethead was closed down for repairs. I was still a bit put off from my experience with the *60 Minutes* disaster. However, this guy seemed much more friendly. I agreed to the segment and we set up plans for the following week.

The crew from NBC spent four days following me around. Besides myself, they spent time interviewing my grandfather, my daughter, Mike Moore, my grandmother and assorted friends. They wanted something from the shopera so we got the band together and they filmed us ripping through a particularly hot version of "Rat Like Me." Dave's pompadour looked like a large exotic bird.

The producer mentioned that he wanted to take the cameras inside the shop to film me on the Rivet Line. Sheesh, what a comedian. I explained to him that I was hardly GM's favorite son and that getting clearance to film inside the factory would be about as likely as receiving permission to film the Pope taking a crap. The producer remained unfazed. He represented America's top-rated morning show. Confidently, he drove straight down to GM headquarters in Detroit for the go-ahead.

The next day he phoned me. "Jesus, you were right on that call," he reported. "The best that I could do was to get permission to film you in the parking lot."

"I warned you." I chuckled. "GM believes a creative mind is a flawed mind."

The producer continued. "All I know is that everything was proceeding fine up until the point when I mentioned your name. From then on, I might as well have been talking to a cement wall."

We arranged to do the shoot in the parking lot. I told the producer to have his film crew ready and waiting at 9:24, our lunchtime. I showed them exactly where they should set up—surrounding the back of Al's pickup camper. I told several of my linemates to show up. At first break Al and I went out and bought three cases of beer. We threw them on ice so they would be nice and chilly for the filming.

Once again, I was bewildered by GM's sense of logic. All NBC wanted to do was get some uneventful footage of the Rivethead and his cronies going about their jobs. A tidy, innocuous venture into the workaday world of an American assembly line. How harmless. How natural. NBC was gonna parade us before the nation so why not have it situated in a locale where GM could monitor the content? We would certainly project a proud image. With Sanders and Henry Jackson hunchin' over us, outstanding behavior would be guaranteed. It was foolish.

GM probably wound up wondering the same thing. For instead of harmless footage of men going about their workday routines, they were to be eventually treated to the cringin' eyesore of twenty or so shifty rivetlings pile-drivin' cans of Budweiser like parched boat people. I had a hunch that this vision would cause some squirmin' down in Detroit. Tough shit.

The producer had one final idea for the segment. The next evening he wanted me to assemble some of my closet Rivet Line chums and bring them over to Mark's Lounge. He wanted to do a bit on the post-shift conviviality of factory folk. He added that NBC would be pickin' up the tab for all the drinks. For his sake, I hoped he wasn't operating on a thin budget.

The next day I was shaving while listening to the noon news on television. The same old shit came rolling forth about deficits and plane crashes and world turmoil. The anchorman then proceeded into the local news. What came next very nearly caused me to cut my lip off. I ran into the living room unable to believe what I was hearing.

"THE SAVAGE ATTACK ON THE TWO WAITRESSES HAPPENED EARLY THIS MORNING AT AN ESTABLISH-MENT IN FLINT CALLED MARK'S LOUNGE. THE WOM-EN WERE ALONE IN THE BAR WHEN AN UNKNOWN ASSAILANT AMBUSHED THEM, STABBING EACH RE-PEATEDLY. THE VICTIMS ARE LISTED IN CRITICAL CONDITION AND THE POLICE HAVE NO MOTIVE FOR THE ATTACK AT THIS TIME."

I sat there in shock as the television showed the two barmaids being hustled by stretcher into an ambulance. There was much blood. I turned off the set. Who could commit such an act, I sat there wondering. The barmaids of Mark's were our Sisters of Mercy, our faithful nannies. They were on *our* side. The animal who pulled this crap had to be an outsider.

I called the producer. "Forget about the segment at Mark's tonight. Some asshole went through there this morning and sliced up a couple barmaids."

"Christ, that's awful," he responded. "Are they gonna live?"

"It's too early to say. It just went down a few hours ago."

"Shit, I'm sorry, Ben. We'll try to film the segment next month when we come back to town with Betty Rollin. Let me know how this thing turns out in the meantime."

"I'll do that," I replied, still in a daze.

The unspeakable turned out to be true. A worker from our

very own plant had committed the attack. Apparently, the guy was doped out of his tree and just went berserk. Not only did he carve up two of our fair maidens, he also busted into a local pharmacy that very same night and stole an extensive amount of drugs. A couple of days later, two kids playin' in the woods behind the nearby UAW softball complex found his body next to a stream, ODed and blue as a jar of Vicks. Lying next to him was a pillowcase full of pills and streaked with blood.

Bad vuggum had its hooks in me also. Another panic attack struck as I was entering the shop one afternoon. I immediately spun around and got hold of Dr. Kilaru. He put me off work for a few weeks and prescribed another drug called Tofranil, an antidepressant. I took the drug for a few days before tossing 'em down the toilet. The damn shit made my heart beat like a jackhammer.

Dr. Kilaru was becoming more and more insistent that I enroll as an outpatient at the mental health center. I steadfastly refused. He kept at it, mentioning how I could assist myself in recovery through daily regimens of personal therapy, group interaction, seminars, medication, physical therapy and field trips. This meant mixing it up with human beings. That was asking a lot.

The field trip idea especially bothered me. I could just envision myself staring out the back of some old red school bus, crowbarred elbow-to-elbow with a slobberin' gang of manics, loons and schizoids. I could see the smug faces of my high school peers as they drove to their useless jobs, see them bursting into hysterics as I gazed back at them through the morning drizzle and bus fumes. "Hey! It's Benny Hamper! The boy we voted most likely to suffocate on his own vomit. Wave at the poor bastard!" Oh, that I could exchange this strange malady for something more simple—like the heartbreak of psoriasis or venereal warts.

Things weren't going a whole lot smoother for my editor, Mike Moore. After only three issues at the helm, he was fired from his job at *Mother Jones*. The publisher listed several reasons for the sudden axe, the most grievous being Moore's refusal to run an article critical of the Sandinista regime in Nicaragua. The publisher also accused Moore of never being around the office or, for that matter, the state of California.

Mike was rather adept at concocting any excuse to fly back to Flint. But doing battle with that procession of poseurs, who could blame him?

With Moore's firing came my conclusion as a columnist for *Mother Jones*. I would miss the extra income but, otherwise, it was fine with me. I was practically bein' driven out of my skull by the magazine's crew of fact checkers and researchers. These morons would call me over and over asking the most goddamn inane questions. For instance, one morning they rolled me outta bed to ask me if I could give them the phone number of at least one other co-worker who could positively verify the fact that the North Unit parking lot was *indeed* called "the North Unit parking lot."

Moore called me to talk about his dismissal. He told me the publisher was upset with his insistence on letting me have my own column. He also added that the publisher thought my last column—a comical overview of the repulsive *Faces of Death* documentary trilogy—was the most tasteless and offensive piece of bathroom humor he'd ever read.

"Since when does tastelessness preclude good writing?" I grumbled. "I thought that was one of the better things I'd written."

"I thought it was a hoot," Mike added.

"Shit, I swear they oughta change the name of that rag to *Mother Teresa*. I say screw 'em. You'd have more creative freedom writin' for Tass."

"Maybe so," Moore replied, "but it was still a job."

A few days later, I received a letter from the managing editor of *Mother Jones*. In it, he stated how much the magazine would enjoy having me stay on as a columnist. He mentioned that he hoped Mike's firing wouldn't have a bearing on my future contributions to the magazine. He even went on to state that bringing me aboard was one of the best moves Mike had made during his brief tenure as editor. Say what?

The bullshit quota was smellin' darn nasty. Somehow I was bein' wedged in between these two corners and it made me feel uneasy. Not knowing who to believe, nor really caring, I opted to stay out of the matter. I was in it for kicks. This shell game hardly qualified as such. I knew where my allegiance was and it didn't lie within the lap of anybody's *Mother.*

I took the Rivethead over to the *Detroit Free Press* where my chronicles of factory life became an instant hit. Detroit couldn't resist a smartass. I wrote for their Sunday magazine and was allowed all the freedom, space and time I needed. Kathy Warbelow, my editor, was always there to coax and coddle me. Even at this late date, I still needed reassurances that the writing was okay. More importantly, I needed to know I was okay. The Rivethead may have been a slicker, but the guy inside was quivering badly.

My notoriety was anything but a source of pride and pleasure back on the front lines. Sanders and Jackson, the Oreo brain police, were beginning to hawk my every move. Sanders was especially eager to burn my ass. He'd been steamed at me ever since he'd been forced to become my mailman. This humorous development began to occur after my appearance on *The Today Show* and the cover of *Mother Jones*. People started writing to me and, not knowing my home address, some of them simply mailed their letters to: The Rivethead, Suburban/Blazer Line, GM Truck & Bus, Flint, MI. I was stunned that the front office people didn't just incinerate these letters. Instead, they sent 'em down to Sanders for delivery. Christ, you could have fried bacon on his scalp.

Attention such as this convinced Sanders that I had some kind of evil stranglehold over the minds of my linemates. Anytime anything went wrong, he converged on me as if I was somehow orchestrating a mutiny with just a nod of my head. I could only wish that it were true.

One night it all came to a boil. I was sitting at the picnic bench when Sanders stalked over and motioned me into his office. I sat down in a chair wondering what the hell I had done now. My foreman grinned. "I've called you in here to discuss an article you wrote for the *Detroit Magazine*. According to this article, you admit to being off plant grounds at a tavern across the street while the line was in operation."

Now it was my turn to grin. "Yes?" I said.

"As you are well aware by now, leaving plant grounds without prior permission from a member of supervision is in direct violation of..." It went on and on. This woeful bleating. This megaphone of hurt. It was like a strange and intoxicating form of music and I sat there bathing in it. I blew smoke rings around the office and stared out at the guys on the line. There was Eddie and Cam and Schobel and Herman and... "... can not and WILL not be tolerated in as far as the recognition between management and the labor force and the agreement pertaining to the aforementioned transgression..." Something like that.

"Do we have an understanding?" Sanders concluded.

"I understand this," I answered. "I'm gonna write your sorry ass up for harassment. What I do or say outside of this plant is none of your fucking business."

Moments later, my committeeman and Henry Jackson were on the scene. Jackson immediately struck out on the offensive, accusing me of smelling like a brewery. "I could write you up this minute for drinking on the job."

"Do it!" I yelled. "At least I'm not a fuckin' cokehead like my foreman."

Sanders's jaw dropped. I knew more about him that he could have ever guessed. I knew friends that he'd bought coke from. I had seen him snortin' lines right in the supervisor's parking lot.

"Now, settle down," Jackson replied. "Do you realize that I could walk through this department every night penalizing men for drinking and smokin' pot? But I don't. You know why?"

"Hell yes, I know why! Because you know, as well as I, that those guys out there are keepin' your fat ass high and dry. Those drinkers and pot smokers comprise one of the most highly rated departments in this factory. Don't pretend you're doin' anybody any favors, all you're doin' is dodgin' the subject. I want Mr. Cokehead written up for supervisional harassment. He has absolutely no right to lecture me about things that I pursue outside of this factory."

Things settled down. Sanders was made to apologize and agree to never mention my writing. I had Jackson so shook up, he even agreed that Schobel and I should be allowed a bit more slack in our double-up routine. I think Jackson was convinced that I was gonna instigate a total rebellion. He overestimated my power with the rivet crew. They'd have just yawned and gone back to their own private hells. In effect, I was once again holding a trump card that didn't even exist.

It wasn't only Sanders and Jackson puttin' the eye on me.

There were others watching. Doug was the first to notice. One night he pointed out some suit-and-tie spy peering around the boxcars at me. He had a clipboard and a beeper. This went on for a while until I just couldn't stand it any longer. I ran out in the aisle and hollered "Kiss me, you fool!" He immediately disappeared.

This was to become a frequent event. Someone would gesture down the line with their head and, lo and behold, there would be some mystery man peepin' around the corner at me. What the hell did they want? If I made any motion to approach or yell in their direction, they would pivot and vanish. My nerves were bad enough without all this creepy cloak and dagger.

Bad enough that another bout with panic let me have it just after we entered '87, my tenth year at General Motors. This was getting truly distressing. Every few months I would topple over like some rag doll off the shelf. Dr. Kilaru relayed that I was also suffering from agoraphobia—an abnormal fear of being in open or public places. This went a long way in helping explain why I felt that I was being led to slaughter every time I entered a mall or movie theater, to say nothing of an assembly plant so large that it took up twenty city blocks.

Agoraphobia, don't leave home without it. Better yet, just don't leave home. Dr. Kilaru put me out on sick leave and for the next three months I rarely left my apartment. I did nothing but smoke, drink, watch TV, sleep, sleep, then sleep some more. I talked on the phone daily with my new girlfriend in Ann Arbor. I'd met her through a letter she had written me the previous fall during a period when Amy and I were experiencing one of our frequent fallouts. Her name was Jan. She didn't smoke or drink or eat meat. How'd she manage to get stuck with the Rivethead? Some folks just ain't got no common sense.

Jan was the first to suggest that I leave the shop. I explained to her that it wasn't that easy. The factory was all I knew. I was a shoprat, bruised brain and all. I had to forge on.

I went back to the Rivet Line in May. It was a total fiasco. I was hell-bent on keeping the demons far at bay. To do so, I began drinking outrageous amounts of beer and liquor. This did tend to squelch the demons but, at the same time, it was taking a costly toll on my work record. I was being written up on a weekly basis on a variety of counts ranging from insubor-

dination to poor workmanship to immoral conduct. My committeeman was spending more time with me than his wife. Each
time he came around, all I could do was shrug. He would ask
me if I wanted to fight the penalty or enter my own grievance.
I always declined. "Nope, Boogie, I'm guilty as charged."

"Goddamnit, Hamper, you're hangin' yourself. Pissin' in
the fuckin' aisleway? Listen, you have to pull it together or
you're on your way out the door."

My committeeman was an all right guy. I just felt weird
calling him Boogie. The word belonged in an arena full of
metalheads cheerin' on a thundering drum solo. Alas, it was
sorta comical and befitting that my personal liaison between
myself and the GM bureaucratic juggernaut would turn out to be
a guy in a sleeveless Jack Daniel's T-shirt named Boogie. It
was like facing a murder rap with an attorney named Killer.

However, Boogie was right. I had to pull it together. I met
with Dr. Kilaru and he once again suggested that I enter the
mental health clinic. This time I agreed.

I was assigned to the Anxiety and Panic group. Each
morning would begin with a rehash of what we had done the
previous night. The fact that we were all afflicted with varying
degrees of agoraphobia prevented much of a chance for any
amazing yarns. A typical briefing: "Went home, cooked a
frozen dinner, watched the news, took my medication, went to
bed." Next!

The rest of the day was spent attending various sessions:
group therapy, occupational therapy, goal planning, stress seminars, relaxation techniques and, my personal favorite, volleyball. Hell, everybody loved volleyball. We'd break up into
teams and have at it—the loons, the paranoids, the manic
depressives, the weeping old women, the scary young men, the
multiple personalities. We shrieked and cheered. We dove for
wayward shots and belly-flopped across the waxed gymnasium
floor like crazed barking seals. It was just like fifth grade all
over again except this time around the beards were much
heavier and we didn't have as much to lose.

Frequently, I would feel totally out of place at the clinic.
Many of the woman there had histories that were so tragic I
almost felt ashamed nursing my little phobia in their midst.
Women who were abused as children and whose own children

were ragin' miscreants stashed in penitentiaries. Women whose entire families had disowned them and left them to weep away in lonely rooms. When it would come my turn to speak, I'd feel like the world's biggest sham: "My problem? Um, I can't, um, relax at my, um, job."

During my stretch at the clinic, the transfer to my new job in Pontiac went through. On July 17th, I came off sick leave ready to resume my calling. I was unaware that I no longer belonged in Flint. I went down to the Personnel office to hire back in and was immediately pointed southward. The people in the front office seemed especially excited to inform me that my tenure at Flint GM Truck & Bus was at an end. Was it something I had said? They handed me some fuzzy map to my new home at Pontiac East Assembly and instructed me to be at this destination the next day at 6:00 A.M.

As I headed for the door, a strange thing happened. Some white-collar tapeworm came hustling up behind me hollerin' my name. I didn't recognize this person—just another gung-ho errand boy from the bright tomb district. As I paused, he thrust an index card and a pen at me. "Would you mind autographing this card for my wife?" he asked. "Her name is Becky, she's a big fan of yours."

I looked at him incredulously. This seemed beyond the bizarre. The timing was the strangest part. Here I was stridin' out the door for the very last time and my last official duty had nothing to do with spot-welders or axle hoists or rivet guns. Some fly-boy's bored spouse wanted my signature. What the hell. I took the pen and wrote: "Dear Becky, I'm looking forward to death. Best Wishes, the Rivethead." The guy shook my hand and I departed.

Returning to the factory was eerie enough without the added complication of entering a totally new environment. From everything I'd heard about Pontiac East Assembly, the place was pure Gulag City. The jobs were timed-out to make sure the workers wouldn't be allowed a moment's intermission. Anyone caught reading a newspaper or paperback would be penalized. The union was nothing more than a powerless puppet show groveling in the muck. There were as many robots as shoprats.

My sources hadn't lied. Everything about this plant reeked of science gone too far. They set me up on a ferocious maze, something to do with brake boosters. I had so much medication flowing through me that I felt woozy. It had to be that way. I'd promised myself that, no matter what else happened, I would sooner lapse into a drug-induced coma than have another panic attack.

So much for that theory. Driving down I-75 for my second day on the job, I had the grandpappy panic attack of 'em all. I got about halfway down there, near a small town called Clarkston, when the wheels fell off. I whipped into a rest area and took a seat in a bathroom stall. I sat there for nearly two hours, alternately sobbing and deliberating. All the while, construction workers and salesmen and gas haulers, men who keep this country in motion, were grunting and farting in nearby stalls. They were gonna wipe their asses and wash their hands and go get it done. It was only a routine, not much different from breathing.

Finally, I snuck out of my stall and splashed some water on my face. I got in my car and drove over by Lake Orion to my brother Matt's house. He was a shoprat too. The same with his wife. I roused them out of bed.

"What the hell are you doing here?" my brother asked. "Aren't you supposed to be working?"

I walked over and grabbed a beer out of his fridge. "It's over," I said.

"What are you talking about?"

"I'm talking about General Moors. It's all over between us."

Actually, I had been a bit hasty in my remarks with Matt. It wasn't over though it really should have been. The next day I was placed back in the Holly Road Mental Health Clinic. I never worked another day in 1987.

During this period, Jan and I got married. We moved to a small town just south of Flint called Fenton. It was a rather awkward way to begin a marriage. Each morning Jan would set off for her teaching job in Ann Arbor and I would straggle off to the mental health clinic for therapy and volleyball. Not exactly the way Ward Cleaver worked it. Shit, even Herman Munster had a job.

Dr. Kilaru added a new medication to my supply, a combination sedative and antidepressant called Triavil. This drug made me feel extremely sluggish and apathetic. I thanked him profusely. Dr. Kilaru also began advising me strongly against ever returning to work in the factory. He was aware of my writing sideline and suggested that I move in that direction. His intentions were sincere, I had no doubt that he meant well, but the good doctor was missing the whole point and I felt that I should inform him regarding the obvious.

"Doctor, in case you're not aware, all I do is write about the factory. In order to do so, it is absolutely necessary for me to *work in a factory*. Otherwise, I'd be an imposter."

"You could write about other topics of interest," Dr. Kilaru responded.

"I have no other topics of interest. I'd just as soon give the factory one more shot."

And, after seven long months at the clinic, I did just that. I marched back to Pontiac to continue my quest for my thirty-year pin and ten frames of bowling with a certain freckled automotive czar.

My reception upon arrival was hardly gracious. My foreman took one look at me as I entered his office and put his hand to his forehead. "Well, if it isn't the one-day wonder. Tell me, how long do you expect to hang around this time? An hour? A day? AN ENTIRE WEEK?"

"Anybody's guess," I answered.

The job he assigned me was sheer insanity. I had to lie down inside the truck cabs, divide all these tangled wire harnesses, tape the wires along the floorboard in four very specific locations, then bend and droop them through the dash. Once that was done, I had to race over and insert two plastic clips onto the four-wheel drive shifter. This completed, I had to scurry back to the cab and bolt down the shifter with this cumbersome air gun that kicked like a mule and was as large as your basic weed-whacker. It was damn hard work, the worst I'd ever come across. However, I was makin' it. The demons were gnawin' someone else. I had so much Xanax and Triavil in me that a nuclear war wouldn't have fazed me. My biggest obstacle was simply keeping my eyes open.

The workers from Pontiac seemed cold, indifferent, resigned to the fact that their union was nothing more than a charade and that management took full advantage of the fact. The only

guy I ever spoke with was the worker right beside me, a
Pontiac native named Jim. The guy was a total mess. He used
to show up for work drunk—an astounding accomplishment
when you stopped to consider it wasn't even daylight yet. It
wasn't long before the two of us were tippin' together.

I'm amazed I didn't kill myself considering all the medication I was taking. Jim and I would each drink a forty-ouncer at
first break, another one at lunch, then smuggle in a pint or two
of whiskey for the last part of the shift. That was an average
day. I recall the time I inhaled 120 ounces of beer in the span of
a forty-minute lunch break. Even Jim was impressed. The
demons kept their distance.

This behavior was truly absurd, not to mention incredibly
dangerous. It got so bad that I couldn't even remember making
the thirty-five-mile commute back to Fenton each day. It was
as if the Camaro was being watched over by some freeway
guardian angel. My wife was less than happy. I'd regularly
stumble through the door and collapse into bed without bothering
to remove my shoes. The next morning, Jan would ask me if I
remembered driving home the previous afternoon. Driving
home? Shit, I couldn't even recall leaving the plant.

This went on for a while, a very short while. Anesthetizing
one's self in an effort to fend off the dreaded panic was one
thing. However, driving across the median at eighty miles an
hour into oncoming traffic with a booze level that could've
boiled mercury was quite another. It was either drop the
drinking or run the risk of killing innocent commuters. It was a
difficult choice. I opted to stay sober.

Things settled down to a point where I truly believed I
was gonna make it. I still had the occasional flirts with anxiety,
but I was always able to talk my way clear of total panic. I
would bury myself in my job, reinducing my old ploy of pretending
my job was an event in the Olympics. I'd muscle and tussle, all
the while inwardly narrating the frantic action: "We haven't
heard much from Hamper, the ex-riveter from Flint, Michigan,
who provided such a startling Cinderella story back in the '82
games. He appears to be in great shape as he prepares himself
for his latest specialty—the four-wheel-drive shifter installa-
tion. Who will ever forget the stunning triumph he provided his

country...blah-blah-blah." Needless to report, I swiped another gold medal.

I suppose there was always gonna be an April 7, 1988. It just hid there like a heartless sniper behind the diesel haze and the minute hand. It knew my name. It knew my brain. It could smell fear a mile away. Its aim was true. The kill was a clean one.

I felt it on the way down to Pontiac that morning: the numbness, the screwy vision, the hovering dread, the disorientation. I chewed down an extra Triavil and drove on. There would be no rest area bailouts this time around. I was stickin' to the path. I was gonna ride this bastard until it either dissipated or completely felled me.

Inside the plant, I attempted to bury myself into the strenuous labor of my rut. It didn't help matters any that my heart felt like a trampoline full of ferrets. I did my best to avoid eye contact with my neighbors. I was certain that they were all staring me down. I kept trying to hold it together. Just let me hang in there until break. April 7, 1988, would have none of my resistance.

I surrendered. I called the foreman over and asked for a pass to go to the plant hospital. He immediately started bitchin' about how he was short of bodies. I assured him that it was an emergency. Reluctantly, he rounded up the Quality man to cover my job.

It didn't take the hospital nurse long to see I was in bad shape. After taking my blood pressure and pulse, she asked if I had a doctor. When I replied yes, she advised that I leave the shop at once and pay him a visit. She wrote me out a slip to give to my foreman stating that I should be allowed to leave the plant immediately.

I went back to my department and handed the slip to my foreman. My arms and legs felt like they had gerbils running through them. Sweat was pouring down my back. My foreman read the slip and launched into a tirade. Just what I needed.

"I've about had it with you goddamn pussies that don't want to work," he yelled, making sure half the department could hear him. "You're a bunch of sorry bastards and, believe me, I'M GONNA START MODIFYIN' SOME CHANGES

AROUND HERE!" (This guy loved big words, context and meaning be damned.)

"Listen, all I know is that I was supposed to give you this slip. I know exactly what it says so don't try pullin' this bad-example bullshit on me. I'm outta here."

The foreman flew into a rage. He took the slip, wadded it up and threw it at my feet. In another time and place, under a different set of circumstances, I would have enjoyed this tantrum to the hilt. However, right then, I was hardly in the mood for idiot drama.

"Why don't you kiss my ass," I said while brushing past him.

"When you come back, I swear I'm gonna KICK YOUR ASS!"

However, he was out of luck. April 7, 1988, saw to it that he'd never get that chance.

EPILOGUE

A BEAUTIFUL, SUNNY DAY NEAR THE END OF A VERY HOT SUMMER. Since it's Tuesday, the Anxiety and Panic group is out for its weekly field trip. Typically, not all in our group are present. A few have chosen to remain back at the mental health clinic, the thought of mingling about in society simply too abhorrent.

Today's outing is miniature golf. It's not so bad. At least we've received another week's reprieve from cowering through the mall.

By the third hole, we are already down to a fivesome—myself, Pat, Debbie, Marge and our faithful psychologist/baby-sitter, Lenice. Lucy has retired to the van complaining about the heat. We shuffle forth, hole by hole, urging each other on, applauding nice putts. Through the first nine, I am in firm command of the lead. Everything is running smoothly.

However, on the fourteenth hole trouble brews. Pat has smacked her orange ball into some swinging donkey appendage and the ball careens all the way into the parking lot. Everyone, including Pat, is in complete hysterics.

"That'll cost you a penalty stroke, Patty," I announce.

"I'm just gonna play it over," she replies.

"Go for it. It's still gonna cost you a stroke for a ball out of play."

"What DIFFERENCE does it make?" Pat howls. "It's only a GAME! Just like volleyball. IT'S ONLY A GAME! Why do you treat it so importantly?"

I can't answer. There is no answer. Rivet Hockey is now volleyball. Putt-putt is now Dumpster Ball. It only makes sense to win.

We play on. With tremendous ease, I'm able to salvage the victory. Patty cools down. She is old enough to be my mother. I give her a cigarette and we stand beside the van puffin' like fiends. I rib her about how I'm gonna destroy her ass in volleyball when we get back to the clinic.

Lenice parades us into the van. She hands each of us a small envelope containing our four dollars in lunch money. We begin our search for an unpopulated eatery. I take command of the radio and find a Paul Revere and the Raiders tune on an oldies station. The old women in the back of the van crack up as I mimic Mark Lindsay's vocal and pound on the dashboard during the organ solo. The old women love me. They keep repeating that they wish they had a son like me.

Jump ahead a few months. One evening I decide it's time to pay a visit to the Rivet Line. I haven't been back there in a year and a half and I'm curious to see how everyone's doing.

I slide right past the guard booth, right on by the old time clocks, up the stairway and onto the Rivet Line. At first, it feels as if a day hasn't passed since I'd been bangin' away on that lurchin' snake. I can hear the old familiar clang of the carrier chains and the repairman's chisel. I can smell the eternal aroma of grease, sealer paint, smoke and sweat.

I begin walking down the line when it suddenly hits me: the jobs all look unchanged, but the faces are entirely different. There's the pinup jobs, but no Tommy or Earl. There's the frame rollover job, but no Cam or Hogjaw. There's the rail-pull jobs, but no Big Red or Willie. And where are Al and Dougie and Paul? The place looks the same but, from a human aspect, it has been almost totally gutted.

Eddie and Dick are still around. We shake hands and swap

information about our old cronies. I ask them whatever happened to Paul, my double-up sidekick.

"He got laid off soon after you left," Eddie says. "He works plumbing and heating now."

"What about Jehan?"

"Got pulled over with a gun and a mess of dope. He's been in jail for months."

"Well, what about Terry and Matt and Joe?"

"They've been out on the street for nearly a year now," Dick reports. "Ever since they shut down the Pickup Line, it's been here today, gone tomorrow."

I look over at my old job. Some new guy's leanin' there at my bench. My faithful rivet gun dangles at his hip. It infuriates me. It's like seein' your wife bein' kissed by a total stranger. As far as I'm concerned, that damn rivet gun is private property.

I go over to the guy and tell him I'll catch the next job. He looks at me perplexed and says "Be my guest." I grab a front wheel spring casting, four rivets and position old faithful. Click, click, click, click. I still have the touch for whatever that's worth. The rivet gun hums like a contented child. I look over at Eddie and Dick and they're both smiling. It's sad and confusing. I almost feel like I belong here. Almost.

I ask Eddie if he feels like drainin' a few Budweisers at break time. I have a twelve-pack in my Camaro and nowhere else I have to be.

We park it back by the barbed wire fence and the railroad tracks. The stars mingle with the smokestacks and the sky whispers winter. I tell Eddie all about my inglorious swan song. I tell him about the volleyball wars out at the clinic.

"You can't tell me you'd rather be playin' volleyball than bustin' up a shin with some Rivet Hockey." Eddie chuckles between chugs.

No, I can't. Nor can I tell him that the only ones who are gonna survive thirty years on an assembly line are those who can consistently blot out the gradual and persistent decay of the trick. There really isn't anything gallant or noble about being a factory hack. The whole arrangement equals nothing more than lousy prostitution. Thinking tears you apart. Start peering at the walls too closely or leaning on the clock too heavily and the whoremaster reality of all this idiocy will surely gobble your ass up whole. The demons aren't demons. The demons are *you*.

"Just about time for that 'All Aboard,'" I tell Eddie. "I'll drive you up to the gate."

"You gotta drop by more often, Ben. Next time I'll try and swing a double lunch and we can have a go at some Hennessy."

"We'll do that," I lie.

I drive away feeling lucky or something like it.